INSTALLING & REPAIRING PLUMBING FIXTURES

INSTALLING & REPAIRING PLUMBING FIXTURES

PETER HEMP

The Taunton Press

BOOKS & VIDEOS

for fellow enthusiasts

First printing: August 1994
Printed in the United States of America

A FINE HOMEBUILDING Book
FINE HOMEBUILDING® is a trademark of The Taunton Press, Inc.,
registered in the U.S. Patent and Trademark Office.

The Taunton Press, 63 South Main Street, Box 5506,
Newtown, CT 06470-5506

Library of Congress Cataloging-in-Publication Data

Hemp, Peter A. (Peter Addison)
    Installing and repairing plumbing fixtures / Peter Hemp.
        p.   cm.
    "A Fine Homebuilding book"—T.p. verso.
    Includes index.
    ISBN 1-56158-075-9
    1. Plumbing. I. Title. II. Title: Installing and repairing
    plumbing fixtures.
TH6122.H43   1994   94-14108
696'.1—dc20   CIP

ACKNOWLEDGMENTS

A lot of people have contributed in various ways to this book. I'd especially like to express my gratitude to everyone at the Rubenstein Supply Company of Oakland, California, for giving me a free run of their facilities and inventory, and for tirelessly researching my requests for product information. I'd also like to thank Meyer Plumbing Supply and Moran Supply, also of Oakland, and Omega Salvage and the Sink Factory, both of Berkeley, for their unselfish contributions of time, materials and photographs.

I owe an unrepayable debt to Sane Contracting of Albany, California, for allowing me to alter their construction schedules to make room for the book's job-site photos. I'd also like to thank the Kohler Company for providing many of the photographs of plumbing fixtures in Chapter 3. And I am greatly indebted to Berkeley's Homemade Cafe and Oakland's Bay Wolf Restaurant for providing field offices, gratis, for the duration of this project.

Last but not least, the following individuals offered their technical expertise or opened their homes to me, helping make this book a reality. To all of you, my heartfelt thanks:

Sally Aberg, John Adams, Lucy Aquinaldo, Elaine Beatty, Hugh Beatty, Jeffery Becom, Jeff Beneke, Janet Berzon, Norman Berzon, Ragnar Boreson, Barry Branco, Everette Campbell, Jon Carroll, Martha Casselman, Ray Chandler, Peter Chapman, Karen Connelly, Bill Dane, Steve Dobrinsky, Megan Fisher, Don Foley, Katharine Foley, Larry Goldman, Daniel Hemp, Katherine Rearden Hemp, Mary Hemp, Sandy Hodges, Jim Kearns, Tim Kearns, Ron Kyle, Vito Lab, Cornelia Levine, Larry Levine, Alex Levy, Suzanne Lowenthal, Babbette Maccoby, Herb Maccoby, Jim Martellacci, Bobby Mesa, B.J. Miller, Chuck Miller, Steve Mitchell, Andrew Moran, Matt Moran, Neil Moran, Deborah O'Grady, Joanne Okamoto, Roger Patzer, John Paul, David Peoples, Janet Peoples, Bob Rubenstein, Craig Rubenstein, Michael Singman, Lisa Stadelhofer, Isabel Stampp, Kenneth Stampp, Jay Vance, Don Villa, Jimmy Weyhmiller, Owen Whetzel, Michael Wild and Randy Wilson.

And thanks again George Inskeep, wherever you are.

CONTENTS

INTRODUCTION

I'm a residential plumber based in Albany, California, a town across the bay from San Francisco. Some years ago I wrote a basic plumbing repair manual for home owners, and from there I decided to go on and write a book that would attempt to demystify the process of designing and installing a complete residential plumbing system. Well, it eventually became apparent that there was simply too much information for one book alone, so the one book became two.

The first book *(Plumbing a House)* covers "rough plumbing" — the installation of piping systems that serve the plumbing fixtures and plumbing-related appliances in the home — as well as remodeling. This second book discusses "finish plumbing," which takes up where rough plumbing leaves off and covers the actual installation of those fixtures and appliances. I've also included a lengthy chapter on common troubleshooting and repair tasks.

I learned a long time ago when coming to the rescue of friends who had tried to do some of their own plumbing that very often it was the sequence of their attack that got them into trouble. Many times they were close to solving their own problems but did something before they should have. When I first sat down to write this book, this issue of sequence was foremost in my mind. As much as possible, I've presented the information in the sequence I would plumb a new house, which will enable a seasoned builder or tradesperson to work through the process of finish-plumbing an entire house, or certain parts of it. I also hope the book will be useful for the home owner who just wants to find information on, say, installing a lavatory sink, unclogging a toilet or hooking up a garbage disposer.

One thing I've learned in my 20-odd years in the plumbing trade is the importance of using quality materials, whether for the fixtures themselves or for the hardware used to install them. Nowadays, almost anything can be chrome plated, but in most cases you'll find that traditional materials — such as brass rather than plastic for slip nuts — give you the best results. It's always tempting to save a few cents here, a couple of dollars there, but, in the long term, quality materials often work out more economical. Using quality materials also leaves less room for failure and, more important, discouragement.

In some parts of the country, you may not be able to use the materials and practices I recommend here (such as ABS or PVC pipe for waste systems), which is why I've presented several alternate methods of installation throughout the book. For minor plumbing repairs, such as installing a new faucet, you usually won't have to worry about any code restrictions, but for major plumbing projects, such as installing a tub and waste line, it's very important to know what materials and practices are sanctioned in your areas. There are three major national plumbing codes that I'm familiar with, and countless local codes that may have one or more provisions that supersede your major code. If you are a builder or tradesperson considering plumbing a new home from scratch or doing a major remodel, I strongly recommend that you buy a copy of your major code and any local code that might supersede it.

A shortcoming of other plumbing books I have read is the authors' assumption that the reader can see into their minds, filling in the blanks where the text leaves too many unanswered questions. I've tried to err on the side of comprehensiveness, covering the standard approaches in depth as well as offering various optional solutions where appropriate.

In almost every plumbing job, there's invariably more than one way to do the work. What is presented here are methods that have worked well for me and should for you. There's rarely a situation where there's only one right way, one code-approved way, or one way that all building inspectors will like. I've found that plumbing codes, on the whole, are very similar, and the methods I recommend here are usually more than code minimums.

CHAPTER

1

TOOLS

If you do a lot of carpentry, home repairs, wood-working and auto repairs, you probably have a fairly extensive tool collection. But if you are going to get seriously involved in plumbing, you are going to need a wide variety of new tools and different models. In this chapter I'll give you an overview of the tools I consider essential for installing and repairing plumbing fixtures. The selection includes general-purpose hand tools, tools for gripping, cutting and drilling, special-purpose troubleshooting tools, and equipment for safety, comfort and convenience. Most of these tools are available from hardware stores, plumbing supply houses or by mail order (see the Sources of Supply on pp. 178-179 for a list of manufacturers). Where appropriate, I have given the names and catalog numbers of specific brands.

GENERAL HAND TOOLS

Although finish plumbing requires a number of specialized tools, you'll also need to have a good selection of general-purpose hand tools. Many of these tools I'll use when plumbing the rough pipes for a house, too. Whatever the plumbing job, I always car-

ry with me a ballpeen hammer and a claw hammer, which I'll use for pulling the odd nail, tapping wedges under sinks and chipping away mortar and tile cement around in-the-wall tub and shower valves. Although wooden-handled hammers are softer on the user, I've found that they don't wear as well as fiberglass and steel handles.

Wood chisels come in handy when I need to remove stock underneath countertops when the thickness of wood and tile is too much for installing top-mounting faucets. And I may occasionally need a cold chisel to blast away exterior stucco for a heat-vent thimble. I keep a cat's paw and a pry bar on my truck too, for those rare occasions when I might need them — perhaps to lift a tub for removal or just to pry open a painted-shut window to get some fresh air.

Screwdrivers have a lot of applications in finish plumbing, and I carry a number of different sizes with me. When assembling close-coupled toilets and removing old cast-iron wall-hung sink hangers, I'm always glad I have a 20-in. long standard slotted screwdriver. Numbers 1 and 2 offset Phillips and standard screwdrivers are indispensable when servicing old toilet ballcocks and flush-ball wire guides. Another job that they occasionally come in handy for is removing dishwasher front panels.

The once novel four-in-one screwdriver with interchangeable bits is now made by a number of tool companies. Although the various brands look quite similar, there are significant differences in quality. The Pasco brand four-way #4208 is my favorite. My tools are often submerged in water (and worse), and other models have rusted and silted up quickly; the Pasco removable bit shaft and barrel are heavily chrome plated and resist rusting. Also, the Pasco bits are harder and longer, and the squared handle gives better purchase.

An important part of installing plumbing fixtures is making sure that they rest level. I use a 2-ft. level for leveling tubs, toilet bowls, pedestal sinks, freestanding ranges, water heaters, washers and dryers, and for scribing lines on walls for the mounting of wall-hung sinks and wall-hung toilet tanks. A plumb bob can also come in handy, though much more often on rough plumbing than on finish.

TOOLS FOR MEASURING AND MARKING

I use two basic measuring tools — a 1-in. wide 25-ft. tape measure for longer lengths, and a 6-ft. folding rule for measuring close distances. I prefer the white folding rule because it's easier to read inside dark cabinets and down in dim crawl spaces.

A chalk line is handy for marking the position of the 2x4 ledger that is screwed to the studs to support a bathtub along the inside wall. In a pinch, it can also be used as a plumb bob. I use a combination square for laying out holes to drill for faucets that mount on countertops, and a compass for marking the vent hole in the wall for a direct-vent heater.

TOOLS FOR GRIPPING

Plumbing involves a lot of gripping of nuts, pipes and faucets. In finish plumbing you'll use wrenches on two basic shapes — round surfaces and faceted surfaces. The round surfaces are typically those of galvanized and brass nipples, and require wrenches that have gripping teeth on the jaws that dig into the outer surface of the pipe (such as pipe wrenches and slide-jaw pliers). The faceted surfaces include faucet trim, waste slip nuts, angle-stop bodies and hose bibbs. For fittings that are designed to be left to view, I usually use smooth-jawed adjustable wrenches so as not to leave scratches in the flat surfaces. Faucet-mounting hardware and other nuts that will not be visible are usually gripped with a basin wrench (see p. 7), which has toothed jaws similar to those of pipe wrenches.

SLIDE-JAW PLIERS

I use four sizes of slide-jaw pliers: 4 in., 6 in., 10 in. and 12 in. (sizes refer to the overall length of the tool). There are definite differences of design shape among the various manufacturers, and you'll need a mix of brands better to accomplish varying tasks.

I find the 4-in. size, with toothed parallel jaws, very useful for working in tight quarters, as when tightening dish-spray hose connections on the underside of kitchen-sink faucets. This size is also handy for loosening the setscrew that secures old pop-up lavatory lift straps to the pop-up actuator arm, which protrudes out the back of the waste. Also, these petite pliers can grip the sides of corroded screws on valve stems to back them out.

Slide-jaw pliers, in both smooth and toothed-jaw designs, are used for gripping pipes and nuts of various sizes.

The 6-in. size is very helpful for loosening and tightening faucet supply nuts in under-sink recesses where the clumsy jaw of the basin wrench (see p. 7) is too big to fit. I also find it possible to loosen or tighten leaking or stripped packing nuts on tub and shower valves when they are slightly behind the tile surface and a larger tool will not fit in the hole. My preferred brand for both the 4-in. and 6-in. pliers is Channelock.

The 10-in. slide-jaw pliers, which can grasp and hold all pipe and fitting sizes up to 1½ in., is the size I use most frequently. The most common applications for these pliers are the removal and installation of tubular-brass P-trap and waste slip nuts and initial assembly of ½-in. and ¾-in. dia. threaded pipe and fittings. I have tried every major brand of tool in these applications and find that Pasco and Craftsman brands are the best.

I was very disappointed with the 10-in. slide-jaw pliers made by Ridgid, which is the long-time, premier plumbing-tool manufacturer. The jaws on their 10-in. pliers are undersized for tubular slip nuts and standard pipe and fitting sizes, and the slide action in the adjustment process is very cumbersome. Also, the handles are uncomfortable to squeeze at every setting. Since a great amount of a plumber's time is spent dealing with drain and waste components, it's important to have a well-designed tool to work with.

I use the 12-in. slide-jaw pliers mostly for removing kitchen-sink basket strainers; loosening stubborn 1½-in. tubular-brass slip nuts (especially at the wall); and assembling 1½-in. and 2-in. threaded pipe and fittings, prior to a final snugging with pipe wrenches. In this size, I have no complaints about the Ridgid-brand pliers.

In addition to my set of slide-jaw pliers, I also have various sizes of needle-nose pliers, which I use primarily in faucet work for servicing valves.

ADJUSTABLE WRENCHES

I use adjustable wrenches, which have smooth jaws, to grip hexagonal or square nuts that I don't want to mar (sometimes I'll apply masking tape over each jaw for added protection on a mirror finish). If you do only occasional plumbing work, you could probably get by with just two adjustable wrenches, an 8-in. and

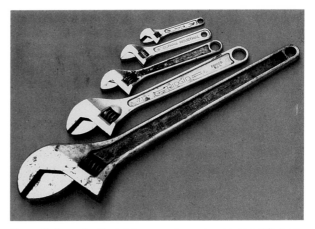

Smooth-jawed adjustable wrenches are used to grip nuts, faucet trim and other faceted surfaces without marring the surface finish.

a 12-in. If you're planning on doing a lot of plumbing, it makes sense to have several additional sizes. My tool box contains a 4-in., 6-in., 8-in., 12-in. and 18-in. adjustable wrench (all Ridgid brand).

The 4-in. wrench is handy for working on closet-bolt nuts, water-heater pilot-light generator nuts and pilot-light tube nuts. It's the perfect tool for turning on and off my acetylene bottle, which I use for soldering copper pipe, and it can come in handy for reaching hard-to-get-at, no-hub coupling bands when the longer torque wrench (see p. 7) will not fit in confined spaces. I use the 6-in. adjustable wrench for tightening and loosening ⅜-in. and ½-in. compression nuts on lavatory, kitchen-sink and closet supplies, and the 8-in. wrench for ½-in. IPS ("iron pipe size") supply nuts on angle stops and faucets when they are easily accessible.

The 12-in. is the wrench for removing large old-fashioned angle stops, for snugging up large closet-supply nuts, and for using with the Ace EX-12 pipe nipple "back-out" (see p. 14). Another application is loosening and tightening many popular sizes of old wall-hung faucet eccentrics and union nuts. I also use the 12-in. wrench on the square shank of my telescoping, Ridgid-brand basin wrench to persuade stubborn, old faucet lock-mounting nuts to let go. I can't recall a time when I've used the 18-in. adjustable wrench on finish work, but I do call it into service occasionally on rough work.

MONKEY WRENCH

Another very versatile wrench is a 14-in., thin-profile monkey wrench. This smooth 90°-jawed wrench has a large-capacity jaw opening that's ideal for grasping thin, large-diameter nuts on toilet "spuds" (the fitting at the back of a wall-hung toilet that secures the flush elbow to the bowl). I also use the 14-in. monkey wrench on wrench flats on toilet flush valves; on wall-hung sink faucet eccentrics; on antique widespread-faucet top-mounting nuts; and on lavatory pop-up waste lock-mounting nuts. Yet other applications include grasping compression angle stops with the upturned 90° jaws, while another smaller adjustable wrench is used to undo the compression nuts; and using with the Ace EX-7 pipe nipple backout when extra torque is required.

PIPE WRENCHES

As the name suggests, pipe wrenches are used primarily on pipes. I always carry at least four pipe wrenches (6 in., 12 in., 18 in. and 24 in.) on my truck. You might think that a 6-in. pipe wrench is too small to be of much use, but a quality-brand 6-in. wrench (I recommend Ridgid) can grasp a ¾-in. iron pipe. I have used mine to stem leaks at tub and shower valve union to iron supply pipe connections when the union was right up against a stud. The 6-in. wrench is also small enough to get into many other areas to break loose or snug up threaded connections.

I use a 12-in. wrench for taking out galvanized test nipples and installing ½-in. brass nipples (see p. 21). The 14-in. size is good for installing ¾-in. nipples at the water heater. The 18-in. and 24-in. brutes are used almost exclusively on rough and remodel work. If you plan on doing a lot of plumbing work, you will find that aluminum pipe wrenches (also available from Ridgid) will save your arms a lot of fatigue.

SOCKET WRENCHES

Socket wrenches are used to service and repair in-the-wall valves. Unfortunately, I have yet to find a company that sells a set of good-quality socket wrenches for plumbing. Most are made of soft, stamped steel, and the precision is so poor that in many cases you end up stripping nuts with them. Forged mechanics' socket wrenches are made to much closer tolerances, and I use them if they fit the nut.

A 14-in. monkey wrench with jaws at 90° to the body is good for gripping thin, large-diameter nuts.

Pipe wrenches have toothed jaws that grip on the outer surface of round pipes.

Use the right wrench and you should be able to snug up any threaded connection, but for a permanent watertight joint you also need to apply one or more sealing materials. These include plumber's putty, Teflon tape and pipe-joint compound.

PLUMBER'S PUTTY

Plumber's putty is used as a sealant to prevent gravity leaks, for example, when setting faucets, kitchen-sink strainers and tub wastes and overflows. Scrimping on putty is the height of foolishness since this material is so inexpensive. Plumber's putty should have a good, elastic consistency. You should be able to roll out little "snakes," pick them up, and not have them break until they have stretched out to spaghetti thinness. Plumber's putty should not be mealy but soft enough at room temperature so that you can pull off the container's lid and work two or three fingers right in with ease. Putty that is too stiff will prevent you from getting enough purchase on threaded parts. Then when the putty eventually relaxes under compression, the threaded parts are all of a sudden too loose and you'll likely get a leak.

Brands of putty that I generally find acceptable include DAP, Hercules, Harvey's and Black Swan.

TEFLON TAPE

Teflon tape is used on male pipe threads as a sealant against pressure leaks. Quality Teflon tape is of uniform thickness, stretches evenly, does not fray when you tear it, and comes off the spool without sliding off at the edges when under tension. Some companies manufacturing quality tape have started coloring their product to differentiate it from the cheap brands. An excellent brand sold nationwide is Pink Plumber's Tape by the Mill Rose Company (see the Sources of Supply on pp. 178-179).

Teflon tape comes in several widths, the most common being ½ in. and ¾ in. For 90% of my work, ½-in. tape is adequate. The ¾-in. tape is useful for 3-in. and 4-in. dia. pipe threads. When buying tape, look on the spool to see how much tape you are getting for your money. A common length is 260 in., but some stores will sell spools with as little as 100 in. at a premium price. When applying the tape, wrap tightly in a clockwise direction and cover all the threads.

PIPE-JOINT COMPOUND

Pipe-joint compound, or pipe "dope" as it is more commonly called, is used as a seal on female pipe threads (and occasionally on male threads, too). My first choice

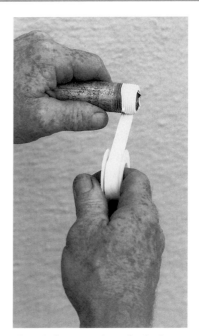

Wrap Teflon tape in a clockwise direction over male threads to provide a watertight seal against leaks.

for pipe dope is Rectorseal #5, which is good for all pipe materials except ABS. (For ABS I use Rectorseal 100 Virgin or Hercules Real-Tuff.) I prefer the consistency of Rectorseal #5, which will "roll" down into cavities. The 100 Virgin and the Real-Tuff are stiffer and require more work (causing more mess) to get into confined areas. Most pipe-joint compounds come in cans that have a brush attached to the screw-on cap (although a squeeze tube would be more practical).

BASIN WRENCH

The basin wrench is used mostly under sinks for reaching nuts that are inaccessible with an adjustable wrench. The Ridgid #1019 telescoping basin wrench is the most adaptable one that I've found. It's available in two sizes — one for faucet supply nuts and the other for tubular-brass slip nuts found on P-traps, continuous wastes and tub waste and overflows.

RUBBER-JAWED PLIERS AND STRAP WRENCH

I often use rubber-jawed pliers or a strap wrench when installing bidets to prevent damage to chrome-finished pipe nipples, unions, couplings, 90° elbows and trim. These tools can also, on rare occasions, come in handy when assembling/disassembling new threaded tailpieces and slip nuts within the confines of the pedestal of a pedestal sink. For these tasks, I prefer the rubber-jawed pliers (which are available with semicircular jaws or with a 90° notch in the middle of the jaws) and have not needed my strap wrench for quite a few years. Buy one only if you find that no other method will work.

NO-HUB COUPLING WRENCH

A no-hub coupling wrench is used to tighten clamps around rubber couplings that join pipes of different materials and/or diameters. In finish plumbing, these couplings are sometimes used on tub drains and on sink drains. The T-handle wrench has a preset clutch that releases when you have tightened the nuts on the coupling's hose clamps. There are two popular designs on the market, one made by Pasco (#7020) and the other by Ridgid. I generally prefer the Pasco wrench (shown in the bottom photo at right) because it is smaller and more comfortable to operate in the forward mode, though the Ridgid works better for backing up the hose-clamp nuts.

STRAINER WRENCH

A strainer wrench is used for removing and installing kitchen-sink basket strainers, tub strainers and bar-sink strainers. There are two basic designs: the standard, malleable-iron Chicago Specialty forked and hollow-cross model, and the new Pasco "aluminum barbell" design (#4554). The Pasco wrench is a good design and provides for excellent purchase with the

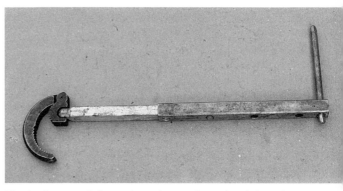

The basin wrench is used to grip nuts in under-sink and under-tub cavities where there is no room to maneuver an adjustable wrench.

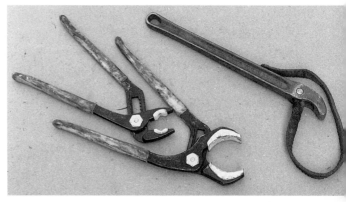

Rubber-jawed pliers and strap wrenches grip nuts, fittings and trim without marring the finish.

A no-hub coupling wrench comes in handy for tightening the clamps that secure rubber couplings.

A strainer wrench (this one made by Pasco) is an indispensable tool for removing and installing strainers in kitchen sinks, bar sinks and bathtubs.

A Rimster wrench is used to fasten the clips that secure a rim-mounted sink to a countertop.

12-in. adjustable wrench, when its pattern is compatible with the slot design and diameter of the strainer. This wrench works on most strainers, but now and then you come across a strainer with a hole pattern that doesn't mesh, and then you have to rely on the primitive forks of the Chicago Specialty wrench. I carry both models with me, which makes it less likely that I'll have to use a more drastic method of removal (i.e., cutting the strainer out with a reciprocating saw).

RIMSTER

If you're installing a kitchen or lavatory sink that is secured to the countertop with a mounting rim, the Rimster wrench is an essential tool. It has a long shaft that allows you to reach up inside the sink cavity, with a mechanism on the end for tightening the clips that secure the rim to the sink.

WATER-METER KEY

If your work involves a structure served by a municipal water service, you will need a water-meter key to be able to turn off the water in the event of an emergency. This key is a simple T-shaped tool with a slot in the end that fits over a small rectangular domino on top of the main water valve. Buy the stoutest key you can find. Usually the cheaper ones are made from small-diameter stock, and some meter valves are so hard to turn on and off that you can twist the cross-handle right off a cheap key.

Some utilities prefer that they be the party to interrupt water service to a structure, probably because their equipment can be damaged by a novice with no direction in performing this task. However, in a large city or large suburban area, it might take a long time to get the utility company to act, and if a burst pipe is flooding a customer's house, protocol isn't an issue. My utility has published a handbill that tells customers how to turn off the water service in the event of an emergency.

MANUAL CUTTING TOOLS

Plumbing entails a lot of pipe assembly, but first the pipe has to be cut. My pipe-cutting tools get used a lot more when I'm rough-plumbing a house, but you will need a selection of saws and other cutting implements when you're installing fixtures and appliances inside the house.

PLASTIC PIPE SAWS

Part of the appeal of working with plastic pipe, which is used more and more these days for fixture wastes and traps, is that it is relatively easy to cut. I use a Pasco #4333-H plastic pipe saw for cutting both ABS (acrylonitrile butadiene styrene) and PVC (polyvinyl chloride) pipe. The tooth set and pitch of this saw are designed to cut plastic pipe without overheating the material and causing the blade to drag. You can buy a wheeled cutting tool designed for plastic pipe that resembles a copper-tubing cutter, but I don't like this tool because it leaves a little lump on the end of the pipe that can cause interference when gluing on fit-

A plastic pipe saw is designed to cut both ABS (shown above) and PVC pipe. Using a miter box ensures straight cuts.

Copper tubing is cut with a wheeled tubing cutter.

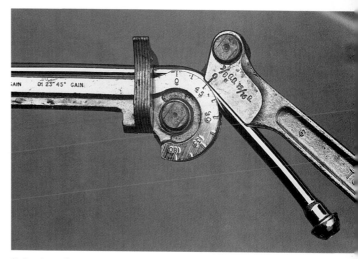

Tube benders are used to bend the supply tubes that deliver water to sinks and toilets.

tings. There's also a scissors-type cutter for PVC pipe up to 2-in. diameter, but I've found that this tool doesn't wear well.

COPPER TUBING CUTTERS

Copper tubing cutters come in various sizes. For finish work alone, you can get by with only one tubing cutter — I'd recommend the Ridgid #151, which cuts anything from ¼-in. copper refrigeration tubing for ice-maker lines to 1½-in. tubular brass. However, the Ridgid #104, which I reverently refer to as "the knuckle buster," is at times required for cutting installed ½-in. and ¾-in. copper tube where there is no swing room for the larger cutter's handle.

For troubleshooting, however, you'll need a variety of tubing cutters because you never know what size pipe you'll encounter — for example, 2-in. copper DWV (drain, waste and vent) and antique toilets' 2-in. flush elbows. I carry at least the Ridgid models #10, 20, 30 and 104. The larger models aren't cheap, but you're throwing away money if you don't buy good quality. Cheap tubing cutters tend to "thread" the pipe instead of tracking in one groove, and they'll also slip off the pipe causing the pipe to deform. If the pipe is out of round, it will be very difficult to get fittings on it and you'll risk leaks after soldering.

I should also mention here the tube bender, which is used for bending supply tubes under sinks and toilets. Tube benders are available in sizes matched to the supply tubes. They are not easy tools to master, so I suggest you practice on scrap tubing first.

HACKSAWS

I carry two hacksaws on my truck — one standard-size model and one mini-hacksaw. I use the standard-size hacksaw primarily on remodel work, for severing sections of old galvanized water lines, cutting thin-walled tubular-brass wastes, and so on. Good-quality hacksaws — there are many satisfactory models — have a rugged, rigid frame and a well-designed mechanism to maintain proper blade tension. One feature that I like on my Lenox brand tool is the ability to set the blade at a 45° angle (which comes in handy from time to time for sawing off old, corroded metal toilet-seat hardware).

The inexpensive mini-hacksaw has a couple of applications for finish work. I use mine to trim closet bolts when installing new toilets, and also to cut the chrome cover tubing that I sometimes slip over a brass nipple at the wall for an all-chrome finish.

AVIATION SNIPS

Aviation snips come in handy for trimming away sheet-goods finish flooring around toilet closet flanges and tub trap boxes. I also use snips to enlarge holes in chromed-brass escutcheons, to remove small (¼ in. or less) amounts of material from tubular-brass trap arms that cannot be cut with a tubing cutter, and to cut my own extra rubber gaskets for tub waste and overflow shoes. Other applications for this versatile tool include removing excess lengths of stainless-steel hose clamp on rubber couplings, cutting vent connectors for water heaters, and removing heavy-duty plastic packaging.

Most plumbing supply houses sell three versions of aviation snips with color-coded handles. A yellow-handled tool is for cutting in a straight line, but can also trim wide arcs. A green-handled tool is for cutting tightly arced right-hand cuts; a red-handled tool is for cutting tightly-arced left-hand cuts. I carry all three, but find that the yellow-handled snips can make almost any cut I need. I also have a large pair of traditional straight-cutting snips resembling scissors whose longer blades do a good job of cutting ⅝-in. and ⅞-in. dishwasher and garbage-disposer drain hose.

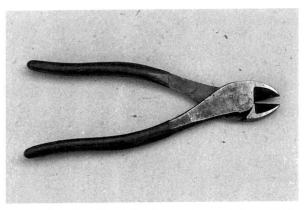

Diagonal-cutting pliers (dikes) come in handy for cutting narrow widths of thin metal, nylon strapping and string packing.

DIAGONAL-CUTTING PLIERS

I use 8-in. diagonal-cutting pliers, or "dikes," in finish work for trimming nylon cable straps that I sometimes use to group together air-gap and dishwasher drain hoses to keep them out of harm's way. When installing lavatory faucets with pop-up wastes I also use dikes to trim the lift strap on the pop-up waste to length (see the photo on p. 109). For troubleshooting and repair of leaking packing nuts on shower valves, I use the dikes to cut the round Teflon string packing that tends to roll when you try to cut it with scissors or a knife.

My 8 in. dikes are made by Diamond Tool. Klein Tools also make a good pair that are arced on the flat side, which gives your hand good clearance to make flush cuts.

POWER CUTTING AND DRILLING TOOLS

In addition to my manual cutting tools, I also have a jigsaw, a reciprocating saw and various drills. All these tools see much more service when I'm rough-plumbing a house, but there are a number of fixture-installation tasks where you'll need to reach for a power cutting tool or drill.

JIGSAW

In finish plumbing, I use a jigsaw to cut holes in fiberglass shower stalls and tub surrounds for single-handle tub and shower valves, and for cutting out countertops for sink installations. For these chores, I place some wide masking tape (and sometimes felt) on the saw's shoe so it doesn't scratch the finish as it cuts. There's also a scroll blade made just for plastic (with the teeth pointing down, instead of up), which prevents the plastic from chipping around the cut. Since these chores are not particularly demanding, any light-duty, two-speed jigsaw works just fine.

RECIPROCATING SAW

I use a reciprocating saw to cut any studs or joists that interfere with tub and shower drains, to cut countertops along a backsplash and to enlarge holes in cabinets that can't be accessed by a drill. On troubleshooting jobs, this saw gets used for cutting inspection holes in existing walls. When you need it, nothing else will do. I have tried every brand there is, and I keep coming back to the Milwaukee Sawzall. For plumbers, the Dual Range, Trigger Speed Control Sawzall (#6508) is an excellent choice for rough and finish work.

DRILLS

The heavy-duty Milwaukee Hole Hawg (right-angle drill) that I use extensively on rough plumbing has more power than I need for most finish work, but since I own one, I use it. (If you're not planning on doing any rough work, you could get by with a variable-speed, reversible ⅜-in. or ½-in. Milwaukee Hole Shooter drill motor with thread-on side grip handle.) You'll need a right-angle drill for boring holes in countertops, in fiberglass or acrylic shower stalls and through cabinet backs and walls for piping access.

Other companies besides Milwaukee make right-angle drills, some with a built-in clutch that releases when severe torque threatens property and limb. However, I find that these competitors are not as compact as the Hole Hawg for getting into tight spots, and do not have its power. I like the fact that the Hole Hawg has a constant slow turning speed, which is best for drilling holes larger than 1 in. in diameter. Also, the right-angle drill is flat sided, al-

A right-angle drill, with hole-saw and drill-bit attachments, is used for boring holes in shower stalls, countertops and cabinets.

lowing it to lie flat in kitchen-sink cabinet bottoms for drilling the holes in cabinet sides for running dishwasher drain hoses and water supply (which I like to include in one hole if possible).

A cordless drill is a convenience, not a necessity. I have one that I use for screwing the nailing flange on plastic bathing fixtures to the framing. It also comes in handy for drilling pilot holes in countertops, shower stalls, and so on. Anywhere you would use a ¼-in. or ⅜-in. AC drill for low-torque applications, the cordless (with a fresh battery) will usually work fine.

One other power tool I keep on my truck is a hot-glue gun. Troubleshooting will invariably involve opening up walls to get at pipes, so it's a good idea to carry with you a scrap of drywall and a glue gun for making wall repairs. I keep a 2-ft. square piece of ½-in. drywall on my truck for filling any holes that I must make in drywall. When I have finished a repair, I cut 4-in. wide strips of drywall and use the hot-glue gun to glue these strips around the inside edge of the hole, leaving a 2-in. lip. The hot glue sets up in seconds, and then I glue the original piece that I cut out of the wall back in place onto the 2-in. lips. I also use the glue gun to glue cardboard strips to the bottom of self-rimming sink edges for making a cutout template.

SPECIALIZED TROUBLESHOOTING TOOLS

Most of the tools I've discussed up to this point have uses outside the realm of plumbing. In this section, I'll introduce you to those tools that are used almost exclusively for plumbing, primarily for troubleshooting. You'll find detailed discussion of how to use these tools in Chapter 10.

PLUNGER

The plunger, also known as a force cup or plumber's helper, is the first line of attack against clogs in toilets and drain lines. Plungers come in different sizes and shapes, which translates into different degrees of effectiveness. Theoretically, the larger the cup, the more force you can project with it. If the cup's rubber is too soft, though, regardless of how large it is, it will not have the strength necessary to shove any generated shock waves forward. The stick handle will just go up and down, and you'll get nowhere. If the cup is too stiff, it will not conform to different-shaped fixtures and, again, forces will go sideways and not forward.

I like to use a plunger that has a thicker back and more pliable sides and a fold-out skirt on the bottom. My number-one workhorse is a Toilaflex (shown in the top photo at right), which is a Sealmaster product manufactured by the Radiator Specialty Company (see the Sources of Supply on pp. 178-179). This design gives good projection and provides a better seal on the compound angles found at the bottom of a toilet bowl. And the fold-out lip just fits inside a kitchen-sink basket strainer.

CLOSET AUGER

A closet auger is a tool that works like a corkscrew to retrieve items such as cloth diapers, paper towels and combs from the internal trap of a toilet bowl. My favorite closet auger is manufactured by General Wire and Spring (model #3FL-DH). Its beefy construction makes it indestructible. It has a long cable of heavy wire that will not kink when wound up tightly within the confines of a toilet's trap, and the retrieving hook on the end of the cable can pull out even difficult items like toothbrushes.

A plunger is an indispensable tool for removing clogs from toilets and drain lines.

A closet auger can be snaked down into a toilet trap to retrieve hard objects that are causing a stoppage in the toilet.

SNAKES

There are two basic types of "snakes," or drain augers, for clearing stoppages in drains. At one end of the scale is the standard home owner's hand-powered snake, which sells for just a few dollars. I've never found this tool effective, unless the clog happens to be head on — to get deep down into a drain line the snake has to turn corners, and the human hand simply can't turn the thing fast enough. At the other end of the scale is the powered mechanical snake, which is sold with various retriever-head and root-cutter attachments. This is a professional drain-clearing tool that sells for up to $1,000 or more. If you have a stoppage that a plunger or closet auger won't budge, I'd recommend you call a drain-cleaning contractor.

A seat wrench is used to remove worn valve seats from faucets.

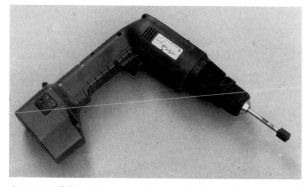

A seat-polishing stone can be used by hand or mounted in a drill to grind damaged valve seats.

A faucet-handle puller is used for removing faucet handles. (Photo by Bill Dane)

MECHANICAL FINGERS

I use mechanical fingers to retrieve small objects such as rings from traps that would be difficult to take apart. The tool has a long flexible cable, which houses the spring-loaded fingers; when the knob at the operator end is compressed, the fingers come out of the housing and can be manipulated to grab the object (see the photos on p. 161). These handy tools break easily, and I usually end up buying three or four a year. My present tool (#MPU24) is imported from Taiwan by Great Neck Saw Manufacturers (see the Sources of Supply on pp. 178-179).

SEAT WRENCHES AND STONES

A seat wrench, which is used to remove worn or damaged valve seats, is a round metal rod, bent to 90° in the middle with stepped thicknesses on each end. One end is hexagonal and the other is square. Seat wrenches are available at most hardware stores, and there are no significant differences in brands. I also carry a valve-seat assortment kit of 60 seats, made by the Chicago Specialty Company.

If a seat wrench can't extract the seat, you can try grinding the damaged seat with a seat-polishing stone. This tool can be operated by hand by turning the crank handle, or you can remove the handle and mount the shaft in a drill (see the bottom photo, above left). I use a Sealmaster polishing stone (Radiator Specialty Company), though, again, there are no significant quality differences among brands.

Another tool that you'll need for working on faucets and tub and shower valves is a faucet-handle puller. This tool is essential for removing faucet handles without damaging them when you need to troubleshoot leaks caused by failed valve seals, packing or stem washers.

A pipe nipple back-out is used with an adjustable wrench to remove damaged nipples from the wall.

PIPE NIPPLE BACK-OUTS AND PIPE TAPS

If you need to extract corroded or leaking nipples for angle stops and wall-hung kitchen-sink faucets, you will need an "easy out" or nipple back-out. There are a number of designs and brands, but I have found the Ace line to be the best (the Ace EX-7 is the size you'll need for ½-in. pipe).

If you're installing a water heater, you might need to use a ¾-in. pipe tap to rethread the female threaded connections on the top of the appliance (see the photo on p. 143). These are the connections where the hot and cold nipples are installed.

HAND PUMP

I use a small hand pump to empty water from toilet tanks in preparation for replacing tank parts, and to remove water from the tank and bowl before lifting the toilet. I pump the water into a bucket or a conveniently located tub. My tool of choice used to be a boater's plastic bilge pump, which worked fine until I backed over it in my truck. Now I rely on a Parr Brass Utility Hand Pump, manufactured by Jabsco.

SAFETY, COMFORT AND CONVENIENCE

Like any trade, plumbing has its share of potential risks. Although there's generally more danger of physical injury while running the rough pipes for a house, there are measures you should take when installing plumbing fixtures to ensure your safety. Some appliances require gas and/or electrical connections in addition to standard plumbing connections, and you should never perform this work unless you know what you are doing. Also, always turn off any appliance before you service it, and use electrical tools only in grounded outlets. Now let's look at some of the equipment available that can make your work safer and more comfortable.

PROTECTIVE GEAR

Eye protection should be taken seriously, especially when using power saws, drills and cold chisels. You should also wear safety eyewear whenever you're lying on your back threading on nuts and washers underneath a sink. Personal preference should reign in the selection of proper and effective eyewear — that way, you'll use it. I prefer to wear safety glasses with side shields rather than goggles, which tend to fog and scratch easily. I also wear a dust mask and ear plugs when necessary.

Hand protection is important for plumbers, both because of where we have to put our hands and because of the harmful chemicals found in sealants and fluxes. These days, many plumbers wear disposable gloves. If your skin reacts badly to the powders in latex gloves, you can purchase unpowdered latex gloves. Another choice is to use disposable vinyl gloves.

I once came close to a leg amputation because of an infection acquired from kneeling on contaminated floors while installing toilets. Since then I have worn knee pads. In addition to preventing contact with dirty floors, knee pads are also kind to old bones (and to finish flooring). I like the felt-lined, leather variety.

Plumbing can be hard on the back. Lifting heavy, bulky fixtures can really strain your muscles. Once it was unheard of for "real" men to admit a compromising physical condition, but now that vulnerability is accepted the sight of the back support (worn on the outside) has become almost chic.

Safety equipment for a plumber includes safety glasses, gloves, knee pads and a back support.

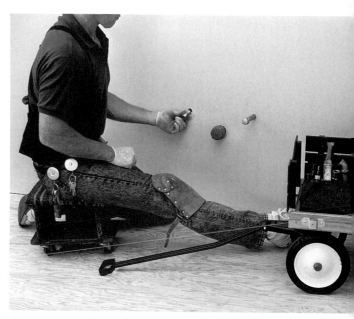

A toy wagon is handy for carrying materials, and a stool on casters is easy on the back and knees.

Wearing a head lamp allows you to work with both hands free in poorly lit areas.

One other piece of equipment that I find very convenient on large finish jobs is a Radio Flyer toy wagon, which greatly reduces trips to the truck and keeps nipples, angle stops and other materials close at hand. My little stool on casters (see the top photo at right) saves a lot of pain in the knees and back from stooping and kneeling.

And, finally, flashlights. I've tried every major brand and type and have yet to discover one that I consider well suited to all of a plumber's needs. One that I do use a lot in finish plumbing, however, is a head lamp, which allows me to work with both hands free in poorly lit areas. Mine's simply a small penlight (a "Mini-Maglite") attached to a Velcro strip that wraps around my head. You'll really appreciate one of these when you're lying in a dark kitchen cabinet trying to tighten up a faucet mounting nut in back of the sink.

CHAPTER
2

MAKING CONNECTIONS

Finish plumbing is all about installing fixtures and appliances. But before you can hook them up, you have to make the connections with the rough plumbing. This is where nipples, angle stops, escutcheons and bibbs — the nuts and bolts of finish work — come in. If you're simply replacing, say, a toilet or a kitchen sink, you may not need to replace these connecting parts. But if you are plumbing a new room or a whole house, the choices you make about nipples, angle stops and other fittings will have an important bearing on the finish job.

A nipple is a length of factory-threaded pipe that attaches to threaded fittings that were installed during the rough-plumbing stage. Nipples are used for pressurized fresh-water distribution, for gravity waste systems, and for connecting fuel gas at water heaters, cooktops and freestanding ranges, wall furnaces and direct-vent heaters, and gas clothes dryers. In this chapter, I'll focus on nipples used for fresh-water distribution. (Nipples for waste and gas systems are discussed in chapters 8 and 9, respectively.)

Angle stops, usually found under sinks and toilets, are small shut-off valves attached to the nipples. They are called angle stops because they change the direction of the water flowing through them from a flat 180° to a vertical 90°. A supply tube delivers water from the angle stop to the faucet or fill valve above. Straight stops are similar to angle stops, except that they don't angle the water flow.

Escutcheons are round discs of metal with a hole in the center that are slid over the nipples to provide a more attractive finish at the wall. Escutcheons are purely cosmetic, but they are an important touch.

Bibbs are simple hand-operated shut-off valves. There are two types: hose bibbs, which are faucets installed on the exterior of the building for hose hookup, and washing-machine bibbs, which are shut-off valves for the washing-machine hoses.

NIPPLES

Nipples are available in various lengths, diameters and materials. They range in length from just under 1 in. ("close" nipples) to 12 in. For fresh-water distribution, we use ½-in. and ¾-in diameter nipples. The ½-in. size is used with angle stops (for sinks and toilets), washing-machine bibbs (shut-off valves), tub filler spouts and shower arms, and sometimes with outside hose bibbs and any under-cabinet point-of-use electric water heaters. The ¾-in. diameter nipples might also be used with outside hose bibbs. For gas

Nipples and angle stops provide the connection between the in-the-wall piping and the supply tubes serving each fixture. The stubbed-off pipe in the foreground is a galvanized test nipple.

An escutcheon provides an attractive finish at the wall.

Threaded brass nipples, shown here in a handy nipple caddy, are available in lengths from 1 in. to 12 in.

distribution, ½-in. nipples are used with water heaters, clothes dryers and gas cooktops. A ¾-in. nipple is sometimes used with a freestanding gas range.

BRASS VS. GALVANIZED STEEL

Nipples for fresh-water distribution are normally made from brass or galvanized steel. While galvanized piping is okay to use in the wall, where it will remain untouched until the house comes down or a remodel occurs, I think it's a mistake to use steel for nipples. Nipples serving valves get a lot more abuse than in-the-wall piping, and brass is much more durable than galvanized steel. Unless your water supply is outright unfit to drink because of excessive concentrations of salts or other corrosive minerals, brass nipples will easily serve a house through three quality faucets — 60 years or more. Galvanized nipples, on the other hand, have a much shorter lifespan, especially if water conditions are poor. Under dielectric corrosion, which occurs when ferrous metal (e.g.,

steel) contacts nonferrous metal (e.g., copper), a galvanized nipple will always corrode faster than the copper fitting or a brass nipple. In my opinion, galvanized nipples are the cause of an enormous amount of plumbing-related damage to houses.

Also, when unthreading the "eccentrics" (the offset threaded fittings that thread onto the nipple) of a wall-hung faucet, galvanized nipples tend to break off flush with the end of the eccentrics' female opening or break off from a fitting inside the wall. When this happens, it is sometimes necessary to break open the finish wall to make the repair.

Brass is softer than steel, and when a brass nipple is threaded into a steel fitting it conforms to the confines of the fitting. When used in conjunction with copper water piping and brass, copper to FIP (female iron pipe) drop-eared 90° elbows (see the drawing on p. 21), brass nipples will last a long, long time, and you will have fewer leaks. The time that you save repairing leaks and the insurance that brass buys for the health of your structure are worth every cent of the price difference between brass and steel nipples.

ANGLE STOPS

When I started out in the plumbing business more than 20 years ago, it was common practice to use unplated brass angle stops for inside-cabinet installations where the angle stops would not be visible. For toilets, wall-hung lavatory basins and pedestal sinks, where the angle stops would be left to view, it was the practice to employ more expensive, chrome-plated angle stops. Today, you'll be hard pressed to find raw-brass angle stops, and if you do they may well cost more than chrome-plated ones. The only unplated brass angle stops I see nowadays are two-port angle stops for use under kitchen sinks (see pp. 22-23).

COMPRESSION VS. THREADED

There are two basic types of angle stops — compression angle stops and threaded angle stops (see the drawing at right). Compression angle stops attach to copper pipe with compression ferrules and compression nuts; threaded angle stops simply screw onto the nipple. Compression angle stops are designed so that they can be fastened directly onto copper pipe without need for a copper to FIP drop-eared 90° elbow. This does save time in the installation, but I prefer to use threaded angle stops because they cause less trouble down the road. If you use the copper to FIP drop-eared or high-set winged 90° elbow ("high-set" meaning that the wings are set higher than normal on the fitting) that I recommend, then you can use only threaded angle stops.

There are several things I don't like about compression angle stops. First, even when you use a soldered copper to copper drop-eared elbow screwed to solid blocking and then come out of the wall with

Angle stops are 90° valves that control and shut off the water service to the faucets and toilet tanks above.

ANGLE STOPS

COMPRESSION ANGLE STOP

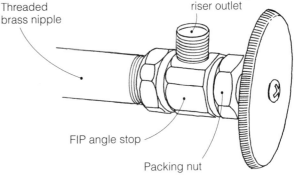

Compression nut

Compression ferrule

Compression riser outlet

Copper pipe

Male compression threads

Compression angle stop

THREADED ANGLE STOP

Threaded brass nipple

MIP or compression riser outlet

FIP angle stop

Packing nut

more copper pipe, there's too much movement in the pipe when you install the compression angle stop. The ears on the elbow do not provide the degree of stability that I want on my supply terminations. Second, the compression nut that holds the angle stop in place is also held captive on the pipe stub once it has been installed. If the plumber uses this angle stop for a toilet along with a plated-steel escutcheon that has rusted, you may not be able to get the compression nut off to replace the escutcheon. Also, around toilets the angle stop itself starts to look awfully unattractive all too fast, and it can prove impossible to replace. And compression angle stops in under-sink cabinets are sometimes next to impossible to replace without ruining the cabinet back.

Another problem with compression angle stops is that some designs do not use a standard compression thread pitch. These models usually have a corrugated chromed supply tube soldered right to the angle-stop body (and a unique plastic stem and packing assembly that is prone to leaks). If you use one of these angle stops and then later decide to replace it with a better quality one, you've got problems because the compression nut is captive to the pipe and won't accept a different angle-stop body.

A threaded angle stop, on the other hand, can be removed easily at any time from the brass nipple and be replaced. And, if necessary, you can position the angle stop closer to or farther from the wall by using a shorter or longer nipple, which comes in handy with changes to cabinets or to fixtures such as pedestal sinks and low-boy toilets.

Sadly, today's threaded angle stops aren't made to the same quality standards as American Standard, Crane or Mueller stops from the 1940s. The old stop had about three times as much mass, and the handle was actually designed to fit the human hand. When I find one of these old ½-in. FIP to ½-in. MIP (male iron pipe) stops in the demo piles from remodels, I retrieve them, re-washer and re-pack them, polish them up, and save them for my loyal customers.

While the female end of the threaded stop is ½ in. FIP, the male threaded shaft sticking out the top of the angle stop can be either MIP or compression type. This outlet is where the supply tube connecting the faucet or other valve attaches. With new ½-in. FIP angle stops, you will find four possible supply-tube

Old-style angle stops (shown at back right and in the foreground) have large round handles and are generally sturdier than their modern counterparts.

connection thread diameters and pitches: ½-in. iron pipe, ½-in. compression, ⁷⁄₁₆-in. compression and ³⁄₈-in. compression. For this connection, I like to use an angle stop with a ³⁄₈-in. compression outlet. The little brass ferrule and compression nut work well on the soft, smooth ³⁄₈-in. chromed-brass supply tubes that I like to use (see p. 100). The ½-in. compression nut and ferrule do not work as well with ½-in. supply tubes. They tend to leak at the ferrule because it has a tendency not to stay aligned when you compress it with the nut. One portion of the ferrule's edge peeks out from the hole in the compression nut around the supply tube, which means that it is misaligned. So, I do not use ½-in. supply tubes in new construction. The only instance where I would consider using them is for supplying water to legged tubs on repair or remodel jobs.

Chromed-brass adapters can be used to connect the ½-in. male threads of an old-style angle stop to a ⅜-in. compression fitting.

Chrome-plated brass escutcheons are available in a variety of inside diameters to fit nipples and trap arms at the wall.

If I'm installing a rebuilt old-style ½-in. MIP angle stop with ⅜-in. supplies, I use ½-in. FIP to ⅜-in. compression chromed-brass adapters (see the photo at top). These adapters thread onto the male pipe threads and reduce the connection to ⅜-in. compression. Since the adapters are small and chromed, they look as though they belong with the old angle stop.

ESCUTCHEONS

Traditionally, escutcheons were made of brass and then chrome plated (see the bottom photo at left). Sometime after World War II, manufacturers began making the escutcheons out of steel and plating them with chrome. Chrome-plated steel escutcheons begin to rust in a short period of time, which is why I never use them. I use only chrome-plated brass escutcheons for small-diameter (½-in. and ¾-in.) pipe.

You can't always tell chromed-brass escutcheons from plated-steel escutcheons, though some of the brass ones for ½-in. pipe are flatter. If I have any doubts about an escutcheon I use a magnet to test it. If it's steel the magnet will grab it; if it's brass or stainless steel, it won't. If you don't have a magnet handy, you can scratch the chrome off the back to see if there's brass underneath.

Escutcheons are also used on drainage nipples and trap arms at the wall. However, it is becoming almost impossible to find suppliers today who will stock chrome-plated brass escutcheons in these larger diameters. But it always pays to ask for them anyway. If you can't find them, you will have no choice but to use steel ones.

INSTALLATION

Now that you're familiar with the nuts and bolts of finish plumbing, I'm going to walk you through a typical installation in a new house, beginning with the nipples and then proceeding to all the necessary angle stops, washing-machine bibbs and hose bibbs.

To begin, I shut off the main water supply and open the existing hose bibbs (which I installed during the rough-plumbing stage for the convenience of masons, painters and other tradespersons) and drain the building down. Then I gather together a 10-in. slide-jaw pliers, 10-in. adjustable wrench, 4-in. pipe wrench, Teflon tape, a can of pipe dope (I always use Rectorseal), a tray of various sizes of brass nipples, 12 in. or more of ½-in. chromed-brass covered tubing, a stack of chromed-plated brass escutcheons and an assortment of angle stops.

To keep my work areas clean, I also like to keep a large sponge and a 2-gal. bucket handy. I carry a roll of kraft paper or building paper to lay over the areas where I'll be working. I strap on my cushioned leather knee pads and grab my rolling stool and head for the nearest unoccupied wet room.

As a general rule, I don't install sink cabinets. But I've found it to be good practice to be on the job installing nipples and angle stops in kitchen-sink and lavatory-sink cabinets before any tiled-in sinks, self-rimming sinks, Corian sinks or marble or granite counters have been installed. It's much easier on the back, neck and shoulders to be able to walk up to the cabinet and then just bend over to undo the galvanized test nipples than to try to stuff your body through a small cabinet-door opening.

INSTALLING NIPPLES

When I plumb a new home or an addition, I always use rigid copper pipe for the water lines. I then solder a drop-eared 90° fitting on the pipe, inside the wall, at the fixture locations. Next I thread a galvanized test nipple into the female iron pipe threads of the 90° fitting. (For detailed information on running the water lines, see *Plumbing a House,* this book's companion volume.)

When I come back to do the finish plumbing, I begin by removing the galvanized test nipples and replacing them with permanent brass nipples. A 4-in. long nipple will almost always bring you out far enough past a cabinet back if you have screwed the drop-eared 90s to 2x4 blocking inside the wall. If it's a deeper wall and/or the cabinet back is recessed farther into the cabinet to accommodate a profiled kickboard over a tile cove, you'll need to have a selection of nipples to try. It's cheaper to make a deal with the plumbing supplier and bring a whole stack of various-length nipples to the job and then return the ones you don't use than to run back and forth to the supplier. If you are a builder and will eventually find uses for an assortment, it's nice to have a full nipple tray of, if nothing else, ½-in. brass nipples.

I wrap the threads on all nipples with four layers of Teflon tape, following the spiral direction of the threads. (If you wrap Teflon tape onto the nipple in the opposite direction, you'll merely remove the tape when you thread it into a female threaded fitting.)

MAKING SUPPLY-SIDE CONNECTIONS

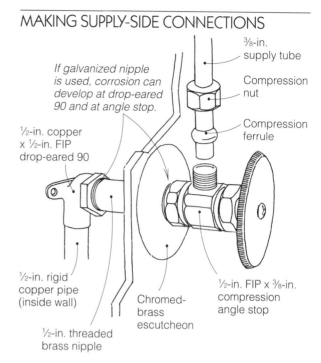

⅜-in. supply tube

Compression nut

Compression ferrule

If galvanized nipple is used, corrosion can develop at drop-eared 90 and at angle stop.

½-in. copper x ½-in. FIP drop-eared 90

½-in. rigid copper pipe (inside wall)

½-in. threaded brass nipple

Chromed-brass escutcheon

½-in. FIP x ⅜-in. compression angle stop

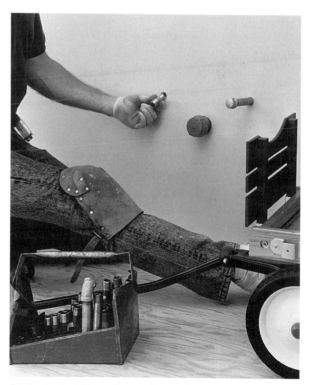

Begin the installation by replacing the capped galvanized test nipples with permanent brass nipples.

I then put pipe dope on all threaded female openings prior to threading the nipple in. Applying the pipe dope is a major step in reducing leaks at these joints.

For now, I leave the galvanized test nipples in the shower-arm and tub-spout drop-eared 90° elbows. These nipples can be removed at any time after the water is back on by just turning off the valves.

INSTALLING ESCUTCHEONS

Once the brass nipple is threaded in place, you can install the escutcheon. The hole on the backside of the escutcheon has a scalloped lip, which is designed to grip the nipple and keep the escutcheon in a true vertical position, up against the wall or cabinet back. These little scallops must point inward slightly to apply pressure to the nipple in order to accomplish their task. When you try to slide the escutcheon onto the nipple, in many cases the scallops prevent you from doing so. To get around this problem, I flip the escutcheon over and shove it onto the nipple backward, with the scallops pointing out toward me. I push it on only a short distance and then wiggle and rotate it simultaneously, which bends the scallops back slightly and makes it easier to install the escutcheon when I flip it back over. When handling escutcheons, always be careful of the outside edge, which can be sharp.

INSTALLING ANGLE STOPS

With the nipple and escutcheon installed, the next step is to mount the angle stop. If you want the escutcheons, angle stops and supply tubes to have matching trim, you may need to cut a short piece of chrome-plated brass cover tubing to slide over the nipple before threading on the angle stop. Chromed-brass shower-curtain rod often suffices for ½-in. nipples. Be sure to have at least five threads showing past the end of the cover tubing. It's not essential to have the angle stop touching the tubing, hiding every hint of nipple underneath. Getting the cover tubing within ¹⁄₁₆ in. of the angle stop is fine for all under-cabinet trim. Today's angle stops are so much smaller than traditional angle stops that the cover tubing is slightly larger on the diameter than the angle stop. So when they're touching, you'll notice that the tubing wall is exposed slightly at the corners and sides of the octagonal body.

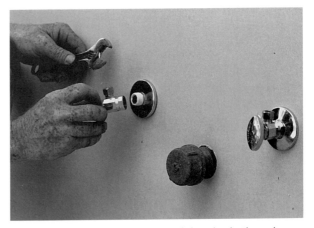

With the escutcheon in place and the nipple threads wrapped in Teflon tape, thread the angle stop onto the nipple.

In the kitchen, you might need to make connections to send water to a dishwasher or an ice maker. Many codes no longer allow the use of angle stops that have two supply outlets and only one handle and stem, which shuts off both outlets at the same time. These angle stops were used primarily on the hot nipple under kitchen sinks to send water to both the kitchen-sink faucet and the dishwasher. Then, as ice makers in refrigerators became more common, plumbers also started putting two-outlet angle stops on the cold nipple for both the sink faucet and the ice maker. In recent years, angle-stop manufacturers have begun producing a double-stem, double-handle angle stop with two outlets that attaches to the hot or cold nipple. This setup allows each of the outlets to be regulated separately, although the valve is attached to just one nipple. In theory these angle stops sound good, but I've had to stop installing them because too many were defective and leaked.

Lately, I have begun to install a brass tee on the end of the brass nipples, with close brass nipples in each barrel onto which I thread individual angle stops (see the drawing on the facing page). I've had much better luck with these than with the two-outlet angle stops. So if you're plumbing a new house, I suggest that while you're installing all the angle stops you install a ½-in. brass tee with two short ½-in. brass nipples on each nipple at the kitchen sink.

ANGLE STOPS UNDER THE KITCHEN SINK

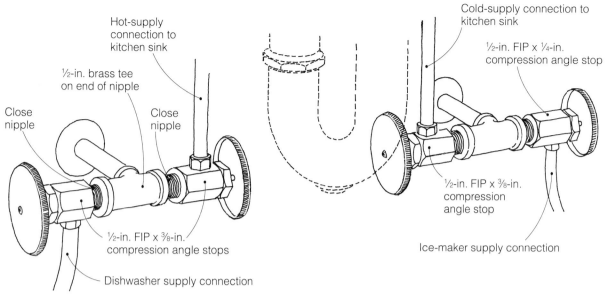

Hot-supply connection to kitchen sink

½-in. brass tee on end of nipple

Close nipple

Close nipple

Cold-supply connection to kitchen sink

½-in. FIP x ¼-in. compression angle stop

½-in. FIP x ⅜-in. compression angle stops

Dishwasher supply connection

½-in. FIP x ⅜-in. compression angle stop

Ice-maker supply connection

Plumbers can run into trouble when they plumb a bathroom strictly according to the details on the bathroom elevation drawings, only to discover on their return visit that the client, builder or architect has had a change of heart and selected a different cabinet. The water lines may now prevent the drawers of the new cabinet from closing, or the nipple may run straight into a back vertical or horizontal support (see the photo at right). If your 4-in. long brass nipples protruding out of the wall would hold the angle stops off the wall farther than they need to be, you could try using shorter nipples. This might allow you to fit behind the drawers, but the local authority might also require that the angle stops be in plain view, over closer to the faucet connections. If you have to move them, you can try threading brass 90° elbows onto the shorter nipples. Then you could use cut-to-length copper tube with male iron pipe (MIP) adapters soldered on each end. Thread one end into the brass 90s and re-thread the angle stops onto the other ends that are now poking in closer to the sink area. If this ploy doesn't work satisfactorily, you'll just have to have a carpenter remove the cabinet and then you can open up the wall and move the piping over to where it now has to be.

Water lines may need to be run away from the backs of drawers if changes were made to the cabinetry after the bathroom plans were drawn up. (Photo by Bill Dane)

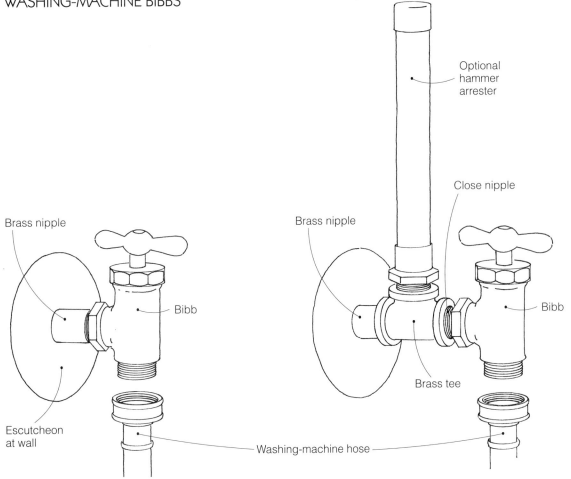

Optional hammer arrester

Close nipple

Brass nipple

Brass nipple

Bibb

Bibb

Brass tee

Escutcheon at wall

Washing-machine hose

INSTALLING WASHING-MACHINE BIBBS

In the laundry room, replace any galvanized test nipples with brass nipples, and add escutcheons and cover tubing and washing-machine bibbs. Washing-machine bibbs differ from ordinary hose bibbs in that the threaded hose connections hang straight down. This design keeps the hoses closer to the wall and re-lieves damaging pressure on the hoses at the metal connections. If you use hose bibbs (and you can if you have the room), the appliance hoses, besides hanging much farther out from the wall, may de-velop premature cracks at the metal connections be-cause the weight of the hoses bends the rubber on such a tight arc at the swaged metal connections. Usually, you're fighting for every inch of available depth for washing machines installed in the typical alcove off a hallway or country kitchen. If you want

to hide your bibbs below the top of a console, they should be on nipples that protrude no more than 1 in. past the escutcheon.

If you're not worried about the bibbs being vis-ible, you can rough them in higher (above the con-sole where you'll be able to keep an eye on them for drips), let the nipples run longer and use chromed-brass cover tubing, escutcheons and generic, dull-chromed washing-machine bibbs. Using the longer nipples gives your hands much more room to actu-ate the valves, and it's easier on your knuckles too. You can even find deluxe polished-chrome washing-machine bibbs that look great exposed on the wall (available from the Chicago Valve Company — see Sources of Supply on pp. 178-179). If you have a full-sized laundry room or a deep alcove where the ma-chines could sit well out from the wall, then you

Hose bibbs and washing-machine bibbs, which do not require angle stops, are threaded onto nipples or directly to the in-the-wall piping. The bibbs shown in the top row are an FIP no-kink drain valve, a standard FIP hose bibb, a long-shank standard hose bibb and a standard MIP hose bibb; at bottom are two washing-machine bibbs.

have room to use a washing-machine water-hammer arrester (I recommend the Watts #150HA) on the back hose connections of your machine. This device prevents the annoying pipe noise caused by the abrupt opening and closing of valves.

One final note on washing-machine hookup: If you are supplying the washer's supply hoses, make sure you buy hoses with solid-brass threaded connectors. Some companies sell washing-machine hoses with plated-steel connectors, which frequently rust and leak.

INSTALLING HOSE BIBBS

Once I've installed the washing-machine bibbs, I go around the perimeter of the building and pull out any remaining test nipples and install hose bibbs. I try to set the sill flanges or copper to FIP drop-eared adapters (¾-in., ½-in. or reducing) to a depth that allows the installation of long-shanked hose bibbs. In this way I can thread the bibb right into the fitting instead of using another brass nipple and FIP hose bibb, which is just one more avoidable joint. In cold climates, you should install freeze-resistant hose bibbs, the lengths of which are determined by local

HOSE-BIBB INSTALLATION

STANDARD HOSE BIBB

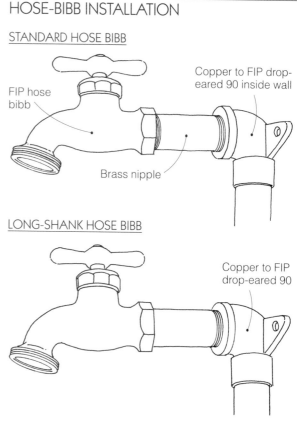

FIP hose bibb

Copper to FIP drop-eared 90 inside wall

Brass nipple

LONG-SHANK HOSE BIBB

Copper to FIP drop-eared 90

conditions. These long-shanked bibbs have a washer and seat at the end of shank, which when installed is inside the heated structure. After all the angle stops and bibbs are installed, go back and check each one to make sure that they are all closed.

If necessary, you can turn the water supply back on now, but if you can wait, go ahead and disconnect the water-heater test loop and install escutcheons and ball valves so you can get the water back on and leave it on (see pp. 140-146 on water-heater installation). In rough plumbing, I loop the hot and cold water stub-outs for the water-heater supply, either with rigid copper pipe or with a flexible water-heater connector. The loop needs to be removed before the water heater is installed. If the loop was made with rigid copper, I saw it away with a mini-hacksaw or cut it with a copper-pipe tubing cutter. If I used a flexible water-heater connector, it will merely unthread from the male pipe adapters that I soldered to the ends of the copper stub-outs.

Before you turn the water service back on, open the hose bibb closest to the main building supply shut-off. This is an important safety measure that will relieve most of the pressure on the house system. You can then take a quick run through the house and check all the new nipples, angle stops and bibbs. With only limited pressure on the system, any leaks or oversights won't cause serious damage before they are discovered.

If there are no leaks or open valves, let the pressure build in the system by slowly turning off the hose bibb. This lets the system stretch and adjust to the incoming pressure comfortably, instead of receiving a hard jolt if you hadn't left a valve open outside. When the outside bibb is fully turned off, I then go back around again and check all the connections for drips.

TOO MUCH PRESSURE?

In closing this chapter, I want to give you some advice about protecting your home from high-pressure water leaks. If you live in a house with high water pressure, there are a number of devices you can install on the water-supply line to reduce the pressure; these include pressure-reducing valves, pop-off valves and temperature and pressure relief valves.

PRESSURE-REDUCING VALVES

If you live in the country and depend upon a private well to supply your home with water, excessively high water pressure is probably not a problem. However, in cities and suburban areas served by a municipal water system, sometimes the water pressure exceeds limits deemed safe by most plumbing codes. As a rule, 80 psi (pounds per square inch) is the top threshold for an unregulated, residential building's water system. Any greater pressure would need to be harnessed by a pressure-reducing valve or regulator, which is a little device that I install when necessary on the water-supply line at an exterior wall. (In cold climates, the regulator should be installed in the basement or cellar to protect against freezing.)

Most pressure-reducing valves are preset at the factory to reduce the incoming pressure to about 50 psi to 60 psi. The pressure-adjustable valve has an adjustment screw on top, which when threaded inward (clockwise) relaxes its controlling effect and allows water at a higher pressure to pass through. When the adjustment screw is unthreaded (counterclockwise), the regulator increases its control, lowering the pressure of the water passing through it.

Most pressure-reducing valves use a rubber diaphragm in the process of reducing the pressure. Eventually this diaphragm will rupture, and the valve will no longer be capable of maintaining the lower pressure. The higher the water pressure the valve is controlling, the sooner this usually occurs.

POP-OFF VALVES

Because pressure-reducing valves pose a threat of failure, you might want to add another line of defense if you need to harness dangerously high water pressures (80 psi and above). (In one particular neighborhood near me, I replaced valves less than a year old that were trying to control water pressures of 150 psi.)

A temperature and pressure relief valve provides an extra measure of security against high water pressure.

A pressure-reducing valve installed on the water-supply line helps to protect a structure from high-pressure water leaks.

This backup device is known as a pop-off valve. The pop-off valve doesn't reduce the water pressure but has a calibrated spring inside that is overpowered by high pressure. When the water pressure exceeds the design limit of the spring, the valve "pops off" and abruptly dumps the high-pressure water, thus relieving the pressure on the house's piping. Pop-off valves can be bought either with a single, preset pressure rating (my preference) or with a variable pressure rating.

In temperate climates, the pop-off valve can be installed on a tee's branch in front of an outside hose bibb, or at the exterior terminus of a separate branch line run from the house's main cold-water line to the perimeter of the building. Pop-off valves are not freezeproof, and in cold climates should be installed only where they will not freeze. The discharge port of the pop-off valve has FIP threads, into which you can attach piping and create a discharge line to run to the outside of the building.

TEMPERATURE AND PRESSURE RELIEF VALVES

On a few occasions I have found that pop-off valves did not stand up to the pressures for which they were intended, but leaked at a lower pressure or did not actuate until a considerably higher pressure was attained. As with all mass-manufactured items, now and then you'll come across a dud. If it happens more than once, I may then install a temperature and pressure (T&P) relief valve on the cold-water line. The T&P valve is similar to the pop-off valve in that it is supposed to release water for excessive temperature and/or excessive pressure. Although the temperature-regulating aspect of the valve is wasted for this application, the T&P valve tends to be more dependable than the pop-off valve for cold water only. (For a discussion of the use of T&P valves on water heaters, see pp. 143-145.)

FIXTURES AND FIXTURE MATERIALS

Plumbing fixtures are available in a wide variety of materials, and choosing the best material for each fixture is an important part of quality plumbing. Over the long term, quality fixtures are actually more economical to install because they require replacement far less frequently than inferior models. And if you're choosing fixtures for new residential construction, now's the time to install the best you can afford. Getting a quality fixture that will last a lifetime into the house before all the stud walls are up is a lot easier than having to maneuver around solid walls to replace a defective fixture a few years down the road.

When I refer to fixtures, I mean bathtubs, manufactured shower stalls and shower pans, combination tub/showers, sinks, toilets and bidets. Faucets, valves, tub waste and overflows and sink wastes are not considered fixtures and are discussed in later chapters.

PORCELAIN

Porcelain, or vitreous china, is a timeless material, one that we've grown accustomed to and comfortable with. In its luster and brittleness, porcelain is like glass, and we learn quickly that it is fragile. But, given that it is treated with relative care, porcelain ages more gracefully than iron, steel or plastic.

The most common plumbing fixtures made of porcelain are toilets, bidets and sinks. Built-in and full-sized porcelain bathtubs are very rare, and because of this material's vulnerability to shock, kitchen sinks are no longer made from it in any significant quantity. A dish dropped on edge can and did destroy many a porcelain kitchen sink. But a porcelain lavatory sink bowl, which is much less likely to be hit by a heavy falling object, is still a very viable choice. And, although you might not be able to detect a sink's composition, a porcelain sink seems to present a warmer, more regal air than its iron, steel and plastic competitors.

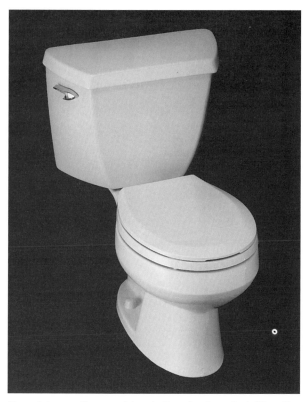

Porcelain, or vitreous china, is the classic material for all styles of toilets. (Photo courtesy of Kohler)

Like toilets, bidets are made almost exclusively of porcelain. (Photo courtesy of Kohler)

TOILETS

Toilets are made almost exclusively of porcelain. A few companies have tried manufacturing residential toilets out of cast iron, cast aluminum and, most recently, plastic, but none of these designs has been well accepted. Porcelain remains the ideal material for creating a complex, doubled-walled shape.

All porcelain toilets have a glazed, lustrous exterior finish. Better-quality toilets also have a glazed internal passageway, which provides for less friction of fluids and wastes flowing through it (but costs more to fire). Quality porcelain tanks and bowls are also made with generous wall thicknesses (regardless of price, none of today's offerings equal the thicker quality of old-style toilets). Another feature of a good flushing toilet is a large-diameter outlet. There is a raised ring, or "horn," around the bottom outlet of a toilet bowl. The older, better-flushing toilets of yesteryear had an inside horn diameter of 3 in. or more. Today, you are lucky to find a toilet with an opening greater than 2⅜ in.

BIDETS

Bidets, which like toilets are almost exclusively porcelain, can be relatively expensive to buy and to install. The more expensive bidets have an in-the-wall valve with a sprinkler, or "rose," in the bottom of the pan. The least expensive have a shelf-mounted valve, with no sprinkler (see pp. 74-75). In my opinion, owning one of these fixtures dictates that the customer be a real enthusiast, and one whose budget keeps pace with his or her worldly tastes. Hand-held-shower manufacturers, such as Alsons Co. (see the Sources of Supply on pp. 178-179), offer bidet attachments with quick-disconnect features that allow you to change from a hand-held shower head to a hand-held bidet fitting in seconds. I advise my customers to try one of these before deciding that they want the floor-mounted model.

Porcelain is a popular choice for all styles of lavatory basins, including self-rimming (top), wall-hung (middle), underhung (bottom) and pedestal (right).
(Photos courtesy of Kohler)

SINKS

Porcelain sinks are available in many styles, which are defined by how they are installed: cabinet-mounted (including self-rimming, rim-mounted, tiled/mudded-in and underhung), wall-hung and pedestal. The vast majority of lavatory basins for new homes are cabinet mounted, and of these the self-rimming style is generally the easiest to install. The pros and cons of the various methods of sink mounting are discussed at greater length in Chapter 6. A big factor in deciding whether to buy a porcelain basin is whether or not small children will be around, since porcelain will chip if hit hard enough. On the other hand, cabinet-mounted porcelain sinks generally cost less than basins made of other materials. An additional advantage of the self-rimming sink, which does not require a metal mounting rim to hold it in the cabinet, is that it is easy to replace.

If you are considering installing a new, commercially manufactured wall-hung or pedestal sink, porcelain will probably be the only material that you'll find being used for this sink design today. (Cast iron was used in the past.) Things to look for in a pedestal sink are the quality of the material, how well the bowl mates to the pedestal and how well the finished product maintains a trueness of shape. Imports now dominate the pedestal-sink market. I've found that Northern European designs are generally on a par with domestic brands, whereas Asian imports tend to be inferior.

CHECKING FOR DEFECTS

Porcelain fixtures have a high rate of failure in the manufacturing process. If the defect is not obvious, the manufacturer will many times ship the fixture anyway. So, you should always unbox your purchase at the supply house and check it over very carefully before accepting it. The most common defect for porcelain fixtures is physical deformity, followed by flaws in the finish. A defective toilet might have a bowl that doesn't rest flat on the floor, a bowl rim that sags at some point or a tank that doesn't rest level on the bowl. A pedestal-sink reject might have a pedestal that doesn't stand plumb, a bowl rim that sags, a depression in the bottom of the bowl that collects water that doesn't go down the drain, or a faucet shelf that isn't level.

All manufacturers make duds, but the more prominent name brands usually have better quality control, have a vested interest in protecting their name, and cull more of the bad ones before they escape to market. Kohler, American Standard, Eljer and Universal Rundle are some of the domestic brands that tend to be the most reliable, but I tell my customers to check any porcelain fixture before they buy it, regardless of the brand name. The less the item sells for, the greater chance you'll find some deformity.

Enameled cast iron is the most durable and comfortable material for bathtubs. (Photo courtesy of Kohler)

ENAMELED CAST IRON

Enameled cast iron has long been the most popular choice for bathtubs in quality construction, both for its durability and comfort, and it is also an excellent choice for kitchen sinks and lavatory basins. Cast iron heats up uniformly and holds the heat well; it maintains its shape, and is durable and quiet in use. It is also the heaviest fixture material, which can cause problems in installation. All things considered, I think that cast iron offers the best value for money of all fixture materials.

BATHTUBS

The old cast-iron legged tub is still the number one choice for serious bathers. New legged tubs such as the Kohler Birthday Bath and the Porcher import are good tubs, but they're no match for the original article that can still be found at affordable prices in plumbing salvage yards.

If you really like soaking in long, hot baths, I'd recommend that you install a floor drain, tile the floor and all the walls and hunt down the biggest old legged tub you can find. Use a modern in-the-wall tub and shower valve and forgo a curtain — you don't need one with the floor drain and tile walls. If you don't want to go to this extreme, the standard 17-in. deep built-in cast-iron tub should serve you well (see the photo above). And if you intend to use your tub primarily as a shower receptor, you can get by with the shallower, less expensive 10-in. deep tub.

Self-rimming kitchen sinks (top) and lavatory basins (bottom) in enameled cast iron are durable, attractive and easy to install. (Photos courtesy of Kohler)

well built and the tile professionally set or water will get under the quarter-round or bullnose tile, the wood will rot, and the weight of the cast-iron sink will cause the cabinet to sag.

For both lavatory basins and kitchen sinks, enameled cast-iron self-rimming sinks are my first choice. I like the durability of the cast iron, its heat-retaining property, its quietness of use, the color options available, and the self-rimming sink's ability to keep all splash water on top of the counter, without letting it leak down into the cabinet. Rim-mounted cast-iron sinks are also a good choice, as long as they are mounted on a smooth-surface countertop. Another advantage of cast-iron kitchen sinks, of any mounting, is that they are rigid enough to hold a garbage disposer in place without the risk of leaking.

CHECKING FOR DEFECTS

Care must be exercised when handling any fixture, and cast iron is no exception. Tubs (and many times kitchen sinks) are shipped in a wire reinforced crate, and it's a good idea to ask the supplier to uncrate the fixture for your inspection before you accept it. Shipping damage usually shows up as a chip on any of the upper and lower outside corners, but give the entire surface a good once-over while it's all easily visible.

When inspecting a cast-iron bowl for defects in the porcelain finish, pay special attention to the inside corners, which is where most enameling fails. If the sink is colored, the darker the color, the more susceptible it is to flaws in the corners. What you don't want to find are fracture lines in the color, below the top translucent surface. Many times you won't notice these lines when viewing the bowl in a poorly lighted warehouse, but when you get it installed in a well-lighted kitchen, the tiny fractures will be all too obvious. So, take a good flashlight with you when you inspect a sink and position yourself over the bowl, moving the light around at different angles and paying close attention to the upper corners. The fractures will appear as bright streaks that get deeper as you pass the light over them.

SINKS

In days gone by, enameled cast iron was used fairly extensively for wall-hung sinks and pedestal sinks, but today cast-iron sinks, both lavatory and kitchen, are almost exclusively for cabinet installation.

As with porcelain sinks, there are three methods for securing the cast-iron bowl to the cabinet: self-rimming, mudding-in (with tile or stone over the lip) and rim-mounting. As far as a watertight installation is concerned, the best performer is the self-rimming bowl. However, many people like a flat surface from countertop to sink so that splash water and food messes can be swept directly in, without being stopped by a raised edge. A mudded-in sink overcomes this obstacle because the sink is below the level of the countertop. However, on mudded-in installations, you'd better make sure that the cabinet is sturdy and

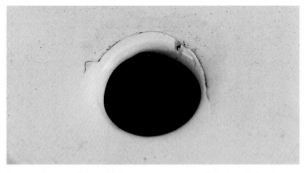

Enameled cast-iron fixtures are susceptible to defects around the faucet-mounting holes and drain hole.

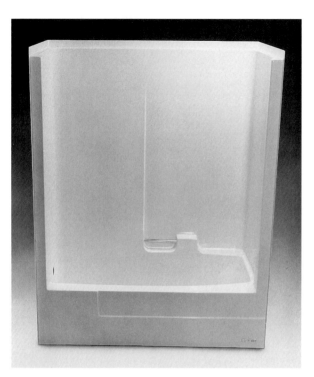

One inspection that you can make without uncrating the tub is to check the drain hole. Make sure that there's no dimple or bump on or around the edge of the hole, which would prevent the tub strainer from resting flat in the hole and result in leaks. Similarly, on a kitchen sink, look out for any bumps around the edge of the drain holes that will interfere with a good fitting of the basket-strainer lip or garbage-disposal flange. Also look for bumps or fractures around the faucet-mounting holes.

Once the cast-iron fixture has passed your inspection, I recommend that you have the supplier deliver it (if they offer this service, and especially if it's a tub). If anything happens to the fixture en route, it's the supplier's responsibility. When I'm doing a remodel, I usually try to time the delivery of the tub so that the driver and helper can take the old one away (for a fee, of course).

FIBERGLASS

The 1955 Chevy Corvette is the first fiberglass object that I can remember. Since then, the material has found its way into many areas of our everyday lives. As for plumbing fixtures, it's in shower stalls and combination tub and shower enclosures that fiberglass claims the biggest market. You'll be able to find a large price differential among producers, and even within their individual model lines. Since fiberglass fixtures require a labor-intensive installation, it simply isn't worth buying anything less than the best quality you can find.

Fiberglass combination tub/showers (top) and shower stalls (above) are generally less expensive than other bathing receptacles, but they are time-consuming to install and prone to failure. (Photos courtesy of Florestone)

Regardless of quality, however, I feel that fiberglass tubs generally make poor bathing receptacles. Not only are the shapes of most fiberglass tubs poorly suited to the reclining body, but because of fast temperature loss the water doesn't stay warm for very long. In addition, noise amplification from running water into fiberglass fixtures can prove a nuisance to those occupying adjacent rooms. Another drawback of fiberglass fixtures is that they cannot be cleaned with generic household cleansers — you need to use "soft-scrub" liquids and rub out the finish.

The supposed attraction of fiberglass fixtures is that they are less expensive than fixtures of more traditional materials. However, although the initial cost may be relatively low, installation costs can be greater than the cost of the fixture itself. And fiberglass fixtures have a much higher rate of failure than other fixtures. Very few fiberglass fixtures remain in service for a decade or more without requiring maintenance or replacement that would have been unnecessary had the fixture been of a more durable material.

The weakest point of any fiberglass shower stall or tub and shower enclosure is the floor, since plastic is inherently more flexible than iron or concrete. I've had to replace many fiberglass shower stalls and tub and shower enclosures (getting them out by sawing them into small pieces) because the floor flexed too much and the drain fitting wouldn't remain tightly sealed in the unit, thus producing leakage and water damage to the building. This problem is especially common when the fitting is plastic and the fixture users are heavy. Some manufacturers recommend that you mix up a batch of concrete and pour it on the floor before you set their fixture to add structural integrity. In essence, the manufacturers are asking you to complete a process that they should have completed before they took your money.

CHECKING FOR DEFECTS

My reservations notwithstanding, I know that a lot of people are going to buy fiberglass tub/shower fixtures (and I will concede that a plastic bathing fixture may be the only one you can maneuver up three flights of stairs). Here's some advice about what to watch out for before you buy. First, take a close look at the nailing flange that will hold the fixture in place. At the supply house, the fixture will likely have 1x4 wood spacers nailed across the front opening (as

Fiberglass shower stalls are often shipped with 1x spacers across the opening. Before buying, check for any cracks caused by the nails.

shown in the photo above). Look to see if the nails used to install the shipping spacers have caused any cracks that extend over and around the corner onto the wall of the fixture. Also check for any small chunks missing from any portion of the nailing flange.

Next, check the back of the nailing flange for flatness. If the flange has lots of lumps on it, it won't lie flat against the framing members (nor will the drywall that covers it). The nailing flange should also be in the same plane as the wall of the fixture. Lay a wooden yardstick against the inside walls to see how parallel the nailing flange is to the walls. If the flange turns inward, when the fixture is nailed or screwed in place it can crack or even break away from the wall. If the flange turns outward, it can be difficult to get the fixture into the framed opening.

Another thing to watch for is the thickness of the enclosure wall, which determines the structural integrity of the fixture. Manufacturers cut costs by reducing the wall thickness, but it can be difficult to gauge the thickness since it is common practice to spray the backsides and underside of the fixture with flat black paint. Use a flashlight to check for any thin spots in the wall, which can puncture and crack after installation. Also look closely at the front outside lower corners of a tub's skirt wall. These fixtures have been slid around from the time they left the factory, and any chips and cracks developed along the way are likely to appear here.

You should pay close attention to the drain hole (and the overflow hole on a tub/shower combination). After the fixture has finished curing at the factory, it's someone's job to take a hand-held grinder and grind a flat surface at these points to provide a flat mating surface for the rubber gaskets of the tub shoe and overflow riser (see pp. 45-46). Sometimes you'll find a groove on the surface that will make it difficult to obtain a watertight joint. Reject any fixtures that do not have well-finished surfaces at these points. One final inspection point: On the inside of the tub, there should be a recess around the drain hole. This recess allows for the depth of the tub strainer so that no standing water is left that cannot roll over the top of the strainer's flanged lip. Many fiberglass fixtures do not have a well-defined recess, and standing water collects around the drain hole as a result.

ACRYLIC

Acrylic plumbing fixtures have been competing with fiberglass for a share of the market for almost two decades. In its early days, acrylic did not enjoy the reputation that fiberglass had garnered. It eventually found its greatest acceptance in jetted bathtubs, or whirlpools, and now big-name domestic manufacturers are moving strongly with acrylic into the standard-sized household tub market. I seriously doubt that acrylic will prove any more durable than enameled cast iron, but if forced to choose between acrylic and fiberglass tubs, I would opt for acrylic.

Acrylic fixtures are cast from a liquid material, not unlike molten iron. The cast plastic's end product tends to be more dimensionally precise than fabricated fiberglass and generally has fewer shape defects. Its weight is also greater. But as with fiberglass, man-

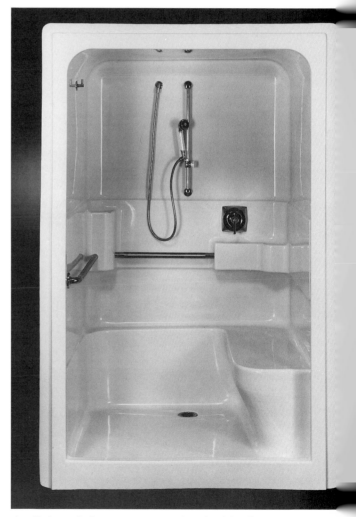

Acrylic is a relative newcomer to the plumbing-fixture market and is used for whirlpools (top) and barrier-free showers (above). (Photos courtesy of Kohler)

Acrylic is a durable material for shower pans and other small fixtures. (Photo courtesy of Kohler)

Two-piece enameled-steel tubs, which are more common than one-piece units, are prone to rusting along the joint edges.

ufacturers will often cut costs by producing thin-walled fixtures. Acrylic scratches very easily, so check carefully for shipping damage before purchasing a fixture of this material.

Acrylic has also been used for lavatory basins, although I haven't seen any of these bowls in my area for some time. I suspect that it is because their finish, though initially attractive, doesn't hold up to the wear and tear of prolonged use. Otherwise the base material is extremely strong in small shapes such as lavatory basins (and bar sinks and shower pans).

ENAMELED STEEL

Enameled steel used to be the material of choice for developers on low-budget construction. With the surge in popularity of fiberglass and acrylic tubs and showers, stainless-steel kitchen sinks and solid-surface, synthetic-marble lavatory basins, this material has lost a lot of its former market share.

BATHTUBS

Steel bathtubs are not my idea of a good material application. Like fiberglass fixtures, they are cold and noisy and prone to strainer leaks from a floor that flexes. Additional problems include rust and chipping. Most steel tubs are not fabricated out of a single piece of material, but made up of two or more pieces, which is why you rarely see a straight-sided one. The majority have a ledge that tucks under on the exposed skirt side, and from under this return another piece forms the skirt wall. These two-piece tubs are prone to rusting. The rolled-steel stock from which these fixtures are made is, by nature, much smoother than the surface of a cast-iron fixture prior to enameling. As a result, not as much porcelain is required to produce a smooth, finished exterior on steel. And a thinner surface, in turn, is more easily chipped.

Steel fixtures are shipped in cardboard boxes, not wooden crates. Sinks usually survive the trip and warehousing without many losses because they are smaller and lighter, but tubs suffer damage at a much higher rate. As with cast-iron tubs, steel tubs are prone to chipping on the outside corners and on the top flange that runs along the back wall side of the tub. You can walk into almost any plumbing supply house and find a stack of chipped steel-tub rejects. In many instances, the chip wouldn't be visible once the

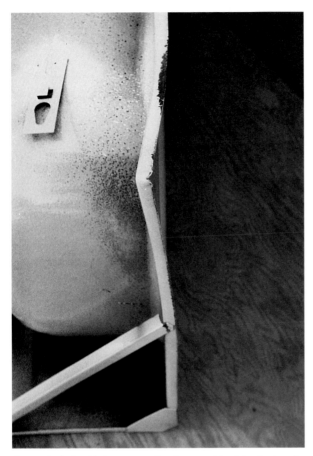

Enameled-steel tubs are easily damaged in shipping and should be inspected closely.

noise, heat loss and garbage-disposer problems. In the case of the latter, the bottom of the sink can both flex and ride up and down when the disposer starts up, which has a tendency to shake and twist tubular-brass wastes, in turn loosening up slip nuts and causing leaks.

Enameled-steel lavatory basins have an additional handicap with the overflow passageway. The overflow is the sealed channel that is supposed to catch any excess water introduced to the bowl and deliver it to the sink waste, below the stopper, before the water can flood the basin. On cast-iron, cultured-marble and acrylic sinks, this passage is molded or cast as an integral part of the bowl. On enameled-steel sinks it is a separate, stamped piece of steel that has been spot-welded to the bowl to form the passage, prior to enameling. The junction between the two invariably rusts out and starts leaking, and the bowl has to be replaced.

STAINLESS STEEL

In residential plumbing, the only stainless-steel fixtures you are likely to work with are kitchen and bar sinks. Stainless steel is rarely used in lavatory basins, in part for aesthetic reasons, but also because of the need to add an overflow channel.

There is a wide spectrum of quality in stainless-steel sinks. If you are considering the purchase of a stainless-steel sink on the premise that it requires less upkeep or is more durable than other material choices, you will realize these attributes only if you purchase a top-quality sink, which can cost at least as much as, and sometimes even more than, a high-quality enameled cast-iron bowl. Top-quality stainless steel has a higher percentage of nickel and chromium, which gives it superior strength and an attractive high luster. A top-quality stainless sink will be made of 18-gauge material, be fully undercoated and have no warp. It will lie flat in the hole, with the entire arc of all four corners touching the countertop even without the mounting clips installed.

Inexpensive stainless sinks are very dull, looking somewhat like pewter. They are made from lighter material, 22 gauge or less, and have no undercoating. The finish will be coarsely brushed, which streaks

tub was set and the wall system installed. Since the suppliers cannot sell them as "perfect" fixtures, most will give you a good deal on a chipped steel tub.

SINKS

Enameled-steel sinks are either installed with a mounting rim or mudded in. I have always felt that it was foolish to have a professional tile job done over an enameled-steel sink, because if the sink needs replacing (usually because of chipping), the tile will have to come up too. The expense for the tile setter will far outweigh the original savings for using this type of sink. A rim-mounted enameled-steel sink on a smooth plastic-laminate countertop is the only combination that I wouldn't try dissuading a customer from. Enameled-steel sinks share the same negatives as stainless-steel sinks (see below), namely

Top-quality stainless-steel kitchen sinks, shown here in underhung (top) and self-rimming designs (above), are durable and attractive fixtures. (Photos courtesy of Kohler)

badly. The inexpensive offerings are noisy and have poor thermal qualities. The bowl or bowls will be shallow, and the rim will not lie flat on the countertop, no matter how many extra clips you install.

One of the biggest customer complaints about stainless-steel kitchen sinks is noise, caused both by the water running into the sink from the faucet spout and by the sliding and colliding of dishes and cooking utensils in the sink. One way sink manufacturers try to compensate for this factor is to apply undercoating. A good undercoated sink reduces noise and holds heat better. Some sink manufacturers stick little pads of sound-absorbing material to the bottom of the bowls, but these are not as effective as the sprayed-on undercoating.

Another problem with a stainless-steel sink is its less than perfect adaptability for hosting a garbage-disposal unit. Waste-piping leaks, caused by vibration from garbage disposers, occur far more often in stainless-steel sinks than in cast-iron ones. Also, because of the relative thinness of stainless steel, the mounting flange of the garbage disposer has a tendency not to stay put or centered as well in the drain hole of a stainless-steel sink. You'll often need to add a second flat rubber mounting washer under the disposer flange when it is installed in a stainless-steel sink, because the flange's mounting screws are too short (see pp. 129-133 for more on garbage-disposer installation).

Stainless-steel sinks, though called "self-rimming," mount with the same process and clip design as rim-mounted sinks (see pp. 88-89). They are best installed on smooth plastic laminate over ¾-in. plywood or particleboard. If they are installed in conjunction with tile, they are best mudded in (i.e., set under tile with no extra rim or clamp system). When you consider the cabinet damage that can occur as a result of rim leaks, mounting a stainless-steel sink on top of tile that is not professionally set is a big gamble.

OTHER FIXTURE MATERIALS

In addition to the traditional fixture materials, such as porcelain and cast iron, and the newer plastics (fiberglass and acrylic), there are also a number of specialized natural and man-made materials. These include terrazzo, ceramic, marble, fused quartz and various metals.

TERRAZZO

Terrazzo, which is composed of marble chips embedded, ground and polished in waterproof concrete, is my favorite material for shower pans. In its natural color and finish (usually a yellow to beige or a light bluish-green marble chip in a white-sand concrete), it's certainly not as attractive as custom tile, but it has the best no-leak record of any shower floor. The drain fitting is cast into the material and uses a brass and neoprene compression joint (see p. 54). If you choose, you can have color-complementing tile set on top of the terrazzo. However, this should be done before the shower is used so a soap film doesn't inhibit the adherence of the thin-set tile adhesive.

A terrazzo shower pan, which comes with an integral solid-brass shower drain, is extremely rigid and won't flex under heavy loads. (Photo courtesy of Florestone)

Terrazzo pans are heavy — a 36-in. by 42-in. pan weighs about 380 lb. — so you'll need some help lifting and setting these brutes. Terrazzo pans are shipped in wooden crates, and I've rarely had a problem with any defective units. The one area you might check for damage is along the front edge.

CERAMIC

In recent years, vacationers returning from Europe and South America have been bringing back with them ceramic (earthenware) lavatory bowls. With their bright or one-of-a-kind color and patterns, these ceramic bowls are hard to resist. I've found that the Northern European varieties have usually been properly fired and possess a near-good temper, whereas the South American bowls are usually not as well fired and are generally softer. Great care must be taken when installing the waste and faucet on these pieces of usable art. One quarter-turn too many on the waste lock nut or the faucet-mounting nuts can pop the sink in half. Ceramic bowls are invariably too irregular for standard-sized mounting rings, and have to be custom-mounted to the countertop. These colorful plumbing fixtures make for a nice, cheery guest-room bath, but I wouldn't recommend them for high-traffic, family bathrooms.

CULTURED AND SYNTHETIC MARBLE

Cultured marble, which is primarily onyx or limestone chips mixed with polyester or polyurethane resins, has captured a large portion of the lower-end market for lavatory basins. One of the advantages of this material is that it can be cast into a sink and countertop as one piece, which eliminates the need to mount a separate bowl to a countertop and also gets rid of a common splash-water leak source. Cultured marble was being manufactured by small-shop operations for some time before DuPont saw the potential of such a system and began manufacturing their own much more expensive version. DuPont's product (Corian) is technically a synthetic marble rather than a cultured marble, but the end result is the same — a one-piece bowl and countertop. Whereas cultured marble is preferred by many do-it-yourselfers, synthetic marble is often installed only by specially trained and certified installers.

As with all fixture materials, there are some drawbacks. Cultured-marble sink/countertop combinations tend to have a rather thick cross section at the point where the predrilled factory holes for the faucet are located. Although this thickness makes the unit nice and strong, it can present problems for mounting some faucets that have shorter than normal fau-

Cultured marble can be cast into a sink and countertop as a single unit. (Photo by Peter Hemp)

cet connections (like Price Pfister's mini-widespread). You also want to make sure that the surface around the underside of the drain hole is level and smooth, with no large pits. Early versions of cultured marble would scratch, burn and stain very easily, though some manufacturers now produce a product that is sandable to remove blemishes. And finally, the plastics in some cultured-marble products are incompatible with plumber's putty, which will stain if used. In this case, you'll have to use some form of caulking instead when installing the faucet and waste.

FUSED QUARTZ

A beautiful, recent addition to the list of sink materials is fused quartz. Sinks of this material are composed of ground-up quartz or other minerals that are molded to a shape and then fired in a super-heated kiln until the materials melt and are fused into a solid. Moen makes a version called "Moenstone." There are several domestic manufacturers. Although the finished product is very attractive, I'm not yet convinced of the long-term durability of fused quartz. These sinks are expensive.

METALS

In designers' showrooms you may find some very beautiful, hand-crafted metal basins made from brass, bronze, copper and aluminum. Before you buy one of these beauties, consider the following potential drawbacks. For one, they are often incompatible with standard mounting practices, such as clamp-down rims that are made for industry-size standards. These sinks often don't have an overflow, which may be mandatory where you live, and their drain holes also may not be a standard size for existing manufactured wastes. In which case, if allowed to use one, you'll be paying top dollar for a one-of-a-kind fabricated waste, which may require a special inspection process. So check first with your local authority before purchasing one of these sinks. And, for installation, carefully follow the manufacturer's instructions.

CHAPTER
4

TUBS AND SHOWERS

On new construction, I begin finish plumbing in the bathroom, with the installation of the big, bulky bathing fixtures: the standard single-unit tub, plastic tub/shower combination, plastic shower stall or pre-fabricated shower pan. It's easiest to tackle these large fixtures before you have anything else in place in the bathroom, but even in an empty room they can present some installation headaches. In this chapter, I'll explain how to install bathing fixtures as painlessly as possible, both on a slab floor and on off-ground construction.

PROTECTING THE FLOOR

In addition to the difficulty of installation, another problem to be overcome with bathing receptacles is how to set each fixture so that its splash water doesn't find its way to the subfloor. On new construction, most builders want to get the bathing fixtures set in position before the finish floor is down. Unfortunately, this means that the floor installer has no option but to run the floor up to the fixture and then caulk or grout along the joint between them. Over time, this joint will inevitably open up and water will seep down to the subfloor.

A much more logical sequence, to the plumber at least, is to lay the finish floor down first from wall to wall and only then install the bathing fixtures (see the drawing on the facing page). By setting the tub and shower on the waterproof finish surface, you've blocked the splash water's path to the subfloor. You can caulk around the fixtures, and if in time the caulking fails any spillage will stay on top of the floor, not be pulled straight down to the subfloor. I realize that this sequence of completing the bathroom depends on the cooperation of the builder and owner; it may not be possible in every case because it involves rearranging not just the plumber's usual finish schedule but also that of other trades. If you're working on your own house, however, I strongly recommend that you work this way. Then you won't have to worry about having to tear out fixtures and walls in years to come when you need to repair a rotted subfloor.

When you're working on a finished floor, it's important to lay something on top of it for protection. I use a layer of paper — either water-resistant building paper or red rosin paper (both available in rolls of various widths from lumberyards and building-supply stores) — and a layer of Masonite. I carefully vacuum the finish floor in stocking feet before laying down

SETTING BATHING FIXTURES ON FINISH FLOOR

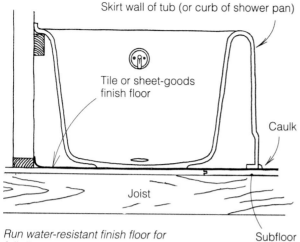

Skirt wall of tub (or curb of shower pan)

Tile or sheet-goods finish floor

Caulk

Joist

Subfloor

Run water-resistant finish floor for full dimension of room. Set fixtures on top of finish floor.

the paper. Leave a generous overlap between meeting sheets and tape the joints with a wide, high-tack masking tape.

Because there is nothing in this studwall room at this stage, and because most bathrooms are rectangular, it's a quick job to slice up the ¼-in. Masonite and lay it out on top of the paper. You will have to take care when cutting an access hole through the Masonite for the closet flange and the void in the floor for the tub waste. Making these cuts is the only slow part of the entire process. I tape the butted Masonite joints with silver-fabric duct tape. Now other tradespeople can come in with their equipment and supplies and work in the room without any harm to the finished floor.

SETTING A SINGLE-UNIT TUB

Installing a standard single-unit bathtub entails setting the fixture in place in the framed opening, hooking up the tub waste and overflow (W&O) and connecting the W&O to the trap and drain. (The trap is the bend in the drainage pipe that provides a water seal to prevent sewer gases from backing up into the

house.) The sequence of installation for a tub differs depending on whether you are working on a slab floor or off the ground. If you're installing the tub on a slab, you'll need to install the W&O on the tub before setting the fixture in place since you'll have no access from below once the tub is down. If you're setting a tub on a first floor over a crawl space or basement or on multi-floor construction (see pp. 52-53), you can position the tub first and then install the W&O from below.

INSTALLATION ON SLAB

To provide room for the trap under a tub on slab construction, a void has to be left in the slab at the time the concrete is poured. Inside this void there's a round or square tub box, or "trap box," which is either factory-made or constructed on site. During the rough-plumbing stage, the drain line was run through a knockout in the side of the box then stubbed off and sealed. When we come back to finish-plumb the house, it's down in this small box that we have to hook up the P-trap and make the W&O to P-trap connection. (The drawing on p. 51 shows all these connections.) But first, the W&O has to be installed to the tub.

INSTALLING THE WASTE AND OVERFLOW   On slab construction, where replacing the W&O on an existing tub can be an expensive proposition, it makes a lot of sense to purchase a top-quality W&O to begin with. I like to use a brass pop-up stopper type (see the drawing on p. 44). This W&O has a large internal passageway, which allows for a faster-draining tub and leaves a cleaner fixture. The internal lift-bucket variety is less expensive, but has a smaller passageway. Most plastic W&Os, which I would use only in very accessible locations, are either a toe-tap or lift-and-twist design. For more on tub W&Os, see the sidebar on p. 47.

To install the W&O, first maneuver the tub close to its final position in front of the framed opening. You can work with the tub either up on its skirt-wall side (on a piece of clean carpeting) or on a four-wheel piano dolly that allows sufficient ground clearance. If the tub is on its side, I install the tub shoe first, which acts as a support to build the rest of the system on. If the tub is upright, I begin by installing the

WASTE-AND-OVERFLOW OPTIONS

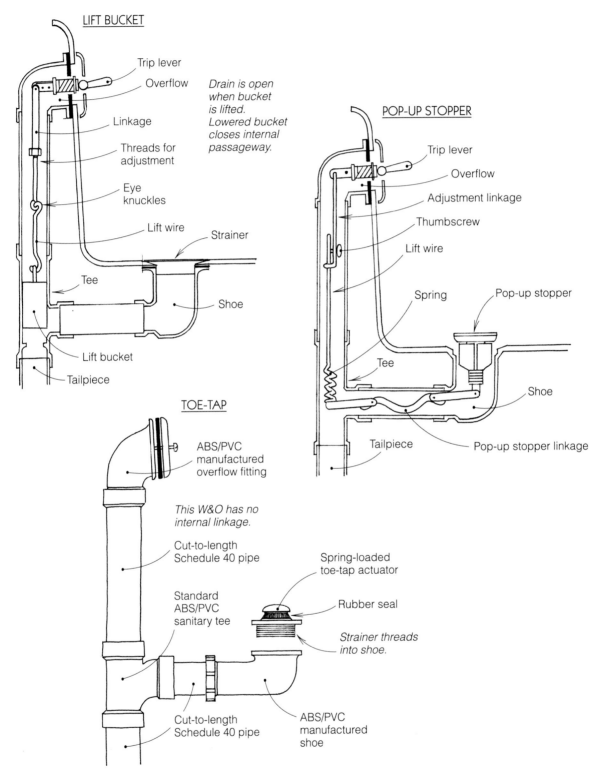

LIFT BUCKET

Trip lever

Overflow

Linkage

Threads for adjustment

Eye knuckles

Lift wire

Strainer

Tee

Shoe

Lift bucket

Tailpiece

Drain is open when bucket is lifted. Lowered bucket closes internal passageway.

POP-UP STOPPER

Trip lever

Overflow

Adjustment linkage

Thumbscrew

Lift wire

Spring

Pop-up stopper

Tee

Shoe

Tailpiece

Pop-up stopper linkage

TOE-TAP

ABS/PVC manufactured overflow fitting

This W&O has no internal linkage.

Cut-to-length Schedule 40 pipe

Standard ABS/PVC sanitary tee

Spring-loaded toe-tap actuator

Rubber seal

Strainer threads into shoe.

Cut-to-length Schedule 40 pipe

ABS/PVC manufactured shoe

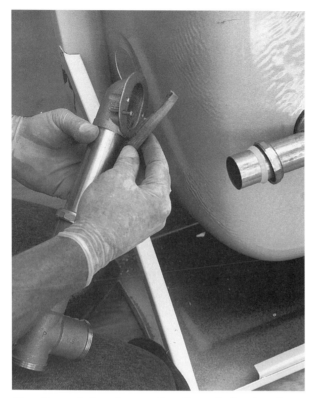

Place the gasket on the overflow flange before hanging the overflow tube. Make sure that the thickest part of the gasket is in the correct position.

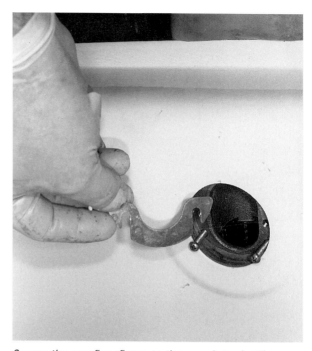

Secure the overflow flange to the opening using the hardware provided with the W&O (here, two screws and a yoke).

overflow tube. Whichever method you use, you must first do a test assembly to determine how much you need to trim from the tub-shoe tubing.

First, install the rubber overflow gasket to the top flange of the overflow tube (as shown in the photo above). One end of the gasket will be thicker than the other to accommodate the slope of the tub head or the angle of the face of the overflow tube's flange. You have the gasket positioned correctly when the overflow tube hangs closest to plumb. Then temporarily secure the overflow tube to the opening on the tub. Depending upon which W&O you are using, the method of attachment might be two screws and a yoke (see the photo above at right), a large, thin, threaded nut, or some other means.

If you're installing an extra-deep tub (anything over 17 in. deep), you'll need to attach an overflow-tube extension to the original overflow tube. This extension will be supplied with the W&O. Some extensions have a 1½-in. male-threaded end and slip nut

and slip-nut washer; others have a belled-end tube with extra O-rings to install in grooves on the original overflow tube. Slide on a slip nut and slip-nut washer on the bottom of the overflow tube (or tube extension), and then push on the longer-barrel end of the tee. Hand-tighten the slip nut to the tee.

With the shoe in one hand, slide it into the branch of the tee, making sure that the overflow-tube gasket is flat on the back of the tub. Then see how far away you are from having the drain hole in the tub match up with the threaded hole in the shoe. Tub-shoe tubing tends to be a little long for most installations, and you end up trimming it down a little. If you have any doubts, trim the tubing off little by little until the holes line up. Then take everything down and put Teflon tape on all the male threads and pipe dope in all the female threads (and in the slip nuts too). Now you're ready to install the W&O permanently.

Roll out a snake of plumber's putty about 6 in. long and ½ in. to ¾ in. thick. Wrap the snake under the lip of the strainer and gently press the strainer into place. Put pipe dope on the top flat lip of the shoe and on both sides of the flat washer that lies between

Brush pipe dope onto the lip of the shoe and onto both sides of its washer before installing the shoe and strainer (shown in the foreground) in the tub drain hole.

the shoe and the bottom surface of the tub. Push the strainer into the drain hole in the tub. If there's an etched name on the strainer, it looks best if the name is right side up when you finish the installation.

Using a strainer wrench in one hand to hold the strainer still, thread the washer and shoe onto the strainer with your other hand (see the photos at right). Tighten the shoe until the strainer is deep in the tub's drain-hole recess and the flat rubber washer is tightly compressed, leaving the shoe's tube pointing in the correct direction. Be careful not to tighten the two pieces so tightly that the washer squirms out of place between the tub's bottom surface and the lip of the shoe. This is easy to do if the washer is too soft. (I buy flat, corded, rubber-diaphragm stock from a wholesale rubber jobber to make custom washers for W&Os that come with unusually poor-quality, super-soft washers.)

Thread the shoe onto the strainer with one hand (top) while holding the strainer still in the drain hole with a strainer wrench in the other (above).

TUB WASTE AND OVERFLOWS

A tub waste and overflow (W&O) is the fitting installed at the tub head that carries waste water away from the tub, either through the tub shoe or through the overflow port. As with most plumbing fittings, my preference is for a brass W&O, of which there are two basic designs: pop-up and lift bucket.

In years gone by, Kohler, Crane and American Standard all made good pop-up stopper W&Os. Unfortunately, Crane stopped making them, and both Kohler and American Standard have recently changed their all-brass waste linkage to a partial-plastic linkage design. The shoe and strainer housing of the Kohler W&O is difficult to fit in anything but a Kohler tub, but their W&O is the most durable one available. It's worth taking the time to enlarge your tub's drain hole with a round file to accommodate it. Gerber makes a more affordable and smooth-operating pop-up style W&O. Similarly, Price Pfister manufactures a relatively inexpensive lift-bucket type W&O.

Regardless of brand, always read the installation instructions that come with the W&O — fixture manufacturers are constantly changing the design of their products, and you may have to modify the general installation

Tub waste and overflows are available in various materials and designs. Shown here (from left to right) are the top-of-the-line Kohler brass pop-up; Price Pfister's plastic lift-and-twist design; Casper's plastic (Schedule 40) W&O with toe-tap drain; and Price Pfister's brass lift-bucket design.

procedures that I outline in the text (see pp. 43-46, 48).

The only all-plastic (ABS or PVC) W&O I would recommend using is one made of a 1½-in. Schedule 40 sanitary tee and cut-to-length pieces of Schedule 40 pipe that you cement together. Gerber is the only company I know of that makes a plastic W&O with internal linkages serving lift-bucket and pop-up stoppers — all the rest are the slower-draining toe-tap or lift-and-twist style. The Casper W&O shown in the photo above is one of the better toe-tap designs.

Some ABS and PVC W&Os are made with a lightweight plastic tubing that's the same thickness and outside diameter as a tubular-brass tailpiece. Unlike the cemented Schedule 40 W&Os, this style threads together with plastic slip nuts and nylon slip-nut washers. I cannot justify using this product for an application that's so inaccessible once completed. Sometimes a professional drain cleaner will send a powered mechanical snake down through the overflow port on a tub to access the tub drain line, and these super-lightweight W&Os are so flimsy that they can easily break. If you're going to install a plastic W&O, make sure it's the Schedule 40 variety.

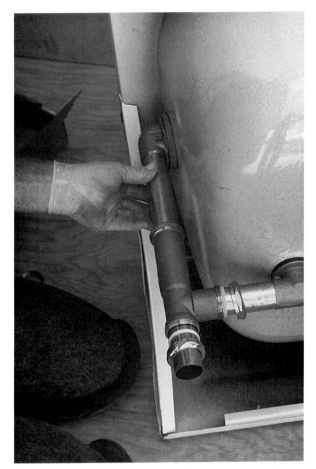

Assemble the shoe, tee and overflow, then secure the overflow tube to the tub opening.

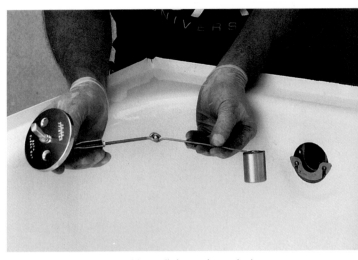

Install the lift bucket and lever linkage through the overflow opening after the tub is set and trapped.

Now slide the overflow tube into the Teflon-tape-wrapped tee and hand-tighten the slip nut. Slide another slip nut onto the shoe's tube and follow it with the slip-nut washer. Most of these washers today will be beveled nylon — make sure that you have the bevel pointed toward the tee. Slide the tee onto the shoe's tube and hand-tighten the slip nut. Then lift up the overflow tube and get it secured again to the tub, this time for good. Use the slide-jaw pliers and really snug up all the slip nuts. If you think that you (and a helper if necessary) can get the tub rolled over and set in place without letting the W&O contact the floor, you can install the tailpiece now. If it looks risky, wait until the tub is sitting over the void. You might as well wait until the tub is set and trapped before installing and adjusting the linkage and pop-up

or lift bucket because you need water to know when it is properly set. The instructions for your particular brand of W&O will illustrate how to do this.

SETTING THE TUB AND HOOKING UP THE WASTE
Once the waste and overflow is installed, you can set the tub in the framed opening. First, lift the Masonite out of the alcove and pull back the paper. I just fold the paper back and tape it down. (After the tub is set and the waste hooked up, you can flop the paper back up and cover the skirt wall with it. Then cover the tub with cardboard and plywood to protect the fixture from other tradespeople working in the bathroom.) Depending on the weight of the fixture, you may need a helper to maneuver the tub into position. The ledge of the tub should rest on 2x4 stringers nailed to the stud walls. You may need to notch the top edge of the stringers to accommodate the radius of the tub (alternatively, you can install 1x4 stringers in this case).

Now comes the tricky part: hooking up the waste inside the tub box. You invariably have to be a bit of a Houdini to reach through the valve wall down into the void — sometimes it seems that you can never get your head in just the right spot to see things as you would like to. And, if someone has unwisely designed a back-to-back (valve-wall-to-valve-wall) tub configuration, the installation will be a lengthy one.

Once the W&O is installed, set the tub onto the 2x4 stringers in the framed opening. Be careful not to damage the W&O as you maneuver the tub into position.

ABS pipe and fittings are joined with a one-part solvent cement, which is applied to the mating surfaces. (Joining PVC requires the application of a primer before the cement.)

Because the confines of the factory tub box are so small (see the drawing on p. 51), it's easier to be joining ABS or PVC plastic rather than no-hub iron or DWV copper in such tight spots. If ABS or PVC is not allowed by code in your area and you have to run no-hub iron, you'll probably have to adapt over to DWV copper so you can work with physically smaller fittings. Various options for hooking up the waste in all three drainage materials are shown in the drawing on p. 50.

If you're working with plastic pipe on slab construction, you don't want to install a trap with a union nut because the trap will be inaccessible for service in the finished structure (the union nut allows the trap to be opened for cleaning). Instead, you should use a "solvent-weld" P-trap, which has the trap-arm 90° fitting and riser cemented into the J-bend. Cementing the trap components ensures that they will never separate and cause water damage to the foundation.

Because of the body hair and fats from soaps that go down them, the drains for tubs (and all bathing fixtures) are prone to stoppages. Most codes allow traps and trap arms of 1½ in. diameter, but I prefer to plumb tubs with a 2-in. trap system because they drain faster and stay cleaner. If you're using a 2-in. P-trap, you'll need to use an increasing adapter between the 1½-in. tailpiece and the trap.

Ideally, the tailpiece from the W&O will drop straight down into the trap's top leg, but sometimes you'll have to use change-of-direction fittings to make everything line up. For instance, in order to reach your trap's top leg, you might have to use two vertical, offset 45° fittings from the bottom of the tailpiece over to the trap. Sometimes you might have to swing the W&O off plumb to make room for or to reach a fitting. A little offset is acceptable, but if you move it too much, the linkage in a trip-lever W&O can hang up and the tub won't drain properly. You'll probably have the trap and fittings in and out of the tub box a couple of times before you're ready to cement everything together permanently.

TUB DRAINAGE OPTIONS

ABS OR PVC

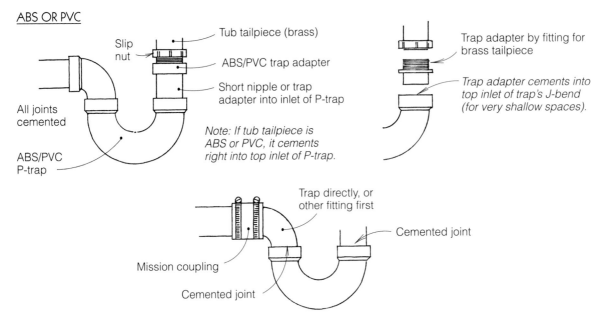

Slip nut

Tub tailpiece (brass)

ABS/PVC trap adapter

Short nipple or trap adapter into inlet of P-trap

All joints cemented

ABS/PVC P-trap

Note: If tub tailpiece is ABS or PVC, it cements right into top inlet of P-trap.

Trap adapter by fitting for brass tailpiece

Trap adapter cements into top inlet of trap's J-bend (for very shallow spaces).

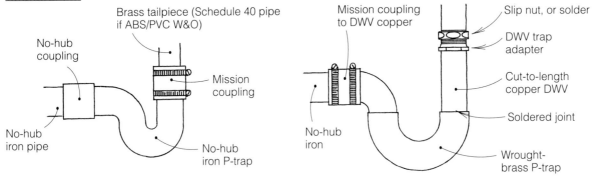

Trap directly, or other fitting first

Cemented joint

Mission coupling

Cemented joint

NO-HUB IRON

No-hub coupling

Brass tailpiece (Schedule 40 pipe if ABS/PVC W&O)

Mission coupling

No-hub iron pipe

No-hub iron P-trap

Mission coupling to DWV copper

Slip nut, or solder

DWV trap adapter

Cut-to-length copper DWV

Soldered joint

No-hub iron

Wrought-brass P-trap

DWV COPPER

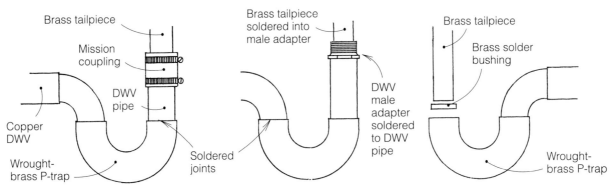

Brass tailpiece

Mission coupling

DWV pipe

Copper DWV

Wrought-brass P-trap

Soldered joints

Brass tailpiece soldered into male adapter

DWV male adapter soldered to DWV pipe

Brass tailpiece

Brass solder bushing

Wrought-brass P-trap

Tricky though it can be, connecting an ABS or PVC system in a void in the floor is much easier than working with no-hub iron or DWV copper. However, with a bit more patience, the latter two can be done. The no-hub iron trap is one piece and doesn't swivel at the juncture of the trap-arm 90° fitting and the return bend, so the alignment with the W&O has to be near perfect. Depending on your local code, you might be able to use a rubber coupling (referred to as a "Mission coupling" in my area, after the most prominent manufacturer) to join iron to DWV copper. The DWV copper trap does swivel, and you can mark the two pieces down in the void and then lift them out for soldering. (For a comprehensive description of the process of soldering, see *Plumbing a House*, the companion volume to this book.) On DWV soldered traps, you could also use a copper-pipe-to-copper-pipe rubber coupling on the trap arm and a coupling for pipe to bathwaste on the W&O's tailpiece.

Regardless of the piping material you are working with, the actual connection to the tailpiece of a brass W&O most often is a slip nut and slip-nut washer.

Rubber couplings banded by stainless steel are sometimes used to adapt different materials at the tailpiece-to-trap connection.

SETTING A TUB ON SLAB

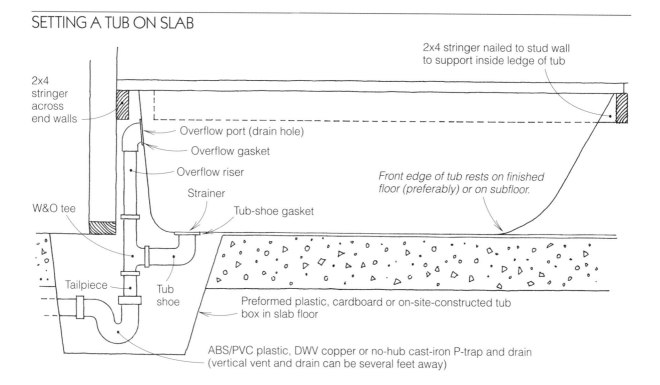

2x4 stringer nailed to stud wall to support inside ledge of tub

2x4 stringer across end walls

Overflow port (drain hole)

Overflow gasket

Overflow riser

Strainer

Tub-shoe gasket

Front edge of tub rests on finished floor (preferably) or on subfloor.

W&O tee

Tailpiece

Tub shoe

Preformed plastic, cardboard or on-site-constructed tub box in slab floor

ABS/PVC plastic, DWV copper or no-hub cast-iron P-trap and drain (vertical vent and drain can be several feet away)

(But check with your local authority first — some may not allow the use of slip nuts in the void, in which case you could use a Mission coupling.) The connection to the W&O tailpiece is a good location *not* to use a rubber slip-nut washer, since the rubber gripping the tailpiece is the weakest link. Instead, whenever possible, I like to use a nylon washer. Also, I use solid-brass slip nuts rather than die-cast slip nuts, which will corrode and start leaking, and solid-brass rather than plastic slip nuts. Plastic nuts have a high crack rate, and it's not worth the risk of using them on ABS or PVC traps under slab floors. When using a solid-brass slip nut with ABS or PVC traps make sure you don't cross-thread the nut and the male threads of the plastic trap adapter. It's a good idea to thread the nut on and off the adapter several times before trying to assemble it in the hole to make sure that the parts marry without any difficulty.

Wrap the male threads of the plastic trap adapter with Teflon tape, and apply a thread-sealing compound compatible with ABS/PVC (such as Rectorseal #100 Virgin or Hercules Real-Tuff) to the brass slip nut. To tighten the nut in the hole, you can many times use the Ridgid #1019 telescoping basin wrench (see p. 7). It's the same extension body used on the #1017 basin wrench, but the claw is sized for larger 1½-in. slip nuts.

On slab construction, I like to know as soon as possible if there are any leaks in the W&O or the trap before moving on. So I adjust the W&O linkage as best I can estimate and then put some water into the tub to see if it holds. If it doesn't, I adjust the linkage until it does. If the tub valve and spout are usable (see pp. 58-61 for installing the tub trim), I turn the valve on, fill the tub to overflowing and test the W&O. If necessary, I use 5-gal. buckets to perform this chore. Then I let the water out of the tub and check the trap and drain connections.

OFF-GROUND INSTALLATION

When setting a tub on off-the-ground construction (i.e., over a crawl space, a basement, or on multi-floor installations with ceiling access), your job is considerably easier than when working on a slab floor. With a 1-ft. square hole cut in the subfloor at the tub's head, you can wait until the tub is set in position to install the waste and overflow. You can reach up and complete overflow connections from below, and you

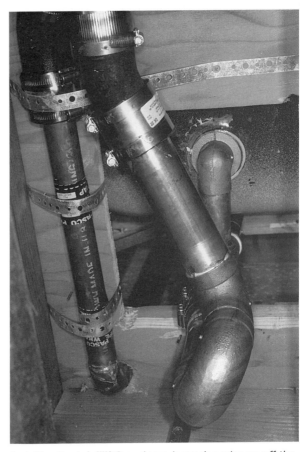

Installing the tub W&O and trap is much easier on off-the-ground construction because visibility and working room are so much better than on a slab floor.

don't have to worry about damaging the W&O when sliding the fixture into position. Installing the trap to the W&O tailpiece and drain line is also a snap.

The key to installing the W&O by yourself after the tub is in position lies with the overflow tube. If the tub's valve wall is an interior wall, and one without drywall on it as yet, you can reach through and hang the overflow tube on the tub temporarily. Then from underneath, lift up the tee and shoe portion and mark how much shoe tubing has to be trimmed. Trim the necessary pieces and then put the entire W&O together. Re-hang the assembly from the tub's overflow hole with the aid of screws or a nut for this purpose, and then, from above, screw in the strainer.

There are two types of strainer wrenches for installing the tub strainer (see pp. 7-8). If you are installing a pop-up W&O, you won't be able to use the

Chicago Specialty strainer wrench to thread the strainer into the shoe because the strainer for this type of W&O doesn't have a cross in it. Instead, it has two lugs that are cast as an integral part of the side walls. I've found that Pasco's aluminum strainer wrench, which has slots on each enlarged end, works with most pop-up strainers. Otherwise, I use an "internal spud wrench" (available from plumbing-supply stores) or make a tool from a piece of 1¼-in. or 1½-in. pipe with two notches in the end to fit over the lugs. Two helping hands will make the job much easier because they can hold the strainer still while you rotate the shoe from underneath. Also, a helper can tell you when the overflow-tube flange and overflow opening match up. You can stay underneath and do the necessary trimming, then snug up the W&O's slip nuts with the slide-jaw pliers and, if necessary, a basin wrench.

SETTING A SHOWER PAN

A factory-made shower pan is the separate floor basin of a shower system. The walls will be separate pieces (ceramic tile, cultured marble, fiberglass panels, etc.) installed by others. Where I live, these pans are most often fiberglass or some other plastic (see pp. 33-36) or terrazzo (see pp. 39-40). You may also come across baked enamel on sheet-metal shower pans. I prefer the terrazzo shower pan, manufactured in my area by Florestone (see Sources of Supply on pp. 178-179), because it is extremely rigid and won't flex under heavy loads. An additional advantage of the Florestone terrazzo pan is that it comes with an integral solid-brass shower drain. One drawback is that the pan is too heavy to install by yourself.

There are some good-quality all-fiberglass shower pans on the market that should last a long time without leaking. The heavier the pan, the better it will survive. Just make certain that whatever fiberglass or other plastic pan you purchase, there is no need to complete any work not done by the manufacturer, such as mixing up a setting bed of mortar. Shower pans that are so thin or weak that they flex when you stand on them will develop constant leaks around the drain fitting or around the riser in the drain fitting. If the pan needs mortar, I recommend that you choose something else.

INSTALLATION ON SLAB

Setting a factory-made shower pan on slab is a relatively simple operation compared with setting a tub. First, there is no overflow to contend with, and, second, if the manufacturer's schematic that you used to rough in the shower was accurate, the drain hole should be directly over the opening in the P-trap.

SETTING THE PAN As with a tub on slab, the waste connection for a shower pan is made in a tub box below the fixture. The shower pan requires a 2-in. trap and drain. With ABS or PVC drainage, I use a solvent-weld P-trap. (With copper or no-hub iron, the drainage connections are the same as for a bathtub.) With the trap pushed all the way onto the drain line, I swing the J-bend this way and that until I have it centered (using a tape measure) with the pan's drain hole. To determine the length of the riser needed, I measure from the bottom of the socket in the P-trap's J-bend up to the bottom of a straightedge lying on the floor across the void. I add the distance for the thickness of the pan from the edge that rests on the floor to the top flush surface of the pan. Then I subtract about ¼ in. so there is a space between the snap-in hair strainer and the top of the pipe. If I have someone around to help me, I lift the pan down in place and see how accurate my reckoning was. Usually I will have a little adjustment to make in height or swing. Then I carefully lift off the pan and use a silver pencil to mark the sides of the trap's J-bend and trap-arm 90° elbow before cementing them together.

I can remember more than one occasion when trying to use only a schematic to arrive at the exact location for the riser that I was off by just enough that the riser entered the pan's drain fitting at a slight angle, which made it difficult to get the rubber sealing bushing down into the drain fitting. This misalignment distance was often less than any possible correction attained with two change-of-direction fittings. On these occasions, I found that by severing the riser and installing a rubber coupling on the riser, the thick rubber wall allowed for a better alignment and relieved the stresses. This ploy should be used only if a glued, soldered or no-hub connected fitting correction is not attainable.

SHOWER-PAN INSTALLATION ON SLAB

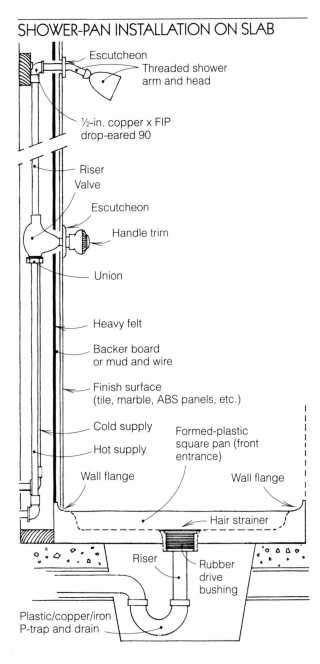

Escutcheon

Threaded shower arm and head

½-in. copper x FIP drop-eared 90

Riser

Valve

Escutcheon

Handle trim

Union

Heavy felt

Backer board or mud and wire

Finish surface (tile, marble, ABS panels, etc.)

Cold supply

Hot supply

Formed-plastic square pan (front entrance)

Wall flange

Wall flange

Hair strainer

Riser

Rubber drive bushing

Plastic/copper/iron P-trap and drain

DRAIN FITTING FOR TERRAZZO SHOWER PAN

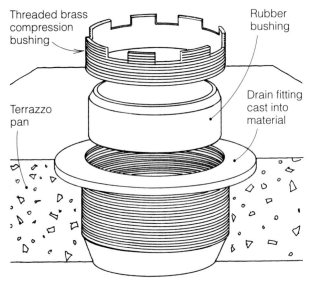

Threaded brass compression bushing

Rubber bushing

Terrazzo pan

Drain fitting cast into material

There are two basic types of bushings for drain fittings: drive bushings and compression bushings. A drive bushing is usually tapered for its entire height and has very defined, stepped ringed edges on its circumference. You merely pound this rubber bushing down into the fitting after getting it on the riser. For the most part this design works fairly well, but when I'm called in to do repairs on leaking pans, they invariably have this type of fitting. If I'm installing a pan with a drive-bushing drain fitting, I carefully seal over the bushing and up onto the surrounding metal surface of the fitting with clear silicone sealant before any moisture is allowed on the pan.

The compression bushing (as used on the Casper's design) provides a surer seal. It has a separate brass retainer ring that threads down onto the rubber bushing to provide a permanent seal on the riser pipe.

OFF-GROUND INSTALLATION

As with trapping a tub, installing a shower pan on off-ground construction is a much quicker operation, because it doesn't require any of the guesswork that's involved when working on a slab. Once the pan is down over the hole in the floor, it stays down — you don't have to worry about lifting it up again if the riser isn't just right.

DRAIN FITTINGS Fiberglass shower pans usually come with either an integral drain fitting formed out of the same material as the pan or a separate drain fitting that is set in the pan by the installer. This separate fitting will be either plastic or brass. The terrazzo pans that I like to work with have a Casper's brand brass drain fitting, which is factory-installed when the pan is poured.

SETTING A SHOWER STALL

As I explained in the previous chapter on types of fixture materials, I have strong reservations about using fiberglass and acrylic plumbing fixtures. Not only are plastics less durable than other plumbing materials, but the fixtures themselves can present some real installation headaches.

The first problem is that you cannot trust the schematic you receive from the distributor to lay out the drain location for a one-piece or even two-piece shower stall. You need to have the actual fixture on site to measure from. The actual dimensions of the fixture can differ as much as ½ in. from the schematic's listing, and this margin of error can mean hours of frustration, not to mention having to use rubber joints on the riser or trap arm to get the necessary alignment. In addition, getting the fixture stuffed into a preframed enclosure can require the use of an adz to shave the rough opening, because the fixture is more often oversized than undersized (which is why I recommend waiting to frame for a fiberglass fixture until the actual fixture is on the job site).

Another problem when installing shower stalls is maneuvering the fixture past the valves. To avoid having water on the bathroom floor when turning on and adjusting the shower valve prior to entering the stall, most people will want the valve on one of the side walls of the stall, not on the back wall facing the opening. Because the valve is positioned on a side wall and part of the valve must penetrate the wall of the shower once it is in place, you will not be able to block in the valve solidly and then slide the stall past the valve stems. You might be able to get a thin-walled stall past the stems by setting the valve closer to the entrance and higher off the floor and radically distorting the plumbness of the stall in the valve wall. The choice of valve can make a big difference to the difficulty of the installation. A single-handle mixing valve such as the Moen valve has a much shallower profile than a conventional two-handle valve with hot and cold stems, and you do not have to shove it back into or out of the wall as far in order to get the stall past it.

To simplify installation, if the valve wall is an interior wall, try to get the framer to install two studs, 12 in. on center, centered on the valve location. (If the studs are the standard 16 in. o.c., there will be a stud right in the way of the valve and riser pipe.) Don't block in the valve when you run the rough pipes, but let it hang or sit atop the supply lines. Also, if you have drywall inside the framed enclosure (it's a great noise reducer) have the drywall installer cut a piece of drywall to fit the 12-in. o.c. studs and screw it in place. When it's time to set the stall, unscrew the narrow panel of drywall, pull out on the valve from the back of the valve wall and tie off the valve so that it's completely clear of the stall enclosure. Then slide the fixture in, being careful not to ram the trap's riser.

With the stall sitting plumb in the enclosure, screw a half-dozen galvanized screws through the nailing flange into the framing. Remove the test nipple in the shower-head riser, which is usually above the top edge of the fixture, and then let the valve come forward to contact the stall. Now with a very small extension bit in a drill motor, drill a hole through the fiberglass at the valve-stem contact points. Tie the valve off outside the wall once again and bore larger holes for the valve stem(s) with a hole saw from inside the stall (which prevents big chips from forming

After first drilling pilot holes for the valves from the back side of the stall, use a hole saw to bore larger holes from inside the stall.

SHOWER STALL ON SLAB

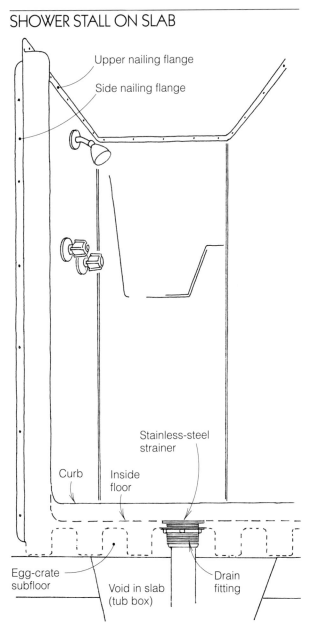

Upper nailing flange

Side nailing flange

Stainless-steel strainer

Curb

Inside floor

Egg-crate subfloor

Void in slab (tub box)

Drain fitting

Prefabricated plastic stalls are plumbed and supported by anchoring unit to framing with nails or screws through nailing flanges. Stall rests on front bottom edge.

in the gel coat around the edges of the holes). To locate the hole for a shower-head arm below the top edge of the stall, make sure to install a test nipple in the drop-eared 90° elbow that contacts the shower wall when the riser is near plumb. Once it contacts the fiberglass, drill about four tiny holes through the

wall marking the circumference of the nipple. Then again from the inside, use the hole saw to make the full-diameter hole. When all the necessary holes are bored, next block and strap the valve from the reverse side and screw the drywall back in place. With the valve installed, finish screwing the nailing flange to the framing.

If the valve wall is an exterior building wall (as is common in warm climates) and the siding or finish surface is already in place, you have a greater challenge. On second or third stories, it can be a matter of such expense that it is cheaper to leave the opposite interior wall preframed and leaning somewhere close by to set in place after the shower stall is in its final position. This way you can go ahead and strap and block your valve and shower head's drop-eared 90s permanently, as you first install them and then set your fixture by moving it into position sideways. Then you set and plumb the opposite wall.

Setting a shower stall (or tub/shower combination fixture) on off-the-ground construction differs from slab for only the drainage. You still face the same drudgery when it comes to maneuvering the fixture into the enclosure and dealing with the valves.

SETTING A COMBINATION TUB AND SHOWER

Installing a combination tub and shower is a job that can't be rushed, and you should anticipate having to slide the fixture in and out several times before getting it right. As with a shower stall, you have to deal with the problem of sliding the fixture into the space past the valve stems. In this case, however, the fixture is even bulkier, and since it's also longer it's easy to get it askew and bound up.

Another factor to compound your predicament is that you have a tub with a waste and overflow to contend with. If the valve wall, which is also the W&O end, is an exterior wall and the finish siding is not yet up, you can often cut the rough siding (on stud) for the stud space covering the valve area and work from outside. In this case, get the fixture in place by leaving the valve unblocked and strapped as we did for the shower stall. You'll probably also

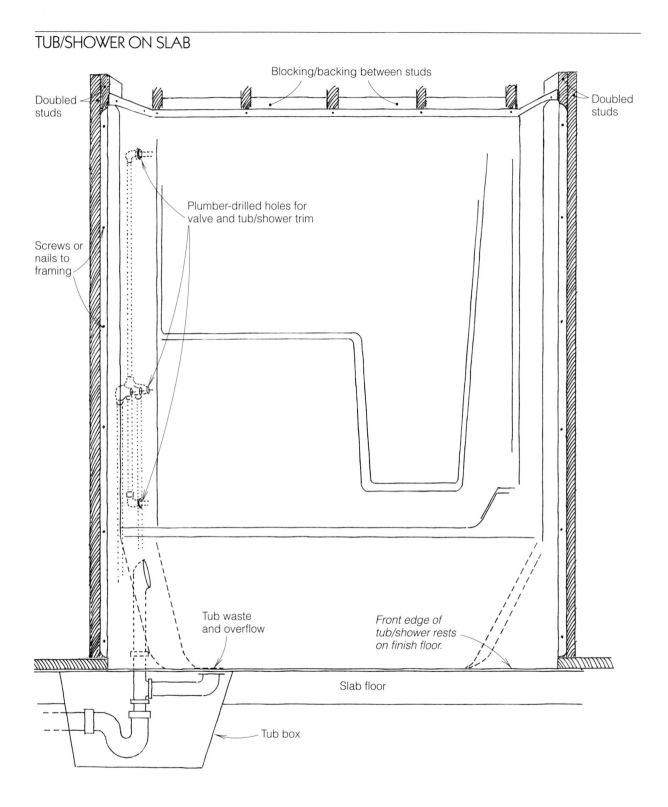

Blocking/backing between studs

Doubled studs

Doubled studs

Plumber-drilled holes for valve and tub/shower trim

Screws or nails to framing

Tub waste and overflow

Front edge of tub/shower rests on finish floor.

Slab floor

Tub box

When installing a combination tub/shower with no access from below or the valve wall, you have to install the W&O assembly to the trap first.

flange into blocking nailed between studs. It takes only two holes on each side flange (one at top and bottom), and two holes on the top flange (one near each inside corner). Countersink the holes and use a cordless screw gun and galvanized drywall screws to secure the fixture temporarily to its plumb position. Then measure the distances between the top overflow hole and the strainer hole in the tub to the mating parts of the W&O, and make adjustments and/or cut and fit new pieces of pipe into the temporary mock-up until you have a match.

Once you get a good match, you can then cement, couple or solder up the final assemblage. Use Teflon tape and pipe dope on and in the threaded parts of the waste and overflow. Set the fixture permanently by drilling and countersinking more pilot holes and driving at least six screws into each side flange and six screws across the top flange. When you are setting the screwheads into the countersink, go slowly so you don't crack the flange when it is sucked down onto the studs and blocking. Screw in the strainer and screw on the overflow/actuator plate (linkage included) and the installation is complete. Once you have the drain hooked up, you can send water into the tub and adjust the linkage for proper handle travel and water-holding ability.

On slab and off-ground installations without ceiling access, I epoxy-putty the joint around the tub shoe's strainer housing to tubing joint because there is often a leak at this factory-screwed or -cemented joint (see the photo at left). You won't be able to see the joint to know if it is leaking when you test the drain for the first time. Some plumbers prefer to solder this joint.

TUB AND SHOWER TRIM

Once the bathing fixture is set and the drainage hooked up, you can go on to install the tub and shower trim — valve handle(s), tub spout and shower arm. This stage usually goes smoothly, though you can run into problems if there has been a change of plan after the valve has been roughed in.

be able to get your trap and W&O connection completed in the void by reaching in from outside. But, when there is no outside access, you have to install the waste and overflow to the trap first, leave it free-standing and slide the fixture in and up to it. For this operation, you can probably anticipate about five slide-ins and slide-outs of the fixture.

To get the W&O in place, first temporarily attach the ABS/PVC, iron or wrought-brass/copper P-trap to the drain stub, then loosely assemble the W&O and attach it to the P-trap (see pp. 48-52). Slide the fixture in and use a 2-ft. level to get it plumb in the rough opening. It helps to have extra hands to hold the fixture still while you pilot-drill some ⅛-in. diameter holes through the side nailing flanges of the fixture into the studs, and a few across the top nailing

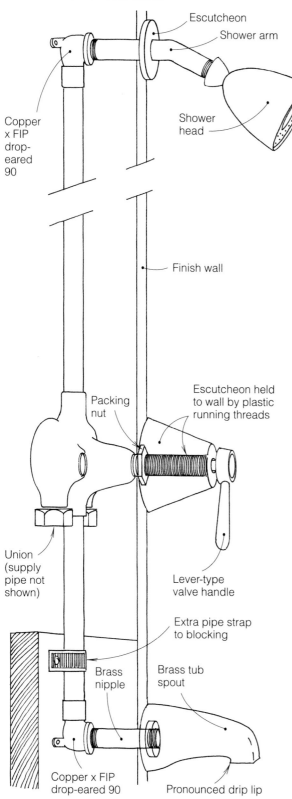

Escutcheon

Shower arm

Copper
x FIP
drop-
eared
90

Shower
head

Finish wall

Packing
nut

Escutcheon held
to wall by plastic
running threads

Union
(supply
pipe not
shown)

Lever-type
valve handle

Extra pipe strap
to blocking

Brass
nipple

Brass tub
spout

Copper x FIP
drop-eared 90

Pronounced drip lip

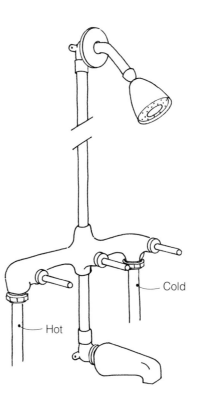

Cold

Hot

VALVES AND VALVE HANDLES

What occasionally happens is that I set the valve depth for a floated wall with tile during the rough-plumbing stage and then when I come back for the finish, I find that the customer or contractor ran out of money and installed water-resistant drywall and a tub surround instead. As a result, the valve is sticking out past the finish-wall surface by ¾ in. or so. In this case, there is nothing you can do but tear off the finish wall and reset the valve deeper, if there is room. Alternatively, if you have drywall on the back side of the valve wall, you can tear it off and pull the valve back from that side.

At the opposite extreme, you may come back to find that the owner or contractor has decided to install a good tile job (float over backer board or lath) instead of the tub surround that was originally indicated in the plans. Now the valve is too deep in the wall by an inch or more. Depending upon the brand of your valve, you may be able to purchase an extension kit. Most of the larger companies, such as Moen, American Standard, Kohler and Price Pfister, make

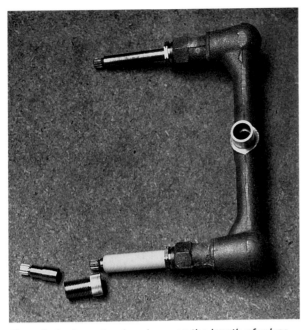

Threaded valve extensions increase the length of valves that were framed in too deep in the wall.

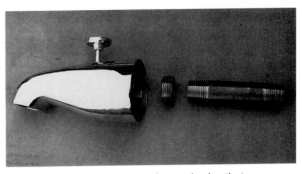

Brass tub spouts thread onto brass nipples that are threaded into the in-the-wall piping. If the tub spout has a ¾-in. mounting hole, use a reducing ring bushing to make the connection with the ½-in. nipple.

extensions to increase the reach of their handles and escutcheon-retaining threads. Some companies make the extensions in more than one length.

I like to install chromed solid-brass handles and escutcheons, because I know they'll last for generations (for more on faucet handles, see the sidebar on p. 95). Many electroplated tub and shower valve handles (and spouts) are not made of brass, but of some form of die-cast metal, or even plastic.

If you are installing a valve with conventional fluted stems and handles, it's a good idea to put some waterproof valve-stem grease on the flutes of the stems and in the handles before screwing them in place. The stem grease prevents corrosion between the handle and the stem, which means that in five to ten years when you need to get the handles off to service the valve, you'll be able to do so without destroying the finish with a pair of pliers. Also, a drop of Loc-tite on the handle screws will guarantee that they do not loosen up, which can cause the handles to loosen up to the point where the female flutes in the handle become stripped.

TUB SPOUTS

If you are working on a tub, the next step is to install the tub spout, or "filler." I recommend that you buy spouts made from solid brass that thread onto brass nipples — stay away from spouts (almost always made of die-cast metal or plastic) that slip over ½-in. copper tube and are held in place by an Allen screw. The tub spout, even though it is not made to function as such, is often used as a safety grab by bathers who have lost their footing or who feel in danger of doing so. You want a tub spout made of heavy brass that is anchored securely in the wall. Also, make sure the spout has a generous pouring lip so that water drips off into the tub and doesn't run down the underside of the spout to the tub and cause premature failure of your tile or other wall surface.

If you are using a brass nipple for the tub spout, you don't have to worry about the depth of the fitting in the wall. Tub valves made from the 1920s to the 1950s were usually shipped with spouts that had ¾-in. female iron pipe threads for mounting. Although some companies still use the ¾-in. opening, the majority now make the tub-spout connection threads in ½-in. female iron pipe. If your spout happens to have a ¾-in. FIP opening, you can purchase a brass ¾-in. by ½-in. reducing ring bushing that is designed specifically to mount in the larger ¾-in. opening and be near flush with the original opening (see the photo above). It's only about ¼ in. deep, and the entire width of the edge is threaded.

You do not apply tools to this bushing. Just wrap the male threads of the selected ½-in. diameter brass nipple and the outside threads of the bushing with Teflon tape, put pipe dope in the inside of the bushing and thread it finger-tight onto the nipple. Put pipe dope in the female threads of the spout and hand-tighten the nipple into the spout. Pack the back cavity of the spout with plumber's putty, then insert the other end of the nipple into the hole in the finish wall. As you tighten the nipple into the drop-eared 90° elbow inside the wall by turning the spout, you automatically tighten the ring bushing into the spout's female threaded opening. To tighten the spout down, you can use a piece of broomstick or other hardwood dowel of the appropriate diameter in the spout hole (if there isn't some form of strainer or stream modifier installed there). Or you can use a strap wrench on the outside of the spout if there's a wide enough portion of uniform diameter. Sometimes I can snug up the spout to the wall with just my hands.

If the back of the spout doesn't rest flush against the finish wall when the spout is tightly turned onto the nipple, back it off and go to a shorter nipple. If you apply too much force to the spout, you can crack the 90° elbow inside the wall. Sometimes you won't be able to find a nipple of the perfect length that will allow the back of the tub spout to contact the finish tub wall snugly. In this case, you can make your own custom nipple out of a short stub of ½-in. Type L or K copper tube and two copper male iron pipe (MIP) adapters. Measure the gap between the back side of the spout and the finish wall, and add this distance to the nipple you tried to use that was too short. Lay out two MIP adapters at this outside-edge-to-outside-edge distance. Then measure the distance between the full bottom depth of each fitting's socket, cut the copper tubing and solder up the three components.

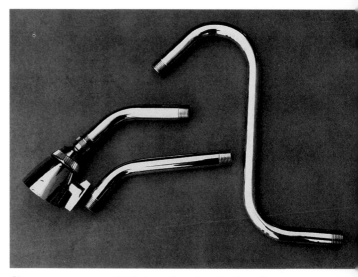

Shower arms are available in various lengths from the standard 6-in. arm to the 'shower-up' extension.

SHOWER ARMS

The shower arm threads directly into the drop-eared 90° fitting in the wall, without use of a connecting nipple. The standard shower arm is 6 in. long with ½-in. threads on the end for the shower-head attachment. (Teflon-tape the threads before screwing on the shower head.) For the shower arm in an extra-deep wall, you can purchase up to a 10-in. arm, though anything over 8 in. might be a special-order item. "Shower-up" extensions are available that allow you to raise the height of a shower head without the expense of running new in-the-wall piping.

CHAPTER
5

TOILETS AND BIDETS

Once I've set the bathing fixtures in the bathroom, I go on to install the toilet and, on rare occasions, a bidet. The three basic designs of toilet — close-coupled, one-piece and wall-hung — each require a somewhat different installation technique. New standard-design close-coupled toilets have never been easier to install, largely because most now come with factory-installed tank bolts and tank gaskets. One-piece "low boy" toilets have always been more of a chore to install, and you'll usually need a helper to work with these heavy, difficult-to-handle fixtures. Wall-hung toilets are the most labor-intensive of all to install because they require an in-the-wall carrier and heavy-duty framing to support the weight of the fixture and the user.

Regardless of the design of the toilet, you usually needn't be concerned about the relative efficacy of the tank components that come with the new toilet. For doctoring aging and worn-out tank components, refer to pp. 158-160 in the troubleshooting chapter.

One other general note on toilets: Unlike other plumbing fixtures, toilets do not require a separate trap and trap-arm assembly. That's because the trap is an integral part of the bowl (see the drawing on the facing page).

TOILET DESIGNS

The close-coupled toilet, in which the tank is bolted directly to the back of the bowl, is the most common toilet design today. Older close-coupled toilets had tanks that held as much as 7 gal. of water, but growing concerns about water conservation have led to the development of low-flush toilets with much smaller tank capacities. In many parts of the country the 1½-gal. toilet is mandated for all new construction. In order for such a small amount of water to produce a successful flush, the close-coupled toilet had to be completely redesigned.

It used to be that only the higher-quality toilet bowls, regardless of the holding capacity of the matching tank, had internally glazed passageways, which made for a great deal less friction and an increase in the velocity of the flush. Now all the newer low-flush toilets have the internal glazing that is necessary to flush successfully with so little water. The bowls on these toilets are also more funnel shaped; the steeper-walled funnel and streamlined passageway and trap increase the velocity of the flush.

CLOSE-COUPLED TOILET

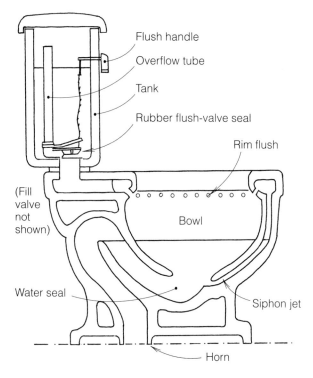

Flush handle

Overflow tube

Tank

Rubber flush-valve seal

Rim flush

(Fill valve not shown)

Bowl

Water seal

Siphon jet

Horn

Modern close-coupled toilets are designed to flush with a small amount of water. (Photo courtesy of Kohler)

Of all the brands of low-flush, or "low consumption," gravity toilets that I've installed, I prefer the Kohler Wellworth Lite model (see the photo at right). It's not the most attractive model, but it is the best performer I've seen. I like its rather tall, large-capacity tank, and the high water column in the tank gives the flush a good "punch." Also, the tank components are very simple. A frequent complaint about low-flushers is that they need to be flushed more than once to clear the bowl, in which case the hoped-for water savings are eliminated. In many cases, however, the problem has more to do with the waste piping than with the toilet itself. The extra capacity in the Kohler Wellworth Lite tank can be tapped for additional amounts of water if necessary to get a complete flush. I do this by repositioning the little float on the flush-valve chain to allow for a longer flush cycle for slow-draining piping. I don't know that Kohler intended this adjustment to be made, but it can save water by keeping people from flushing a second time.

Also growing in popularity are pressure-flushed tank toilets. Whereas gravity toilets flush solely with the water held in the tank, pressure-flushers need the assistance of household pressure. On these units, the toilet tank hosts a pressure tank that is served with water at the same pressure as the building supply. The tank usually has bellows that allow it to stretch a bit, and when flushed the high-pressure tank blasts the waste through the bowl. I have installed a number of these toilets and, though the effort to save water is admirable, I can't recommend them. The water regulators inside the tank are prone to failure, and they are costly to replace. Also, the pressure tanks can leak, in which case they need to be replaced.

I also advise my customers to avoid "low-boy" or low-profile toilets, which are usually one-piece fixtures with the tank cast as an integral part of the bowl (see the photo on p. 64). I know that people like the appearance of these toilets, but they aren't particularly efficient flushers. If you're after looks in a toilet, I suggest you buy an attractive close-coupled model, which can provide trouble-free use for generations.

Low-boy toilets are usually one-piece fixtures with tank and bowl combined. (Photo courtesy of Kohler)

I encourage my clients to avoid wall-hung toilets as well. True wall-hung units, in which both the tank and the bowl hang on the wall, are nice fixtures to live with because the floor underneath can be easily mopped and scum doesn't collect around the base of the bowl. But they are expensive fixtures to buy and to install. Wall-hung toilets can be good performers, but they require heavy-duty framing in the wall — in my opinion, at least 2x10 studs with plywood sheathing under the drywall. I once plumbed a house for an architect who wanted to install three wall-hungs in 2x6 framed walls that he refused to reinforce. I did the best I could under the circumstances, but when you sat on a toilet you could feel it sag. Two of the toilets were in a back-to-back configuration in adjoining bathrooms, and they behaved like a teeter-totter when both were in use.

INSTALLING A CLOSE-COUPLED TOILET

Installation of a standard close-coupled toilet entails three distinct steps: setting the bowl, mounting the tank on the bowl and connecting the supply tubes. The installation is the same for a low-boy toilet, except that there is usually no need to mount the tank to the bowl since most of these fixtures are one piece.

SETTING THE BOWL

When the rough drainage for the bathroom was run, a closet flange would have been secured to the closet elbow at the top of the toilet waste line and screwed to the subfloor or finish floor. It's to this flat flange that the bowl is secured, using a pair of closet bolts. If you laid Masonite across the bathroom floor to protect the finish floor (see pp. 42-43), you'll have to pull it up now in the area of the bowl. Go ahead and cut any building paper out around the flange, too.

Begin the installation by inserting two solid-brass, flat-head, machine-thread closet bolts into the closet flange. Closet bolts are available in two lengths: standard and long. I use only the long, which is a 3½-in. x ¼-in.-20 bolt that costs only a bit more than the standard 2¼-in. bolt (there's also a ⁵⁄₁₆-in. diameter bolt that is used in some areas). On new construction where you have managed to set the flange almost flush with the new floor, the shorter bolt should work on almost every installation, but if you also do repair work and need to reset toilets on all kinds of questionable floors (such as ceramic tile on top of linoleum), the shorter bolt may not be long enough.

On older installations you might find a leaded-on iron flange, but much more common nowadays are steel-rimmed or solid ABS flanges. Other closet-flange materials include PVC, cast iron and brass. If you're working with a steel-rimmed ABS closet flange, the flattened head of the bolt goes into the widened end of the slotted arc and is then centered along the narrow opening. On cast-iron or brass flanges, center the closet bolt in the slot on the side of the flange (see the photo at left on the facing page). Then drop a brass or stainless-steel flat washer down over the bolt and follow it with a chromed-brass or stainless-steel open-top closet nut. Don't use plated-steel nuts and

Insert the closet bolts into the slots in the closet flange. The flange at left is a steel-rimmed ABS closet flange; in the center, an old-style leaded-on iron flange; at right, a no-hub cast-iron flange.

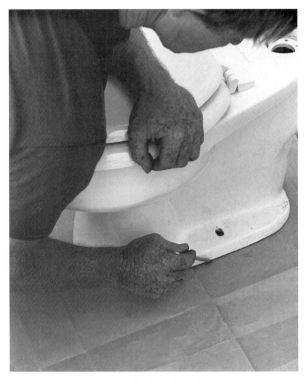

To keep the floor protected while installing the toilet, leave the building paper in place. Trace the footprint of the bowl on the paper and cut out the opening.

washers. Snug up the nut so that the bolt is tight to the flange, then repeat the procedure for the slot in the other side.

You want to keep the finish floor protected while you're installing the toilet, but you'll need to cut out a hole for the foot of the bowl in the building paper. Set the bowl gently down on the flange, with the bolts passing up through the holes in the foot. Then trace the outline of the bowl on the building paper, lift the bowl and cut out the shape from the paper, making the outline about ¾ in. bigger than the bowl. Make sure that the bowl is square to the back wall. If the toilet is in an alcove or next to the tub, make sure that the bowl looks parallel to the wall or tub.

The next step is to install the bowl wax, which provides a leak-proof seal between the bowl and the closet flange. The standard bowl wax is a simple wax ring that lies flat on top of the waste opening. I prefer to use the newer "no seep" style bowl wax, which has a plastic skirt or sleeve on the underside that slips down into the waste line (see the photo at right). These bowl waxes are available in two sizes; the diameter of the closet elbow determines which size you should install. If you have a 4-in. diameter closet elbow, or a 4-in. by 3-in. reducing closet elbow, use a no-seep bowl wax for 4-in. wastes only. If you have a 3-in. closet elbow, use the 4-in. by 3-in. no-seep wax

Set the appropriate sleeved bowl wax into the closet flange.

BOWL-TO-CLOSET-FLANGE CONNECTION

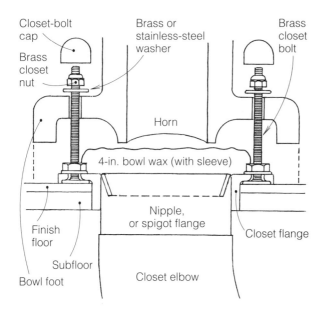

Closet-bolt cap

Brass or stainless-steel washer

Brass closet bolt

Brass closet nut

Horn

4-in. bowl wax (with sleeve)

Finish floor

Nipple, or spigot flange

Closet flange

Subfloor

Bowl foot

Closet elbow

that has a sleeve that necks down to 3 in. This wax would also fit into a 4-in. elbow, but the reduced opening would slow down the velocity of the flush.

Contrary to what you might see or read on the bowl-wax box, don't put the wax on the bottom horn of the bowl and try setting it down on the flange. Instead, set the wax onto the flange, with the sleeve nesting inside the waste line. The two bolts might gouge a slight groove into the sides of the wax, but that's nothing to worry about. When you set the bowl down onto the flange the wax is going to spread out, and the bolts will actually be coming out near the middle of the wax. Use the two long brass closet bolts as locating pins for the holes in the foot and gently slide the bowl down onto the bowl wax.

Don't sit on, stand on or wiggle the bowl once it is in position or you'll overcompress the wax. Drop another stainless-steel or brass washer over each bolt, followed by another open-top closet-bolt nut. Thread the nuts down, going from one nut to the other for about four or five revolutions at a time. Keep turning the nuts until the bowl is resting as flat as possible on the finish floor (but be careful not to overturn the nuts or you can crack the foot of the bowl). If you are setting an antique bowl, there will be four bolt holes

in the foot. Set the bowl as explained above (but using a standard bowl wax), and then use a right-angle drill to drill the holes (use glass and carbide drills for tile) and add two wood-screw-type closet bolts with the bowl in place.

Two words of caution. First, some bowl waxes are shipped with closet bolts, nuts and washers, which will probably be plated steel (use a magnet to test). If so, throw them away and buy brass or stainless-steel hardware instead. Second, your toilet might come with little plastic discs that the manufacturer suggests you install under the closet-bolt washers, on top of the bowl's foot. The discs are designed to hold the snap-on bolt covers in place. Don't use them. If you do, the bowl will seem firm to the floor at first, but as the toilet is used the plastic discs will compress and the bowl will start to rock from one side to the other. After a while, this movement will cause the nuts to loosen up enough so that the bowl is no longer under constant compression with the wax ring underneath, which will allow seepage to begin. Before you know it, water has traveled far and wide under the floor.

INSTALLING THE TANK

Once the bowl is tight to the floor, the next step is to install the tank (leaving the closet bolts long for now). If you are installing a one-piece toilet the flushing mechanism is part of the bowl, so you can skip this section and go straight to the discussion of connecting the supply tube (see pp. 69-71).

Take the tank out of the shipping box, being careful not to drop the lid. Cut one side of the tank box and lay it across the top of the bowl, and then set the tank on the cardboard, back side down. Inside the tank you may find a bag with nuts, bolts and a large, round tank-to-bowl gasket. If the tank bolts are plated steel, replace them with brass ones. Similarly, replace any plated-steel or plastic nuts and washers.

More and more toilet manufacturers are shipping tanks with bolts and tank-to-bowl gaskets already installed. If the gasket was factory-installed, the large flush-valve nut on the bottom of the tank (under the gasket) might have been left loose and will leak unless tightened. In this case, peel back the pre-installed tank-to-bowl gasket and test the tightness of the nut with your 12-in. or 15-in. slide-jaw pliers. Also check that the nut on the fill valve is tight.

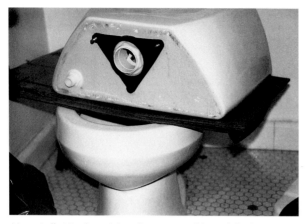

Many toilet tanks sold today come with tank bolts and tank-to-bowl gasket already installed.

Apply pipe dope to the large, round sponge-rubber gasket that goes over the flush valve before setting the tank on the bowl.

Now whether your tank has the bolts already in place in the factory-installed gasket or loose in a bag, you need to wrap little snakes of plumber's putty (about ½ in. in diameter and 2 in. long) under the heads of the bolts. In the case of the factory-installed gasket, there are no washers of any kind under the bolt heads, just an integral part of the gasket, so you put the putty under the brass head. On the traditional loose bolts and gasket installation, you should put putty under the bolt head first, shove the flat rubber tank washers up the bolts and then put the putty under the rubber washers, too. Once you have tested the snugness of the flush-valve nut, push the round gasket on over the bottom of the flush valve and paint it with pipe dope. If there's also a large, flat fiber or plated-steel washer in the bag with the gasket, it goes over the flush-valve threads before the soft rubber gasket.

Next apply pipe dope to the recess in the bowl where the gasket will rest. If you have one of the factory-installed tank-to-bowl gaskets, paint it with pipe dope, too. Now lift the tank and lower it onto the bowl, letting the bolts drop through the holes in the bowl (see the drawing on p. 68). Slide a brass flat washer up one bolt and then thread a brass nut up after it until the washer is almost to the tank. Then do the same for the other one or two bolts (depending on whether you have a two-bolt or three-bolt tank). When you can let go of the tank, insert the tip of a long slotted screwdriver into the slotted head of

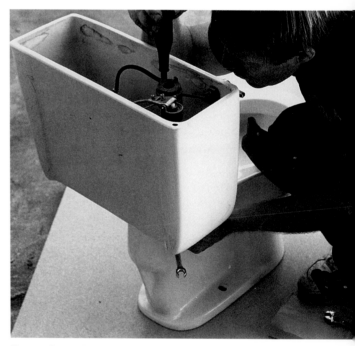

Fasten the tank to the bowl by holding the slotted bolt head still with a screwdriver while tightening the nut underneath with a box wrench.

the tank bolt. Holding the screwdriver still, tighten the nut underneath with an appropriately sized (usually ½-in. or 9/16-in.) box wrench (or mechanic's extension socket and ratchet).

TANK-TO-BOWL CONNECTION
PLUMBER-INSTALLED GASKET

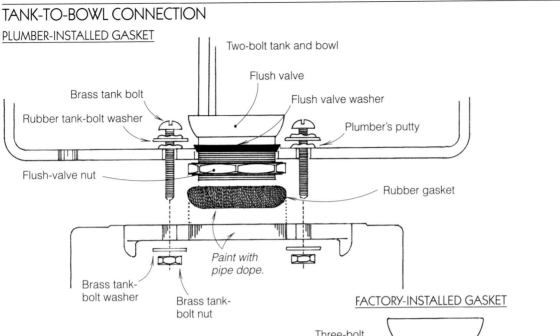

Two-bolt tank and bowl

Flush valve

Brass tank bolt

Flush valve washer

Rubber tank-bolt washer

Plumber's putty

Flush-valve nut

Rubber gasket

Brass tank-bolt washer

Paint with pipe dope.

Brass tank-bolt nut

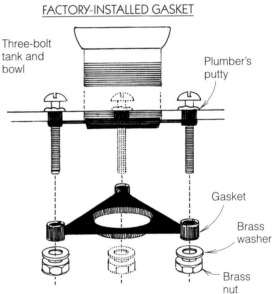

FACTORY-INSTALLED GASKET

Three-bolt tank and bowl

Plumber's putty

Gasket

Brass washer

Brass nut

If you turn the screwdriver and hold the nut still, you can run into problems. On the factory-installed gasket tank bolts, you'll wind up the gasket in the bolt hole of the tank and cause a leak and/or ruin the gasket. On the loose, individually installed bolts, the soft, unreinforced rubber washers that come with the toilet may squirm out from under the head of the bolt and again probably cause a leak. You can use the screwdriver to turn the bolt and hold the nut still underneath (which is much easier) as long as you replace the soft washers with reinforced (corded) flat rubber washers (manufactured by Kirkhill, see Sources of Supply on pp. 178-179). Tighten the bolts up until the tank is firmly fastened against the bowl. It's okay to have a little movement in the tank, but just a little. Don't be in a hurry here; otherwise you can break the bowl or the tank. Tighten each nut a little at a time, going back and forth between them. Work in a warm room to lessen the risk of breakage.

With the tank firmly on the bowl, the next step is to hook up the water supply. But first, it's important to purge any debris out of the water line and angle stop before sending water into the toilet tank's fill valve. To purge the line, I thread the ⅜-in. compression end of a 20-in. to 30-in. long braided stainless-steel toilet supply onto the angle stop (as shown in

the photo on the facing page). Then I hold the supply tube over a 2-gal. bucket and open the angle stop, filling the bucket several times to get most of the excess pipe dope, solder balls, dirt, shavings and other accumulated debris out of the line. (If you have a male hose bibb handy, you can thread it into the end of the supply so you can regulate the water flow.) The toilet bowl is a convenient place to empty the bucket; and, if you're careful not to spill the water while pouring, it can tell you whether you have any leak in the wax to bowl seal.

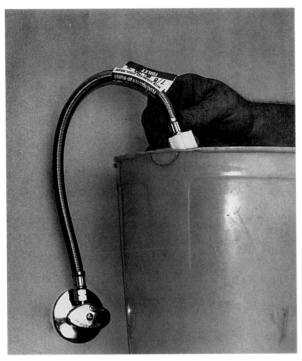

Purge the water line before hooking up the supply so that no debris gets into the toilet tank.

INSTALLING THE TOILET SUPPLY TUBE

Toilet supply tubes (also known as "closet supplies") provide the connection between the angle stop and the threaded fill valve on the tank. These supplies are available in chromed brass, braided stainless steel and polybutylene. Depending on the installation, I'll use either the chromed brass or the braided stainless steel; I don't use plastic supplies.

CHROMED-BRASS SUPPLIES   Chromed-brass supplies are the least prone to leaks, but they can be more difficult to work with because they usually require bending and cutting. They are available in 12-in. and 20-in. lengths, with either an acorn head or a flat head. For standard hook-ups with a plastic toilet fill valve on structures with unregulated high-water pressure, I like to use ⅜-in. acorn-head chromed-brass supplies manufactured by either the Eastman Company or Brass Craft Company (see the Sources of Supply on pp. 178-179). Their trade names are Speedway and Speedflex, respectively. With these supplies I use a standard ⅜-in. rubber cone washer.

TOILET-SUPPLY CONNECTION

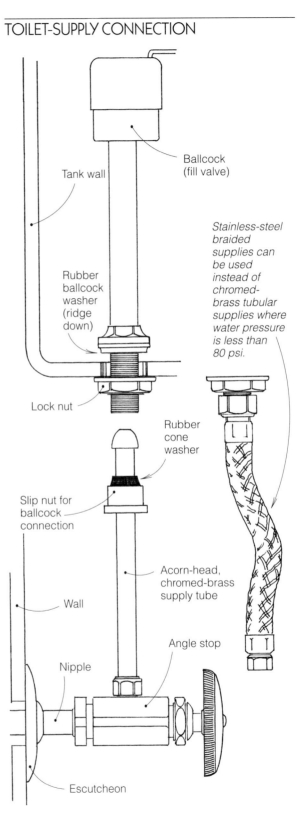

Tank wall

Ballcock (fill valve)

Rubber ballcock washer (ridge down)

Lock nut

Stainless-steel braided supplies can be used instead of chromed-brass tubular supplies where water pressure is less than 80 psi.

Slip nut for ballcock connection

Rubber cone washer

Wall

Acorn-head, chromed-brass supply tube

Angle stop

Nipple

Escutcheon

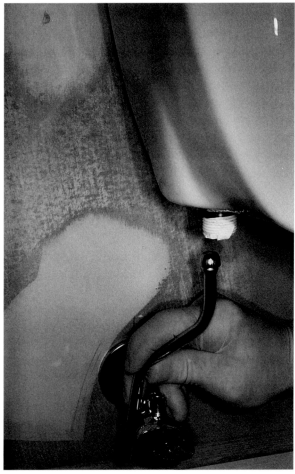

It's not often that the angle stop will be located directly underneath the fill-valve opening, so you'll probably need to bend the supply tube. First insert the end of a folding rule or a small wooden dowel up inside the fill-valve connection to see how far up the recess goes (usually at least 1½ in.), as shown in the top photo at left. Mark that distance on the supply, measuring down from the acorn. Then make the top bend in the supply, either by hand, if it can be done, or using a tubing bender (see p. 11). Shove the acorn up into the fill-valve connection until it comes to a stop, and then gauge how much of an offset to make in the remaining length of supply to bring it down into the angle-stop connection. Make the bottom bend in the supply, slide the acorn back up into the recess, then cut the supply flush with the top edge of compression stub on the angle stop. When installed, the supply will drop down about ⅜ in. into the angle stop, but there will still be plenty of material up inside the fill-valve connection. This extra penetration into the fill valve ensures that the supply will not be blown out of the connection by a surge in water pressure. By allowing you to drop the supply into the angle stop, it's a good savings in time, too.

After bending and cutting the supply, slide the cone washer up to the acorn and then follow it with the brass friction ring and the slip nut for the fill-valve connection. On the bottom end, slide on the ⅜-in. brass compression nut followed by the brass ferrule. Wrap Teflon tape on the male threads of the fill valve, then insert the supply into both openings. Start the threads of the compression nut first, then the slip nut for the fill-valve connection. Finish by snugging up both nuts.

I don't use the chromed-brass toilet supply that has a wide, flat-shaped head surfaced with a plastic sealing pad. This type of supply doesn't slide up inside the fill valve but just seals on the bottom edge of the ballcock connection. If you use this kind, the supply tube has to be absolutely plumb to mate properly with the closet connection. Also, the flat-topped supply tube doesn't seal well on plastic-threaded connections. It needs the greater resistance of brass connections if it is to work at all.

Use a folding rule to measure the depth of the fill-valve connection (top), then bend the acorn-head supply to fit (above).

Braided stainless-steel supply tubes are available for toilets and faucets.

BRAIDED STAINLESS-STEEL SUPPLIES Braided stainless-steel supplies can also be used on standard close-coupled toilet hook-ups, but I wouldn't use them in a house with high water pressure (preferably no more than 55 psi) that didn't have a pressure-reducing valve (see p. 28). For toilets, these flexible supplies come in 9-in., 12-in. and sometimes 16-in. lengths. They have captive nuts on each end that serve as unions, and can be installed in a fraction of the time it takes to install rigid supplies.

I use these braided supplies primarily on low-boy toilet installations in new construction, where it can be difficult to use a chromed-brass supply unless the water-supply rough-in for the toilet was dead accurate. And if I'm replacing a close-coupled toilet with a low boy, sometimes only a flexible supply will fit because the angle stop may be higher up the wall than the fill-valve connection. If a 9-in. flexible supply is longer than needed and kinks when installed, I use one of the longer supplies and intentionally loop it in a complete circle (with the loop under the tank, not out into the room). You can adjust the loop by holding the supply tightly in 4-in. slide-jaw pliers while you tighten the nuts. The Speedflex and Speedway supplies are available in polished brass to complement polished-brass flush handles and other trim that are sometimes used on designer low boys.

POLYBUTYLENE SUPPLIES Polybutylene closet supplies can also be used in some parts of the country, although they are not allowed where I live. These supplies are prone to leaks, and I recommend that you stay away from them. Even plumbers who do install PB water-supply systems tend to use adapters at the wall that allow them to use standard angle stops and braided supplies to hook up to the tank.

CHECKING FOR LEAKS

Once the toilet supply has been connected, you can turn on the angle stop to check for any leaks. Shine a flashlight on the tank bolts between the tank and bowl (for close-coupled designs). You want to make sure the bolts aren't letting water out of the tank (which will drip on the floor and might lead you to believe mistakenly that the bowl-wax seal has failed). Leave the water on low until the tank fills and then open it up all the way. Start flushing and keep checking all the connections.

After about a dozen flushes, if everything looks good you can cut off the excess length of the closet bolts and check the torque on the closet-bolt nuts for the final time. Usually the wax has compressed a little more, and you can afford to tighten the nuts one or two more turns. Next, pack the closet-bolt caps with plumber's putty, leaving about ¼-in. space from the bottom edge, and press them onto the bolts.

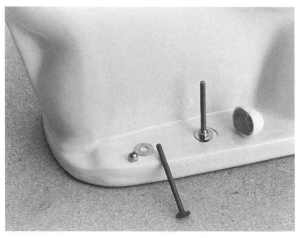

Pack the closet-bolt caps with plumber's putty before setting them on the bolt (which is shown here before it has been trimmed to the correct height).

The putty keeps the caps in place, but they're easy to remove if you should ever need to lift the toilet. Now put the lid on the tank. Some brands come with small, self-sticking rubber pads that go on the tank's top edge to cushion the tank and lid. If you've got them, you might as well use them.

Some codes and some inspectors insist that you seal around the base of the toilet with caulk. I feel that this is a foolish requirement, because if the bowl wax ever fails, water will have no way of getting out and you won't know that it has failed until the floor is rotted. By leaving the edge unsealed, when seepage occurs it will come out from under the bowl and you will know something is amiss.

The one task remaining before you can use the toilet is to install the seat with the mounting hardware provided. For an evaluation of various types of toilet seats, see the sidebar below.

TOILET SEATS

You might think that the choice of toilet seat is a very minor consideration. However, many a toilet bowl is cracked or has to be thrown away because an old corroded steel bolt, nut or washer holding a seat in place cannot be removed.

Toilet seats are generally composed of solid wood (natural finish or painted), pressed wood (wood chips formed to shape with a thin plastic coating) or solid plastic. The solid-wood and solid-plastic seats are the most durable, and the least likely to have problems with corroded hardware.

Pressed-wood seats, which are the least expensive, disintegrate in direct ratio to the number of males using them. On pressed-wood seats, the hinges that are screwed to the seat and lid and are an integral part of the mounting bracket are constantly coated by urine from standing males. The screws used to fasten these brass or plastic hinges are invariably zinc- or cadmium-plated steel, and urine causes them to deteriorate quickly.

The mounting bolts, washers and nuts are also usually plated steel and corrode to the point where removal is next to impossible without damaging the bowl. The plastic coating on pressed-wood seats also scratches very easily. And scratches allow water and urine to get under the coating and further damage the seat. When enough water gets into the area around the hinge screws, the screws can pull loose, and that means the end of the seat.

Solid-wood seats are the most expensive, and often come with brass hardware, including hinge screws. Naturally finished seats are typically cherry, mahogany or oak. I'd recommend that you stay away from the cheaper hardware-store versions of "natural oak" seats. These are made up of several pieces of wood glued together, which will grow to different heights in use, and usually come

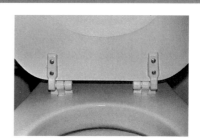

Screws on pressed-wood toilet seats tend to loosen over time.

with plated-brass hardware, which will corrode.

Solid-plastic seats sold through plumbing suppliers are usually available in a range of qualities and prices. A good-quality plastic seat can last a long time and will usually come with solid-plastic mounting hardware, which will never corrode.

Soft or cushioned toilet seats are fairly inexpensive, but they need to be replaced often because the seam in the outer covering splits open. Most of these seats use solid-plastic mounting hardware and will be easily removable during their short life.

INSTALLING A WALL-HUNG TOILET

The tank-to-bowl connection and supply hook-up on a wall-hung toilet are just the same as on a standard close-coupled toilet, but the method of bowl attachment is quite different. Because the wall-hung toilet hangs off the wall, it requires a much sturdier means of support than the floor-mounted model. So instead of using a closet flange to hold the toilet in place, we use a carrier, which is a heavy metal bracket screwed and/or bolted to the wall framing.

Each carrier manufacturer produces different models to fit specific models of toilets in major brand lines, so you must first know what make and model of wall-hung toilet you will be installing. Your local plumbing-supply store should be able to help you choose the right carrier. In general, the carriers with the fewest number of parts offer more rigidity. For residential systems with ABS, PVC or no-hub iron drainage, I like to use the Figure 500 Series carriers manufactured by J.R. Smith (see the Sources of Supply on pp. 178-179).

In addition to the carrier, you'll also need to make sure that the framing is strong enough to support the fixture — I don't like to install a wall-hung toilet on anything less than a 2x8 stud wall, and prefer 2x10 or even 2x12 framing.

Begin the installation by fastening the carrier to the stud wall according to the manufacturer's recommendations. The carrier has a closet extension that connects the opening in the back of the toilet with the fitting in the wall. Wall-hung toilets use a wax-

WALL-HUNG TOILET

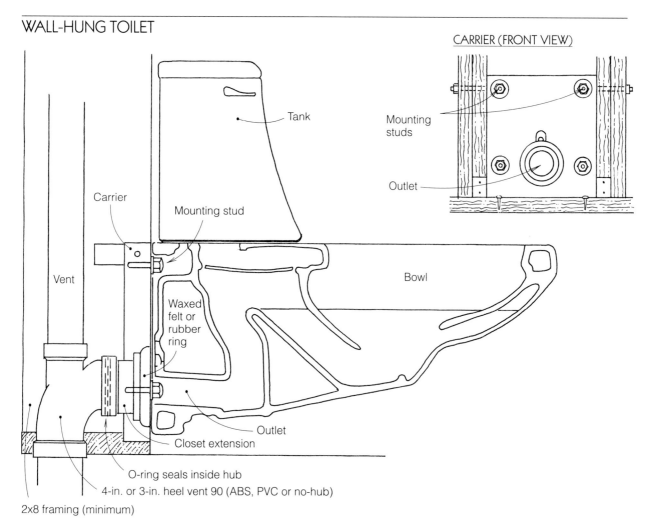

2x8 framing (minimum)

treated felt ring or a rubber ring rather than the bowl wax used on a floor-mounted toilets. Because of the compression exerted at the wall each time someone sits on the toilet, a traditional wax ring wouldn't hold up for long. Install the felt ring on the horn of the bowl, then guide the flange of the toilet onto the four studs of the carrier.

It really helps to have someone hold the bowl while you slide on the washers and start the chromed cap nuts onto each stud. The studs are usually extra long and can be threaded in and out of the carrier for adjustment. By leaving the studs threaded out near the end of their travel, you have locating pins for the bowl. Keep threading the cap nuts onto the studs until they bottom out, and then continue to turn them to thread the studs back into the carrier until the toilet is snug to the wall.

INSTALLING A BIDET

Technically, bidets are classed with toilets because they also convey solid waste, however minute the amount. Depending on the complexity of the valve system, these fixtures can be a real challenge to install. The configuration of a bidet's drainage and valving is far less standard than the configuration of a toilet's drain and supply. You can rough in the drain and the supply for a standard floor-mounted toilet with just an educated guess and be close enough to the mark; but for the bidet you need to follow the bidet manufacturer's rough-in schematic exactly.

DRAINAGE

Twenty years ago, the most popular style of bidet (in California, at least) was one that attached to a vertical drain riser, or tailpiece, from a trap under the floor (see the top drawing at right). The rough-in for the drain pattern would be the same as that used for a shower pan (see pp. 53-54), except that 1½-in. pipe and fittings suffice (rather than the 2-in. minimum required by code for shower drainage). Today, most bidets have a tubular-brass trap within the confines of the fixture, with a long trap arm to reach the sanitary tee in the wall (see the bottom drawing at right). The rough drainage for this type of bidet is almost identical to that of a lavatory basin (see Chapter 8),

BIDET INSTALLATION

SHELF-MOUNTED VALVE, TRAP IN FLOOR

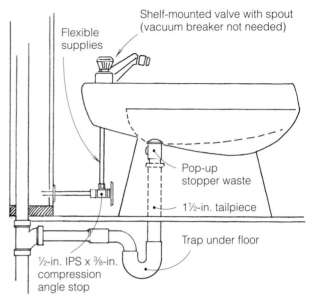

Shelf-mounted valve with spout (vacuum breaker not needed)

Flexible supplies

Pop-up stopper waste

1½-in. tailpiece

Trap under floor

½-in. IPS x ⅜-in. compression angle stop

WALL-MOUNTED VALVE, TRAP IN FIXTURE

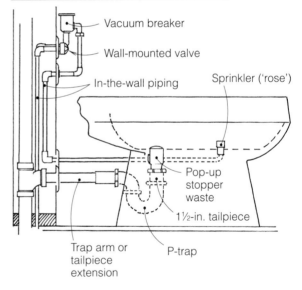

Vacuum breaker

Wall-mounted valve

In-the-wall piping

Sprinkler ('rose')

Pop-up stopper waste

1½-in. tailpiece

Trap arm or tailpiece extension

P-trap

identical to that of a lavatory basin (see Chapter 8), except that the rough-in height of the sanitary tee is lower (usually about 6 in. off the floor).

One possible problem if you're using a tubular-brass trap is finding a trap arm long enough to get to the wall. Whereas a trap arm no more than 10 in. long works under most sinks, on some bidets you might need a trap arm over 20 in. long. If you can't find a trap arm long enough, you can add a tailpiece extension to the arm to get to the wall, but there may be code restrictions here. My code states that I can use only one approved slip-joint fitting on the outlet side of the trap. If I need to use both a change-of-direction fitting and a tailpiece extension to get to the wall, that would be two fittings, and therefore unacceptable.

VALVE SYSTEMS

The valve for a bidet will usually be one of two designs: shelf or deck mounted, or in-the-wall (see the drawing on the facing page). Within the shelf/deck-mounted valve category, there are two ways to disperse the water: from a spout on the shelf or through a sprinkler, or "rose," near the bottom of the bowl. The shelf-spout bidet is by far the easiest to install and is less expensive. This bidet has a valve very similar to a 4-in. lavatory center set (see pp. 92-96), in that the water stream leaves a spout, up on the shelf, and you can use flexible supplies to attach to the hot and cold connections on the valve. The shelf-rose bidet has a valve installed to the shelf, but in the manner of a widespread lavatory faucet, with a vacuum breaker added to prevent back-siphonage from the water in the bowl. Only the handles are visible above the shelf; the valves and connections hang out of sight underneath. The mixed water is piped from a manifold to the rose.

The in-the-wall valve uses rigid connections, usually ⅜-in. or ½-in. polished-chromed, polished-brass or gold-plated brass nipples and unions, to connect the valve inside the wall to the vacuum-breaker in back of the bidet. You need to use a strap wrench or rubber-jawed pliers (see p. 7) to assemble these parts without damaging the finish, and the rough-in height of the supplies in the wall must be very accurately matched up with the connections on the fixture.

For the in-the-wall valve design, the temperature-mixed water is traditionally piped to a rose on the pan of the fixture. Both types of bidet usually have a pop-up stopper in the basin that functions in the same way as a pop-up waste in a lavatory basin (see pp. 106-109). Although the connections for the in-the-wall plus rose design are more difficult to make than the connections for the shelf-spout design, the former is a more practical design.

CHAPTER
6

SINKS AND LAVATORIES

There was a time not so very long ago when people were happy just to have running water in the house, flowing into a wooden or enamel-on-steel basin or a plain tin tub. This "luxury" saved them the trip with pail in hand out to the backyard or village pump. Today, receptacles for running water in the kitchen and bathroom come in a staggering range of styles, materials (see Chapter 3) and mounting methods. Installing these fixtures can be an involved topic, so I have broken the process down into three distinct stages: setting the sink in the counter or on the wall (the subject of this chapter); installing the faucets and supply tubes (Chapter 7); and hooking up the waste and trap (Chapter 8).

SINK STYLES

Although all these fixtures are commonly referred to as "sinks," there are in fact two separate categories: kitchen sinks (which also encompass bar sinks and laundry sinks) and lavatory basins, which are found in the bathroom. Kitchen sinks are generally larger and deeper than lavatory basins, and do not usually have an overflow. The overflow is a sealed channel that is designed to catch any excess water introduced

to the lavatory basin and deliver it to the sink waste, below the stopper, before the water can flood the basin. Other differences between the two styles are shown in the drawing on the facing page. In spite of the differences in style, installation of sinks and lavatory basins is fairly similar.

Lavatory basins are available in three basic styles: mounted on the wall (wall hung), set in a cabinet (cabinet mounted) and freestanding (pedestal). The vast majority of lavatory basins made today are cabinet mounted. Similarly, almost all modern kitchen sinks are cabinet mounted. There are three main methods for securing the bowl to the cabinet: with the lip, or flange, of the bowl overhanging the counter surface ("self-rimming"); with the bowl hung from a mounting rim or from clips below the counter ("rimless" or "underhung"); and with tile, marble or granite over the lip of the bowl ("mudded in" or "counter over"). Whereas self-rimming and rimless sinks are set by a plumber, mudded-in sinks are usually installed by a tile setter.

Older-style mudded-in sinks were usually set below the counter surface by the height of the quarter-round edge tile (see the photo on p. 78). A potential problem with this setting is that over time splash water can cause the grout between the tile and the sink

KITCHEN SINKS VS. LAVATORY BASINS

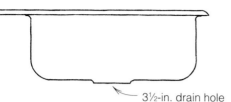

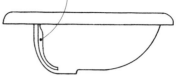

Overflow for excess water

3½-in. drain hole

Most kitchen sinks are deeper than lavatory basins and have a larger drain hole to host a standard-size basket strainer or garbage disposer. Kitchen sinks do not usually have an overflow channel.

Most lavatory basins have a drain hole approximately 1¾ in. in diameter for installation of a standard pop-up waste or rubber stopper, and an overflow channel, which may be on either the front or back wall.

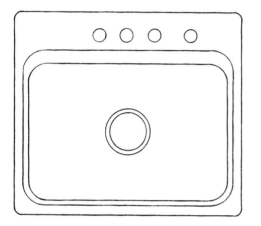

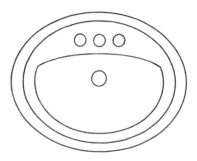

Drain holes on U.S.-made kitchen sinks are usually centered; designer and imported bowls tend to have off-centered holes.

Most lavatory basins have a drain hole near the back wall.

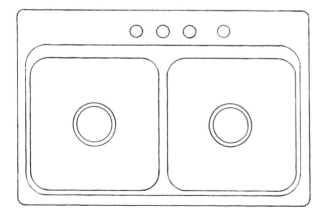

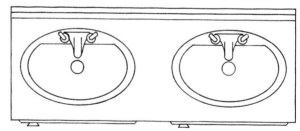

Most kitchen sinks are available in double-bowl designs.

Lavatory basins are single bowl, but are often set side by side on a shared counter.

A 'mudded-in' sink with tile over the lip of the bowl sits below the level of the countertop.

to deteriorate. Today's counter-over designs, using some highly efficient sealants, offer a more watertight installation (see the photo on p. 89).

SINK TO COUNTERTOP COMPATIBILITY

From a plumber's point of view, one of the most important factors in choosing a cabinet-mounted sink for the kitchen or bathroom is the type of countertop it will be secured to. If the seal between the sink lip and countertop is not perfect, splash water will find its way under the lip and down into the cabinet. Up until World War II, out here in the West at least, most kitchen sinks were either cast-iron combination sink and drainboards, on legs or on a cabinet, or sinks mudded in tile; with these sinks, splash-water leaks were seldom a problem. With the development of plastic laminate as a countertop finish material, however, the question of sink to countertop compatibility became an important concern.

PLASTIC LAMINATE

Plastic laminate (Formica is one common brand) provides an excellent mounting surface for sinks of any material, as long as the finish surface is smooth and the substrate for the plastic is ¾-in. plywood. Smooth plastic laminate is the only surface a mounting rim works well with; the laminate seals well to the sink rim and the ¾-in. plywood is well suited for use with sink-rim clips. It also gives plenty of support for self-rimming sinks.

What you should avoid is plastic laminate with a textured surface, which is not a good match for the sink clamp-down rim or for the lip of a self-rimming sink. Water can eventually work its way under the rim or lip and rot the cabinet. Also watch out for thin countertops. Most plastic-laminate countertops today are particleboard, sometimes as thin as ⅜-in. This thinner particleboard can crumble under the rim clips' pressure points, which loosen up as a result and allow water to seep under the rim's lip. Similarly, particleboard cannot support heavy self-rimming sinks (such as cast iron), and the countertop is likely to sag and let water into the cabinet. Not only is the substrate thinner, but the laminate itself often is too. Most modern countertops have a rolled front edge and an integral splash, and only relatively thin laminate can be bent to these tight radiuses.

Stainless-steel sinks, though called self-rimming, require rim clips similar to those used to install rimless sinks. There is a mounting clip available for use with stainless-steel sinks on thin plastic-laminated particleboard, but if the rough opening in the countertop is slightly too large, the edge of the clip can cause the particleboard to compress too much or a chunk to break away — either way, the sink will not stay tight in the opening. If you're installing a stainless-steel sink on plastic laminate, I recommend you use nothing less than a ¾-in. plywood countertop.

TILE

All sinks have potential leak problems when mounted on ceramic tile, quarry tile or any other uneven counter surface. If the tile isn't absolutely flat, splash water will find its way into the cabinet in gaps between the sink edge and the tile. Tile grout that is allowed to deteriorate around the sink edge can also be a conduit for splash water.

Self-rimming sinks can work well on very smooth, professionally laid ceramic tile, as long as they are cemented down on totally dry tile, with a top-quality silicone sealant under the sink lip. Once this sink is glued to the tile, removal of the sink is almost im-

SINK TO COUNTERTOP COMPATIBILITY

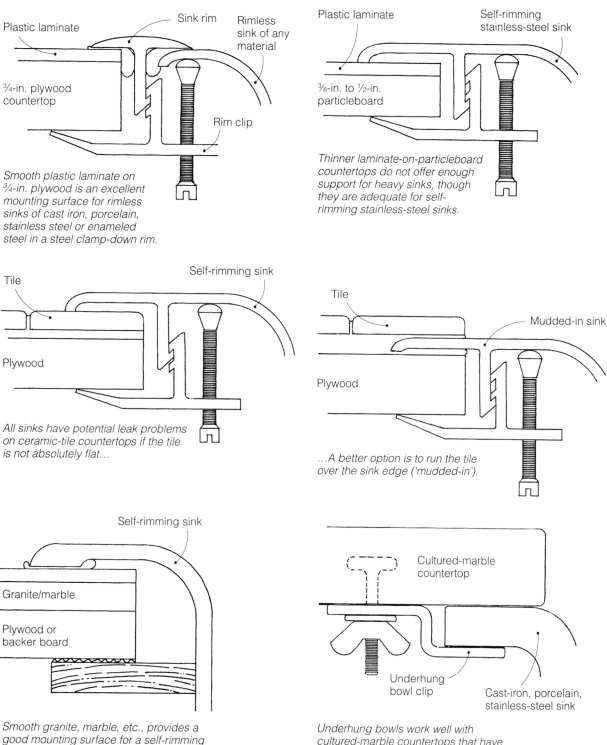

Plastic laminate

Sink rim

Rimless sink of any material

¾-in. plywood countertop

Rim clip

Smooth plastic laminate on ¾-in. plywood is an excellent mounting surface for rimless sinks of cast iron, porcelain, stainless steel or enameled steel in a steel clamp-down rim.

Plastic laminate

Self-rimming stainless-steel sink

⅜-in. to ½-in. particleboard

Thinner laminate-on-particleboard countertops do not offer enough support for heavy sinks, though they are adequate for self-rimming stainless-steel sinks.

Tile

Self-rimming sink

Plywood

All sinks have potential leak problems on ceramic-tile countertops if the tile is not absolutely flat…

Tile

Mudded-in sink

Plywood

…A better option is to run the tile over the sink edge ('mudded-in').

Self-rimming sink

Granite/marble

Plywood or backer board

Smooth granite, marble, etc., provides a good mounting surface for a self-rimming cast-iron or porcelain sink.

Cultured-marble countertop

Underhung bowl clip

Cast-iron, porcelain, stainless-steel sink

Underhung bowls work well with cultured-marble countertops that have cast-in thread bosses for mounting screws.

possible without destroying the tile too. The grout must be expertly installed, because this is the weak link. I recommend the use of epoxy grout, which may be more expensive but is waterproof rather than just water-resistant.

If stainless-steel sinks are installed in conjunction with tile, they are best mudded in (with the tile over the edge of the sink). This installation is more expensive than setting the rim over the tile (and not all tile setters are capable of doing it right), but it's the only way to ensure that there won't be leaks at the sink rim.

GRANITE, SOAPSTONE, MARBLE

Self-rimming cast-iron sinks work well on granite, soapstone or marble countertops, as long as the counter is properly supported on a well-built cabinet. Self-rimming stainless-steel sinks are also a good choice for these countertops if the counters are thin enough to allow use of the standard one-piece sink clips that are employed for ¾-in. plywood. If the stone countertops are so thick that a two-piece extension clip is required (see p. 86), I recommend that you consider a different type of sink.

Underhung sinks also work well with countertops of granite and cultured or synthetic marble. With the trend today toward cultured-marble countertop/sink units, in which the sink and countertop are formed as a single piece, we have come full circle back to the old-style combination sink and drainboard. The beauty of these composite fixtures, of course, is that you don't have to worry about leaks between the sink and countertop (or, indeed, about installing the sink to the countertop).

INSTALLING A SELF-RIMMING SINK

For many years, the standard way to install a kitchen sink or lavatory basin was to use a clamp-down ring to support the sink in the countertop. (We'll look at this method of installation in the next section.) Thankfully, self-rimming sinks (and sinks installed by countertop specialists) are increasing in popularity. With this method of installation, the rim of the sink simply rests on the countertop and there's no need for a mounting rim, rim clips or other paraphernalia that can complicate the installation and lead to problems with leaks down the road.

In this section, I'm first going to explain how to install a self-rimming cast-iron kitchen sink. The installation of self-rimming cast-iron and porcelain lavatory basins is much the same procedure, except for the choice of adhesive used to seal the fixture to the countertop (see pp. 84-85). I'm not aware of any large-scale domestic manufacturer of self-rimming porcelain kitchen bowls. If you find one, or more likely an imported self-rimming porcelain kitchen bowl, the instructions for installing a self-rimming porcelain lavatory basin will serve you well.

CAST-IRON KITCHEN SINK

I begin the installation by setting the sink right side up on the work table (which I usually cover with a piece of carpet or felt). A cast-iron sink is heavy, so don't risk back injury trying to pick up the sink by yourself; get some help to put it on the table. If the countertop is tile, granite or marble, the installer will have left a rough opening for the sink. If the countertop is laminate, however, you'll probably have to cut your own opening. Sinks used to be shipped with a template for laying out the opening, but they rarely are today (more often with a lavatory basin than a kitchen sink). If you don't have a template, it's simple to make one.

MAKING A TEMPLATE   I know many plumbers who use the sink itself as a template, flipped upside-down on the countertop. I don't do this because a cast-iron sink is very heavy and sliding it on the countertop can scratch the sink and/or the countertop. The ten minutes or so it takes to make a template is time well spent. I actually make two templates: The first is a form for making the second, which I use for laying out the lines on the counter.

First, run some masking tape along the outside rolled edge of the sink, then use a hot-glue gun to attach four 6-in. wide cardboard strips to the bottom of the taped edge. Next, use a fine-tip marker to scribe the outside circumference of the sink onto the cardboard, as shown in the photo at left on the facing page. Run a sharp knife between the cardboard and the sink rim to detach the template from the sink, then pull the tape off the edge of the sink. Now cut

Scribe the outside circumference of the sink onto the cardboard template. (Photo by Bill Dane)

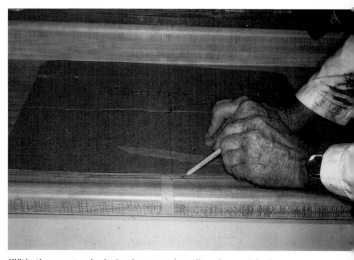

With the center hole in the template lined up with the center hole in the countertop, mark the cutline for the sink opening. (Photo by Bill Dane)

along the line you scribed with a utility knife, and lay the form down onto another large piece of cardboard. Scribe the inside perimeter onto the new piece of cardboard, than draw another line about ¾ in. in. (This ¾ in. represents the counter lip that the sink will hang from.) You can draw the line freehand — it doesn't have to be absolutely perfect. Cut along the inside line and you have the template to apply to the countertop.

LAYING OUT THE ROUGH OPENING   Laying out the rough opening for the sink is not a particularly difficult job, but it's not one that you want to rush: one mistake and you can ruin the countertop. When plastic laminates were first introduced, the counter surface was absolutely flat from wall to edge, with a separate splash and edge strip. Today, with molded cove backs and molded fronts, the total width of the countertop is no longer completely flat. You need to take this reduced width into account when laying out the rough opening.

Begin by marking the center of the cabinet from underneath the countertop. Then, drill a small hole through the countertop at this mark, which represents the exact middle of the sink space, from side wall to side wall and from back to front. Next mark the center of the template and make a small hole so you can use a nail to line up the template with the hole in the countertop. With the template in place

and centered, check to see if the rim of the sink would be resting on a flat surface all the way around (remember to add about ¾ in. out from the edge of the template). If any of it would be contacting a sloping surface near either the front edge or the back, you'll have to reposition the template accordingly. When you're satisfied with the position of the template, flag its outside edge with pieces of masking tape, then lift up the template. Now lay down strips of 3-in. masking tape, using the flags for guides. You want the approximate center of the wide tape to straddle the true perimeter of the sink. Press this tape firmly in place, then put the template back in position and scribe the outside perimeter onto the tape with a clearly visible line.

CUTTING THE OPENING   Now use a small-diameter hole saw to bore a hole through the counter anywhere on the inside of the scribed line (see the top photo on p. 82). Use a jigsaw with a blade made for plastics to cut the rough opening. Alternatively, use a small router. I glue some wood strips or cardboard strips across the corners on the bottom of the counter to support the offcut. The strips prevent the blade from binding and keep the laminate from chipping when the saw cut is complete.

Sometimes the sink opening is so close to the splash wall that you can't use a jigsaw along the back edge. You may be able to make the corner cuts and

Use a hole saw to bore a hole at each corner of the sink opening. (Photo by Bill Dane)

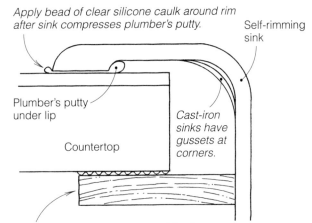

Apply bead of clear silicone caulk around rim after sink compresses plumber's putty.

Self-rimming sink

Plumber's putty under lip

Countertop

Cast-iron sinks have gussets at corners.

Wooden stops glued to underside of countertop keep sink in position.

You may need to use a reciprocating saw to cut along the backsplash.

the long back cut with a compass saw from under the cabinet, where you usually have more room. If not, put a short metal blade in a reciprocating saw and go along the back wall from above. The blade teeth are going the wrong way, but if you choose a fine-

tooth blade and the masking tape is firmly pressed in place, you can complete the cut with just a minimal amount of edge flaking.

With the hole cut, inspect the underside corners of the sink. Cast-iron sinks usually have gussets in the corners that add strength to the bowl (see the drawing above). These gussets can prevent the bowl from lying flat on the countertop, in which case you'll have to enlarge the hole at the corners or cut a groove to provide relief for the ridges.

INSTALLING THE SINK If I'm installing a double-bowl sink, I lift and carry the sink with my gloved fists through the drain holes, which also gives me good control when lowering the bowl. For single-bowl sinks, I lay wood strips across the ends of the rough opening and then grip the basin by the edges, setting one edge down before the other. Then with one fist in the hole, I can lift the sink up far enough to take the strips out, one end at a time.

When I'm happy with the fit of the bowl in the rough opening, I take it out one last time and install the faucet (if it's convenient to do so at this stage of the installation — see the sidebar on the facing page). I don't install basket strainers in the drain holes yet so that my hands will still fit through. Now I remove all the masking tape from the countertop. I then roll out ½-in. diameter putty snakes and arrange them

WHEN TO INSTALL THE FAUCET

In the discussion of sink installation in this book, I talk about mounting the sink first, then hooking up the faucet and supplies and finally installing the waste and trap. However, these three tasks don't always have to take place in that sequence. In fact, I usually prefer to install the faucet to the sink first, because it's easier to get at the faucet's supply and mounting connections. I also sometimes install the sink waste before setting the sink in place.

If the sink is self-rimming, regardless of the material, there's usually no problem installing the faucet before mounting the sink. Sometimes the faucet connections are right up against the rough opening, and you have no choice but to install the faucet first because there's no room to get a basin wrench in to tighten the mounting nuts. And if you need to punch an extra hole in a stainless-steel sink (for an added hot-water dispenser, for example), you'll really appreciate the accessibility that having the sink still free of the cabinet allows.

With other types of sink, however, it can be more difficult to work with the faucet already installed. For example, if you're installing a sink with a mounting

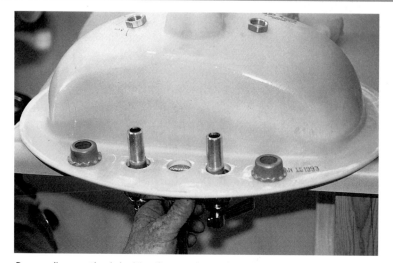

Depending on the job, it's often easier to install the faucet before mounting the sink in the cabinet.

rim, having the faucet connections hanging down (especially when a spray hose is also involved) can be a real nuisance when you're under the cabinet on your back trying to get the rim clips installed. This is especially true when the sink is as big as you can get for the size of the cabinet and there's little room between the sink and the cabinet walls. In such cases, it's a lot easier to work with a bare sink.

Sometimes when setting an underhung bowl in a small lavatory-sink cabinet, I leave the faucet off so it's easier to get the clips positioned under the lip of the bowl. Working with a bare

bowl makes it easier to see what you're doing, and the bowl won't be out of balance while you are trying to hold it in position to get the clips on.

There are a couple of instances when I never install a faucet to a sink prior to setting the sink. One is if the sink is being mudded in by a tile setter. The other is if the sink is being installed with a marble, granite or other specialty countertop. Whatever the countertop material, the installer will not appreciate having the faucet in the way, and there is always the risk that the faucet may be damaged during the installation of the sink.

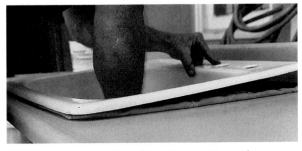

Run a continuous snake of plumber's putty on the countertop, then carefully drop the sink into position.

Carefully trim the putty around the edge of the sink.

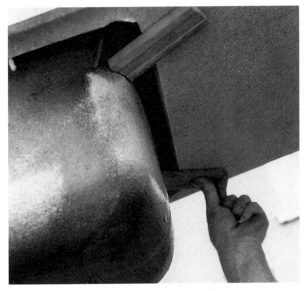

Once the sink is centered, glue some strips of wood onto the underside of the countertop to keep the sink from moving.

around the opening so that the rim will land on top of them. The weight of the sink compresses the putty, some of which will squeeze out past the edge, with the remainder under the lip to act as a splash-water seal. Invariably there are some tiny last-minute centering adjustments to make. When you have the sink where you want it, glue some short strips of 1x2 onto the underside of the counter so that they contact the edge of the bowls. These removable stops keep the sink where you want it.

A very small amount of putty will continue to ooze out from under the edge of the sink for a week or so. I run a pocket knife around the edge to trim it loose — the putty pulls up in very fine strips with the consistency of well-made pie dough. I don't use any type of adhesive caulk on a cast-iron sink because if anyone needs to remove the sink in the future for any reason, it will be impossible do so without also wrecking the countertop. (If it were a porcelain sink, you could use glue and then remove the sink later by draping it in canvas or other fabric and blasting it with a hammer.) I do, however, use silicone caulk as a secondary seal around the underside between the exposed portion of the sink's flanged edge and the countertop.

LAVATORY BASIN

A lavatory basin, whether cast iron or porcelain, is considerably lighter and easier to work with than a cast-iron kitchen sink, but the sequence of installation is much the same. The one difference is in the choice of material used to seal the sink to the countertop. While the weight of a cast-iron kitchen sink maintains sufficient sealing force on plumber's putty under the lip, on smaller and lighter lavatory basins plumber's putty is not the best choice. Instead, I always use an adhesive sealant, which is usually shipped with the better-quality basins. The adhesive needs to be something that will prevent water from seeping under the lip, but it must not be so permanent that it will prevent you from lifting the bowl in the future if you should decide or need to replace it.

I like silicone caulk for some applications, but using this material on a full circumference under the lip of a sink would make lifting the bowl a tough proposition. I once used it for this purpose and later had to replace the bowl. I ended up covering the sink with a canvas sack and smashing the all-porcelain bowl with a hammer. Having learned the lesson the hard way, I now use a general-purpose adhesive caulk. This material is opaque white, so you don't want to apply too much around the countertop hole or it will be visible at the edge of the bowl. After setting the bowl on a very light line of adhesive caulk, I go around the bowl's edge with silicone, filling in the gap between the bowl and the countertop surface. When the bowl is firmly cured to the counter (usually about 30 minutes), you can fill in the void underneath between the bowl and counter with plumber's putty. Adding the putty prevents any water that might get passed the adhesive and silicone from getting into the cabinet or into the underlayment of the countertop. If I need to remove the bowl, I can usually work it loose by inserting a sharp, long-bladed knife between the sink and the countertop.

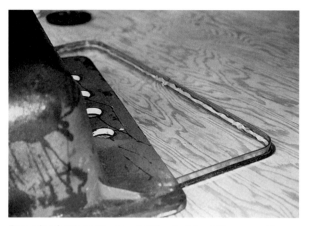

Run plumber's putty around the inside of the mounting rim before setting the sink in upside-down.

Tap in the punch tabs on the rim so that they extend over the edge of the sink.

INSTALLING A RIMLESS SINK

Although most of the sinks I now install are self-rimming, I know that for many years to come people will still be wrestling with sinks that need a clamp-down rim. In this section, I'll explain how to install a rimless kitchen sink. As with the self-rimming designs, the installation of a kitchen sink and a lavatory basin is pretty much the same.

The clamp-down mounting rim used to hang rimless sinks from a countertop, known as a "houdee rim" in my part of the country, is a slightly crowned stainless-steel band with a central partition wall hanging down on the underside. The partition has punch-out tabs that hold the sink in the rim temporarily during initial installation. The bottom edge of the partition is hooked inward to engage matching hooks in rim clips spaced around the circumference of the sink (see the sidebar on p. 86). When the clips are tightened, the sink is held permanently in the rough opening. With proper application of plumber's putty, a watertight seal is made between the sink and the countertop.

If the countertop you're working on doesn't already have a rough opening for the sink, you can make your own template (as described on pp. 80-81) or use the mounting rim as a template. For the latter, set the rim right side up on the counter and trace around the outside of the central partition. Cut out the opening as explained on pp. 81-82.

I begin the installation by laying the mounting rim flat side down on the work table (which you might want to cover with felt or carpeting to protect the finish). I then roll out a snake of plumber's putty about ¼ in. in diameter, and run it along the underside of the rim, inside the partition wall. Next I set the sink upside-down into the rim, and use a screwdriver or a small punch and light hammer to tap in the punch-outs, trying to get the little tab arms as far out onto the edge of the sink as I can. The punchouts in the partition are usually spaced at two dif-

Rim clips were originally designed for a countertop thickness of ¾ in. — the standard plywood countertop base for plastic laminates. But as countertops have gotten thinner, rim clips have become available in correspondingly smaller sizes. A recent innovation is a rim clip designed to fit two thicknesses of countertop. This clip has two hooks at the top, one below the other. The outer hook is for use with traditional ¾-in. thick plywood countertops; the inner hook is for thinner particleboard countertops. If you are using the thinner countertop (which I don't recommend), you need to clip off the outer hook with side-cutting pliers so that the top of the clip doesn't interfere with the underside of the sink.

At the other extreme, extension rim clips are available for securing sinks in countertops that are thicker than the standard ¾ in. These clips are designed for use on countertops of tile over plywood (or granite, marble, soapstone, etc.). In my experience, extension clips don't work for very long before they begin to lose their grip. Over time, splash water works under the sink rim

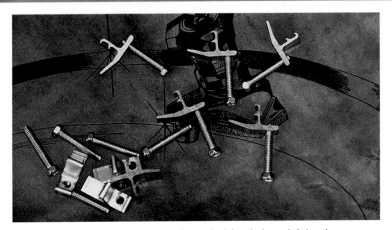

Rim clips hook onto a mounting rim to hold a rimless sink in place.

and can destroy the countertop base and cabinet. If you're using a tile countertop, I strongly recommend you find a good tile setter who knows how to set bowls and quarter round correctly.

Regardless of the design, rim clips are invariably poorly made. The tapped holes in the extruded-aluminum body often have rough edges, which makes it more of an effort to install them. The screws are plated steel and quickly corrode in the clip, making it impossible to tighten them up in the future to improve a failing seal (or to get them off the rim to replace with new ones). It also sometimes happens that the cabinetmaker builds a cabinet that will not ac-

cept the clips without some modification on your part. You end up having to chisel or bore holes into the sides of the cabinet to fit the leverage leg of the rim clip when there's not enough of a lip left by the rough opening.

All in all, I recommend that you think twice before installing a sink in a clamp-down mounting ring. Instead, try to see the advantages of installing a self-rimming or mudded-in porcelain or cast-iron sink, a mudded-in stainless-steel sink, a granite or marble countertop with under-hung bowl, or a solid Corian sink/countertop combination.

ferent heights: Those closer to the flat rim are for enameled-steel sinks and non-self-rimming stainless-steel sinks; the punch-outs closer to the bottom edge of the partition wall are for thicker non-self-rimming cast-iron and porcelain sinks. If I'm installing the faucet before setting the sink in the cabinet, I slide

the portion of the sink with any holes for the faucet off the edge of the work table and, from underneath, get the faucet finger-tight to the sink (see the photo on p. 83). Then I install the waste and pop-up (see Chapter 8) if there's room to drop the sink straight down into the cabinet.

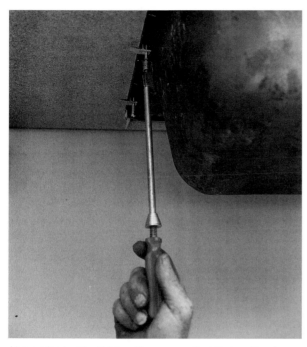

Use a 'rimster' to tighten the screws that fasten the rim clips to the countertop.

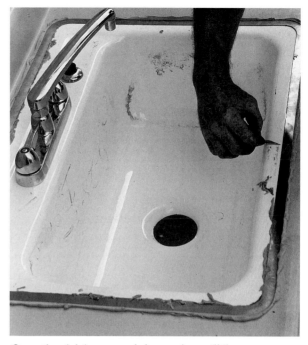

Once the sink is snugged down, clean off the excess putty around the mounting rim with a pocket knife.

Next I run a continuous putty snake along the rim on the outside of the partition, which is the surface that will rest against the countertop. I then pick up the sink, rim attached, flip it over, and set it straight down into the rough opening. The rim overlaps onto the counter and the sink hangs from the punch-outs. With the sink in place, the next step is to attach the rim clips that secure the sink to the countertop. The rim usually comes with 12 clips, which I space out equally along each side. Working from underneath, hang the rim clips from the hooked edge and fasten them in place by tightening the hex-head machine screws. You could use a long slotted screwdriver to fasten the screws, but it's a lot easier and quicker to use a special tool called a rimster (as shown in the photo above). As you tighten the screws, the rim is pulled downward and the sink is driven upward to make firm contact with the bottom of the rim, while at the same time the rim clips grip the underside of the countertop. After making sure that the sink is properly aligned and secure, I make final adjustments to the position of any faucet that I have installed and then snug the sink down tight. Then I carefully clean off the excess putty with a pocket knife.

RIMLESS-SINK INSTALLATION

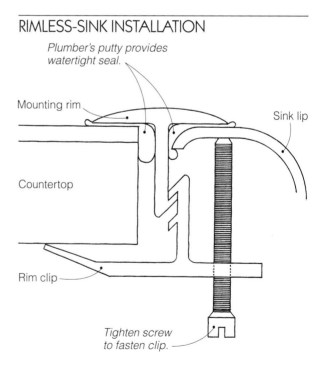

Plumber's putty provides watertight seal.

Mounting rim

Sink lip

Countertop

Rim clip

Tighten screw to fasten clip.

STAINLESS-STEEL KITCHEN SINK

Stainless steel is probably the most popular material used in the construction of kitchen sinks today. Although these stainless-steel sinks are referred to as self-rimming, they require the same rim clips that are used to install rimless sinks. However, the mounting rim that holds the sink in the opening is an integral part of the sink (spot-welded to the underside of the lip) rather than a separate piece.

As with the rimless sinks described in the previous section, the rim clips engage the hooked partition and, as the screws are tightened, draw the sink downward, compressing the plumber's putty between the lip of the sink and the countertop. On stainless-steel sinks, there is an added part for the rim clip — a little plastic boot that is pushed onto the end of the mounting screw after the screw is threaded through the clip (see the drawing below). This plastic boot is supposed to prevent the screw from forming a dent in the stainless-steel rim of the sink when the clip is tightly installed. The boot spreads out and cushions the upward force of the screw. However, just because the screw has the boot, it doesn't mean that you can

tighten the screw as hard as you want. You can still cause a noticeable bump in the sink lip. (This is most likely to be a problem when you're installing a cheap sink that won't lie flat on the counter. As you make that one last turn of the screw to get the gap down to a tolerable amount, the tell-tale bulge appears.)

Some stainless-steel sink manufacturers have developed their own methods of securing their products to the countertop, which, in general, work better than the generic rim clips. One of these is the system used by Elkay, which is a top-of-the-line domestic manufacturer. Their sinks have a channel on the underside of the sink lip. The edges of the channel are hooked inward to support the head of a specially designed screw that is slid into the channel. The bottom edge of the screw is flattened and has a milled screwdriver slot. When installing the Elkay sink, you can slide these screws into the channels before you set the sink in the rough opening (the generic clips on rimless sinks cannot be pre-installed). A U-shaped clip is slid over the screw, and as the screw is tightened the teeth in the top of the clip bite into the underside of the counter.

STAINLESS-STEEL-SINK INSTALLATION

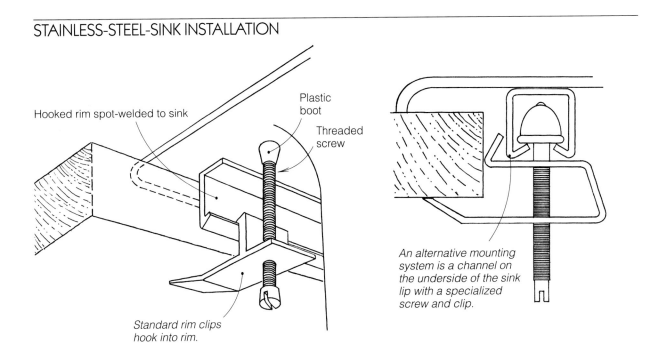

Hooked rim spot-welded to sink

Plastic boot

Threaded screw

Standard rim clips hook into rim.

An alternative mounting system is a channel on the underside of the sink lip with a specialized screw and clip.

What looks like an underhung sink installation is in fact a self-rimming stainless-steel sink on plywood with a Corian counter over the top.

Another domestic sink manufacturer, Polar Sinks (a division of Sterling Co.), uses threaded studs spot-welded to the underside of its bar sinks. A little flat steel clip is slid up the studs followed by a nut and you merely thread the nuts up, carrying the clips with them until they leverage the sink down onto the countertop. A nice feature of this mounting system is that you can use a socket wrench on the nuts, which doesn't slip off as easily as trying to tighten slotted screws. A word of caution, though: I have broken loose the spot-welded studs from the underside of Polar sinks when trying to go for that extra little bit of torque.

INSTALLING AN UNDERHUNG SINK

Sinks can be installed below the level of the countertop either by running tile or stone over the lip of the sink ("mudded in" or "counter over"), or by hanging the fixture from clips attached to the underside of the countertop. The underhung method of installation, which is used primarily for lavatory basins, can be te-dious, but I feel more comfortable with the integrity of the installation than when using a clamp-down rim and rim clips.

The underhung clip is a piece of flat steel shaped into a simple offset. When screwed to the bottom of the countertop, the clip grasps the lip of the sink and holds it tight to the underside of the counter (see the drawing on p. 90). To install an underhung sink, attach four clips to the underside of the countertop, equally spaced around the sink opening. The clips have an elongated slot so that they can be moved back and forth and pivoted out of the way to allow the sink to be lifted up under the counter. Hold the bowl in place, then swing the clips under the bowl and push them forward until they contact the bottom edge of the lip. Then thread the nuts onto the mounting screws. This can be trickier than it sounds, especially if the cabinet is small. It is further complicated if the faucet is mounted to the sink rather than the countertop, which makes the basin heavier and more difficult to balance. I usually leave the waste off an underhung sink until I have it mounted. It also takes several trips from lying on your back inside the cabinet to standing up and checking the position of the bowl for accurate centering.

UNDERHUNG-SINK INSTALLATION

In synthetic marble, the bolt head is often set into the countertop when the mixture is liquid. On other materials, you might find female threads in the countertop.

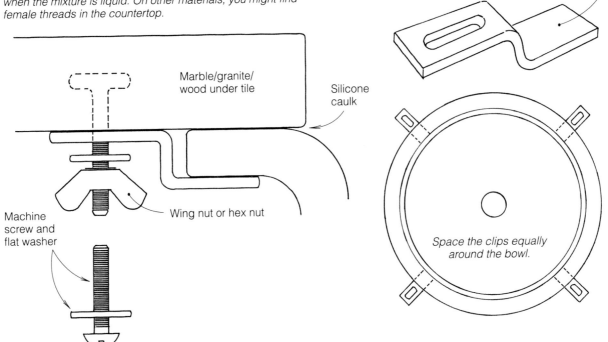

Underhung clip

Marble/granite/wood under tile

Silicone caulk

Machine screw and flat washer

Wing nut or hex nut

Space the clips equally around the bowl.

Once I get the basin in the right position, I loosen the screws a little and run a bead of caulk (clear silicone, or whatever the countertop installer recommends) in between the underside of the countertop and the top surface of the sink's lip. Then I snug up the basin permanently. I use caulk rather than plumber's putty here, because putty tends to keep the bowl held off from the under-counter surface, making it difficult to get the clips in place (unlike rim clips, underhung clips do not have the degree of compression necessary to squeeze the putty flat).

INSTALLING A WALL-HUNG SINK

Wall-hung lavatory basins have lost a lot of their popularity on new construction. (Our vanity has made them obsolete — there's no place to hide all the fountain-of-youth paraphernalia.) They still have their place, though, in tiny full bathrooms or half-bathrooms where a cabinet would make the room too small. A nice thing about the wall-hung installation is that you don't have to spend time cutting out the rough opening, and wall-hung sinks are always easy to remove.

Because there's no cabinet to support the sink, the wall-hung bowl requires some other means to hold the fixture to the wall — usually a hanger. A wall-hung sink also requires adequate blocking in the wall (added at the time of framing) to support the weight of the sink. With the loss in popularity of this style of sink, the quality of hanger hardware has declined.

WALL-HUNG-SINK INSTALLATION

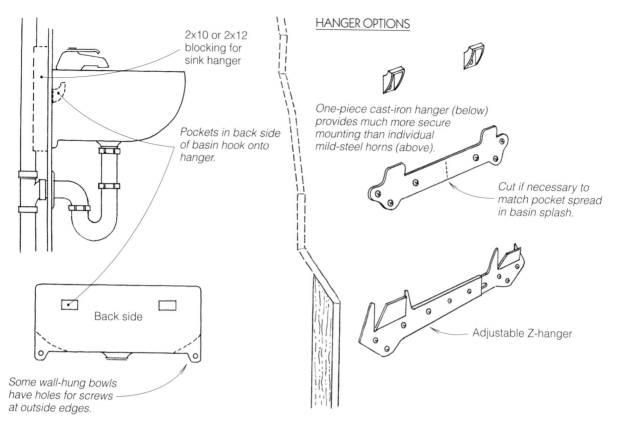

2x10 or 2x12 blocking for sink hanger

Pockets in back side of basin hook onto hanger.

Back side

Some wall-hung bowls have holes for screws at outside edges.

HANGER OPTIONS

One-piece cast-iron hanger (below) provides much more secure mounting than individual mild-steel horns (above).

Cut if necessary to match pocket spread in basin splash.

Adjustable Z-hanger

In former times, when many wall-hung sinks were cast iron and had high back splashes to disperse the forces of support to a large area, hangers were made from forged iron. It required a stout hanger to hold 40 lb. of sink or more on the wall. Modern hangers tend to be lightweight, mild steel, which has very poor rigidity, and the sink has little or no splash. If the hanger doesn't remain rigid once on the wall, the new sink (especially one without any splash or deep sides) will pull away from the wall. If the sink moves, leaks will show up in rigid-tube supply lines and in the waste and trap system.

Because the hangers that some sink manufacturers include with their sinks are so flimsy, I've started saving old horned sink hangers, which are usually at least 12 in. wide. If necessary, I saw the hanger in half to match the pocket spread in the new lavatory-basin splash. There is one old-style adjustable cast-iron horned hanger still on the market today — the Z-Hanger (model #1221) manufactured by Pasco (see

the Sources of Supply on pp. 178-179). This adjustable hanger comes as one piece, with score marks where it can be broken in two and overlapped for sinks requiring a narrower spread.

The actual installation of the sink is straightforward. Mount the hanger an inch or two below the finished sink height (depending on the location of the pockets on the back splash), then lift the sink into place, hooking the pockets onto the hanger horns. Check that the back wall of the sink is level. On older sinks there may be two holes on the bottom edge of the skirt, through which you can add two screws for extra support. I usually mount the faucet to the sink first, because the recess for the connections at the back of the sink tends to be small. If it looks very tight, I'll even install the supply tubes now and trim them to length once the sink is mounted. I don't worry about the waste at this stage — with no cabinet in the way it's easy to hook up once the sink is installed.

FAUCETS AND SUPPLY TUBES

Open a plumbing-supply catalog and you'll find a staggering choice of faucets for lavatory basins and kitchen sinks. In spite of the great diversity of styles, the vast majority of faucets used in new construction are of two basic designs: center-set faucets and widespread faucets.

In the bathroom, the most common type of faucet is one that mounts in holes spaced on 4-in. centers (known as a "4-in. center set"). The majority of 4-in. center sets are faucets whose valve body and spout are formed into one piece during the manufacturing process, either with individual hot and cold handles or a single-handle mixing valve. The bulk of the faucet rests on top of the sink or counter, with water connections that drop down through two holes in the sink or counter. Because the entire valve is above the sink or countertop, the 4-in. center set is often referred to as a "deck-mounted faucet." The deck-mounted design is also the most popular style for kitchen-sink faucets. Kitchen deck-mounted faucets are much the same as 4-in. center sets, except that the water connections are farther apart (usually 8 in.).

Unlike the one-piece 4-in. center set, most widespread faucets are comprised of three separate pieces: a spout and two valves. As the name implies, the valves are mounted farther apart than on a center set

— typically from 6 in. to 16 in. apart. The spout mounts on top of the sink or counter; the hot and cold valves hang down underneath, with just the trim (escutcheons and handles) showing above the deck. I like to think of the widespread design as an "under-deck-mounted faucet." The valves are connected to the spout by a manifold, which used to be a rigid tube on older-style faucets but is now more commonly flexible tubing. Both lavatory faucets and, to a lesser extent, kitchen-sink faucets are available in the widespread design.

In addition to these two basic types of faucets, I've also included some less common designs in the drawing on the facing page. The bar-sink faucet is essentially the same as the 4-in. center set, except that it usually has a high-loop spout. The single-post faucet, which is an old design found mostly on pedestal sinks, has a hot-and-cold mixing valve mounted in a single hole, either on the sink itself or on the countertop. The wall-hung faucet, which was a popular choice for kitchen sinks and laundry sinks in the past but it is not that common in residential construction anymore, is unlike other faucet designs in that it does not have angle stops to shut off the water service to the faucet. Instead, the faucet mounts directly to a hot and cold nipple at the wall (see Chapter 2).

FAUCET STYLES

4-IN. CENTER SET

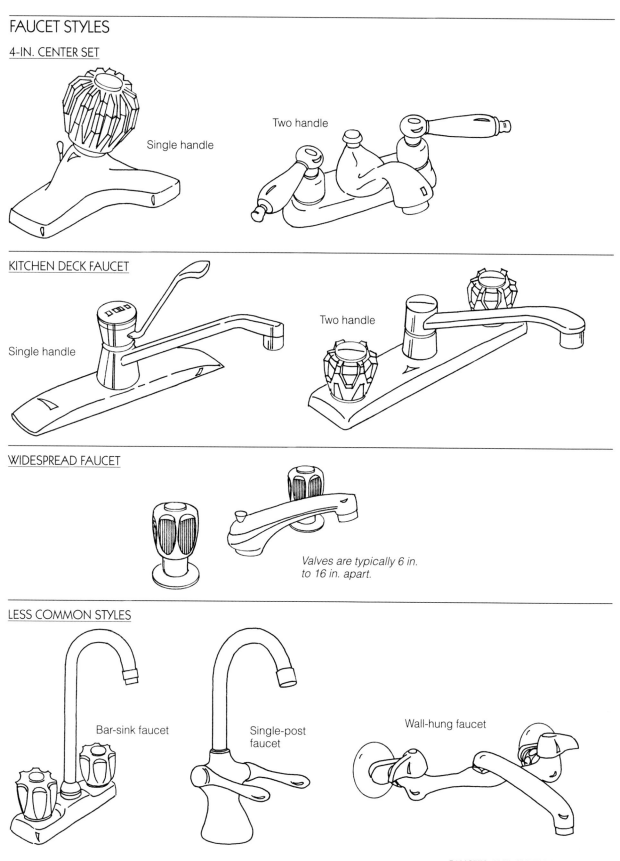

Single handle

Two handle

KITCHEN DECK FAUCET

Single handle

Two handle

WIDESPREAD FAUCET

Valves are typically 6 in. to 16 in. apart.

LESS COMMON STYLES

Bar-sink faucet

Single-post faucet

Wall-hung faucet

Begin the installation of a 4-in. center-set faucet by packing the underside with plumber's putty.

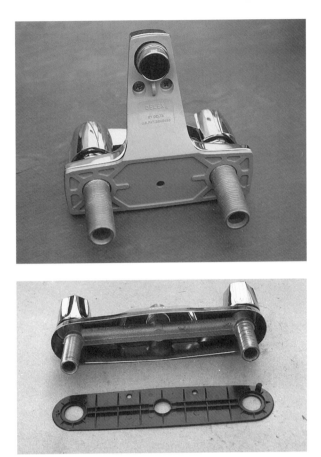

Center-set faucets for lavatory basins (top) and kitchen sinks (above) have different spreads between the thread connections but mount to the sink or countertop in the same way.

CENTER-SET FAUCETS

Center-set faucets are easier to install than widespread faucets since the faucet mounts as a single unit, whether on the sink itself or just behind it on the countertop. The only difference between a standard lavatory 4-in. center-set faucet and a standard 8-in. kitchen-sink deck-mounted faucet is the spread of the thread connections on the underside of the faucet. Here, I'll explain how to install a 4-in. center set, but you could use the same instructions to install a kitchen deck faucet. Whenever possible, I like to install the faucet before setting the sink, and that's the sequence I'll follow in this discussion. For more on setting the sink itself, see Chapter 6.

INSTALLING CENTER-SET FAUCETS

The first step in the installation is to pack the underside of the faucet with plumber's putty. Depending on the faucet you are installing, you might need as much as a full 1-lb. can of putty. Top-of-the-line one-piece cast-brass faucet bodies usually have only a shallow cavity under the faucet. Less expensive hardware-store-variety 4-in. center sets, which have a thin, polished-metal or chromed-plastic outer cover over the manifold and valves, tend to have a much deeper cavity. These economy faucets typically come with a mounting plate of colored plastic or white foam (see the lower photo at left). Don't use the plate, or you'll have a problem with splash-water leaks sometime in the future. Other faucets have a plastic base that is part of the outer housing (see the top photo at left). The base usually has an egg-crate pattern on the bottom to add some needed strength.

For the deep-cavity faucet, fill the underside of the housing with plumber's putty until it is flush with the bottom edge and a little higher in the middle. For the plastic-base faucet (or the cast-brass faucet), put a thin layer of putty on the bottom, making sure to push the putty well into the shallow recesses.

When it comes to buying faucets, the warning "let the buyer beware" is most appropriate. Very often, the glitter substitutes for quality. If there's one piece of advice I can give you when shopping for faucets, it's that brass is best. Nowadays just about anything, even plastic, can be chrome plated, and there's usually no simple way to determine what's under the chrome. Find out before you buy: Check with your supplier or, when in doubt, call the manufacturer of the faucet.

I consider the handles, which get the most movement, to be one of the most important parts of a faucet. They are subject to deterioration much faster than stationary parts, and if they need to be replaced you'll often have to rip out the entire faucet. Handles made of brass outlast all others because brass resists corrosion far better than alloys. Plastic handles have a tendency to lose their grip on stems or other regulating mechanisms. (Plastic leaves a lot to be desired when used in any faucet, whether for the body or the internal workings, so I recommend that you try to avoid all faucets with plastic parts.)

Another problem area is the mounting hardware that accompanies the faucet (usually flat washers and lock nuts). For most faucets, these parts will be plated-steel washers, plated-steel or die-cast nuts, or plastic washer/nut combinations. I recommend that you use only brass or stainless steel. If you cannot find brass hardware at suppliers in your area, write to Homer's Brass, P.O. Box 6541, Albany, Calif. 94706.

With the sink upside-down in your lap or on a work table, set the faucet into the holes in the sink. Now drop the washers down the threaded connections (depending on the faucet, the washers might be flat or cupped) and follow them with the lock mounting nuts. Regardless of the quality or cost of the faucet, I always use stainless-steel or brass washers and brass nuts. Tighten the nuts until the faucet is just barely movable by hand, then flip the bowl over and center the spout over the drain hole in the sink. Flip the bowl again and snug up the nuts. Keep checking the alignment — when you apply the finish torque to the nuts, they have a tendency to walk the faucet out of position. If this happens, loosen up the nuts just enough to reposition the faucet and try again. When you have the faucet in its final position, trim off the excess putty with a pocket knife. If it is physically possible to get the sink into the rough opening in the counter with the pop-up waste attached, I install that now too (see Chapter 8).

Four-inch center sets (and 8-in. kitchen deck-mount faucets) are also now available that mount to the sink or countertop with small-diameter steel threaded studs, large steel flat washers and small hex

With the sink upside-down, install the faucet, washers and nuts.

4-IN. CENTER-SET INSTALLATION

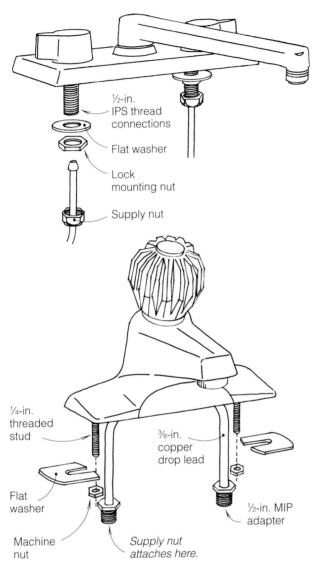

½-in.
IPS thread
connections

Flat washer

Lock
mounting nut

Supply nut

¼-in.
threaded
stud

⅜-in.
copper
drop lead

Flat
washer

½-in. MIP
adapter

Machine
nut

*Supply nut
attaches here.*

Widespread faucets with separate valves and spout are used on all styles of cabinet-mounted sinks and on modern pedestal sinks.

nuts (see the drawing above). The water-supply connections are ⅜-in. copper-tube "drop leads" with ½-in. MIP adapters soldered onto the ends. There are also lavatory and kitchen drop-lead faucets that mount in just one hole. These drop-lead faucets, which are cheaper to manufacture than those with the standard ½-in. IPS thread connections, tend to be more prone to leaks and can come loose on the sink or counter as a result of rusting of the steel nut or threaded stud.

WIDESPREAD FAUCETS

Because widespread faucets are made up of separate components, they are more time-consuming to install than one-piece 4-in. center sets. However, a recent change in the design of the valve-to-spout connection has made widespread faucets considerably easier to install.

On old-style widespread faucets (and a few modern ones) the manifold connections between the individual valves and the spout are made of rigid brass or bendable copper tube. Although these are very durable materials, it can be a very tedious chore trying to figure out the proper lay for the spout connections because the cut lengths have to be just right. The majority of widespread faucets made today have flexible plastic manifold tubes with swaged metal connections, and it's a simple matter to bend or loop the tubing to fit the spread of the valves.

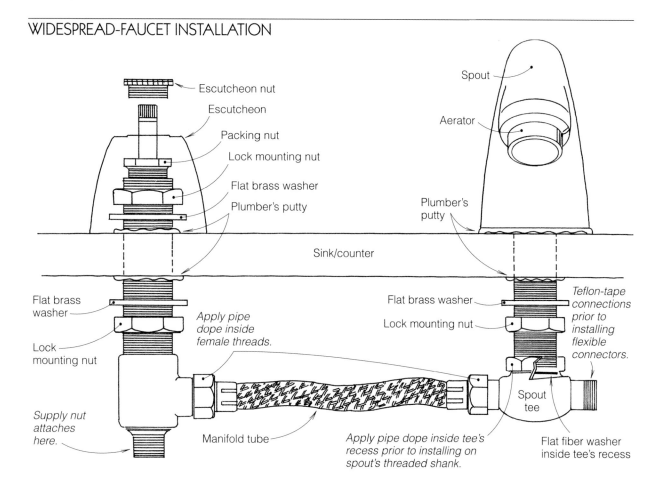

Escutcheon nut

Escutcheon

Packing nut

Lock mounting nut

Flat brass washer

Plumber's putty

Spout

Aerator

Plumber's putty

Sink/counter

Flat brass washer

Lock mounting nut

Apply pipe dope inside female threads.

Teflon-tape connections prior to installing flexible connectors.

Flat brass washer

Lock mounting nut

Supply nut attaches here.

Manifold tube

Apply pipe dope inside tee's recess prior to installing on spout's threaded shank.

Spout tee

Flat fiber washer inside tee's recess

Another thing that I like about flexible manifold tubing is that the connections at the valve and spout are usually ground metal-to-metal joints, which are a great improvement over the slip nuts and rubber cone washers used with rigid manifold tubing (any rubber connection is prone to leaks over time). And unlike supply tubes made from plastic (see p. 103), the flexible plastic manifold tube is not under pressure when the valve is turned off, so there's no danger of the connections blowing apart. Even when the valve is on, the pressure is low because the system is open-ended.

INSTALLING WIDESPREAD FAUCETS

Almost all brands of widespread faucets have essentially the same parts, but because this type of faucet is not a one-piece assemblage I cannot categorically say: "this washer goes here and that nut goes there." You'll have to refer to the instructions for specific installation details. However, I can say that almost all widespreads have a thin flat nut and washer below the sink or counter and another thin flat nut and washer above to hold the valve rigidly in place, as shown in the drawing above. (As with the 4-in. center set, if there are any plated-steel washers try to find brass replacements.) Some faucet companies include thin rubber washers to go under the metal washer on top (and sometimes on bottom) of the sink to prevent splash water from seeping into the cabinet. All brands have escutcheons that thread down onto the valve from above to hide the installation and pack-

SPOUT INSTALLATION

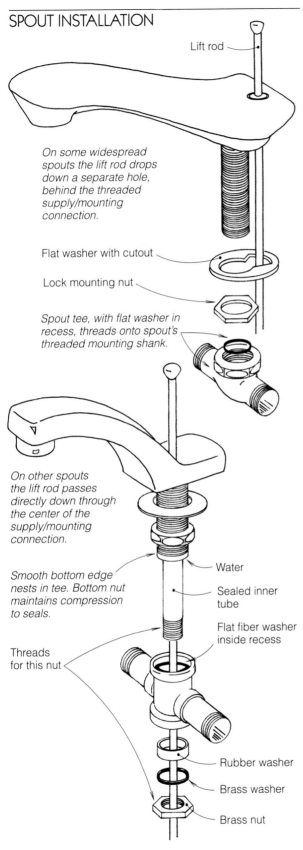

Lift rod

On some widespread spouts the lift rod drops down a separate hole, behind the threaded supply/mounting connection.

Flat washer with cutout

Lock mounting nut

Spout tee, with flat washer in recess, threads onto spout's threaded mounting shank.

On other spouts the lift rod passes directly down through the center of the supply/mounting connection.

Smooth bottom edge nests in tee. Bottom nut maintains compression to seals.

Threads for this nut

Water

Sealed inner tube

Flat fiber washer inside recess

Rubber washer

Brass washer

Brass nut

ing nuts. The biggest above-sink difference between the selection of valves is the stem assembly and how the handle fits onto it, and the shape and type of threaded connections on the escutcheons. Most of the below-sink external differences between brands vanished with the solid-tube manifold and the adoption of the flexible plastic.

Begin the installation with the spout. Apply plumber's putty to the base of the spout, then set it in the center hole of the sink or counter. Slide the large flat washer over the spout's threaded connection, followed by the lock mounting nut. As when installing the 4-in. center set (see p. 95), you'll have to keep checking the alignment of the spout and the drain hole as you snug up the nut. Next thread the spout tee onto the threaded connection. Depending on the design of the faucet, the spout tee may have an opening at top and bottom, or just at top (see the drawing at left). Apply pipe dope (I use Rectorseal) in these recesses before installing the tee.

With the spout and spout tee installed, the next step is to set the valves. Thread one of the large lock mounting nuts and a flat washer down the threaded exterior of each valve, then lift the valves up through the holes in the sink or countertop and add the second nut and washer. I decide in which direction to point the valve's male threads for the flexible manifold connectors depending upon how much room there is under the sink and/or cabinet, how long the flexible connectors are and what kind of handle connections the valves have (some handles can only be installed in one or two positions). Don't tighten the nuts for now, because you may have to reposition the valves slightly after you've connected the manifold tubing.

Apply pipe dope inside the female threads of the manifold tubing and Teflon tape to the male threads of the valves and spout tee. Attach the manifold to the valves first, then loop or bend the flexible tubing as necessary before threading it onto the spout tee. Be careful not to kink the plastic tubing or little or no water will arrive at the spout. Once you've connected the manifold tubing securely, you can snug up all the mounting nuts. Finish the widespread installation by threading the escutcheons over the valves, with plumber's putty under the escutcheon bases, then install the handles.

All sinks manufactured with existing holes for faucets and trim, whether cast iron, porcelain, enameled steel, stainless steel, acrylic, or cultured or synthetic marble, are available with a varying number of holes (most commonly, three or four). In most cases, you'll want to buy the sink that already has the number of holes for what you will be mounting to the sink. In addition to the holes for the faucet itself, you might need mounting holes for a dish-spray hose, a soap/lotion dispenser, an air gap for a dishwasher, or a hot-water dispenser (see Chapter 9).

If you have a stainless-steel or synthetic-marble sink, you can make additional holes yourself, which is handy if you want to add trim after the sink is installed. I use a chassis punch, made by Greenlee, to make holes in stainless steel. It's actually an electrician's tool for punching holes in junction and panel boxes, but it makes a 1¼-in. diameter hole that's just the right size for plumbing valves and trim.

To make holes in synthetic marble, you need a carbide- or diamond-tipped hole saw. Since I don't own either, I have the dealer make any necessary extra holes (for a small charge). There are companies that will, for a considerable charge, make additional holes in cast-iron fixtures. But you can usually buy a sink with the desired number of holes more cheaply than having the extras made.

You can, of course, also mount faucets and trim on the countertop behind the sink. One counter surface I don't recommend for faucet installation, however, is tile. If the tile counter is a thick one, many times the threaded mounting portions of the widespread valves and spout are too short to penetrate the counter and still allow room for the lower washers and nuts. You can spend a lot of time under the counter chipping away supporting wood in order to get washers and nuts on the valves and spout, and you'll be removing what gives the counter its strength. So if you have a choice of mounting a faucet to a drilled sink or a drilled tile countertop, always opt for the sink.

FAUCET SUPPLY TUBES

Once the sink and faucet are in place, you're ready to install the supply tubes between the threaded faucet connections and the angle stops. Faucet supply tubes are available in chromed brass, braided stainless steel and reinforced plastic.

CHROMED-BRASS SUPPLIES

Sinks in use since the 1930s and '40s will usually have ½-in. or ⁷⁄₁₆-in. diameter, heavy-walled, chromed-brass supply tubes with flush-cut ends. These old-style supplies were used in conjunction with rubber cone washers and brass friction rings and attached to the faucet connections with chromed-brass slip nuts. You can still buy flush-cut chromed-brass supplies, but they tend to be of poorer quality than the originals; the metal walls of some cheaper supplies are

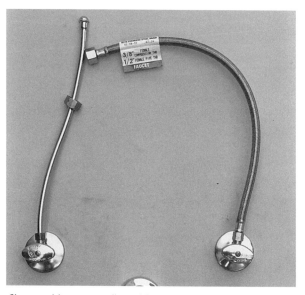

Chromed-brass supplies with an acorn head (left) and braided stainless-steel supplies (right) provide a watertight connection between the faucet and the angle stop.

CHROMED-BRASS SUPPLY TUBES

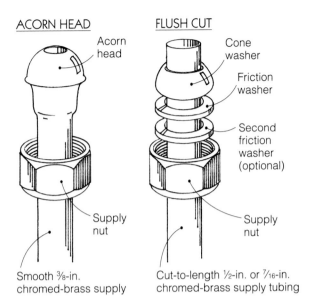

ACORN HEAD

Acorn head

Supply nut

Smooth ⅜-in. chromed-brass supply

FLUSH CUT

Cone washer

Friction washer

Second friction washer (optional)

Supply nut

Cut-to-length ½-in. or 7/16-in. chromed-brass supply tubing

sometimes so thin that they can crack and leak from mere pressure fatigue. (For information on installing flush-cut supplies, see pp. 101-102.)

For kitchen- and bathroom-sink faucets, I prefer to use smooth ⅜-in. chromed-brass supplies that have an acorn head rather than a flush-cut end. The acorn head seals to the beveled opening of the faucet connection, without any need for cone washers and friction rings, and is held in place by a slip nut. If you use the acorn-head supplies with brass FIP to compression angle stops (see pp. 18-19), you completely eliminate the use of rubber washers in faucet installation, which greatly reduces the risk of water leaks.

There are several brands of ⅜-in. acorn-head supplies, but I like to use those manufactured by either the Eastman Company ("Speedflex") or the Brass Craft Company ("Speedway"). I like the configuration of the acorn head of these two brands — once compressed, it very rarely leaks — and the quality of the chrome finish is usually very good. These supplies are available in lengths from 12 in. to 30 in., which can be cut to the length needed. I usually install ⅜-in. supplies, but you can also get ½-in. supplies in the acorn-head design (though they may be more difficult to find in the longer lengths and are harder to bend by hand). You might want to use these larger-

diameter supplies, which allow better water flow, if you live in an area with low water pressure (under 35 psi). With these supplies, you'd need to install ½-in. FIP to ½-in. compression angle stops.

INSTALLING ACORN-HEAD SUPPLIES Begin the installation by sliding the slip nut up the supply tube to the acorn head, then hand-tighten the nut to the threaded connection of the faucet. Now bend the supply tube so that it passes to the outside edge of the angle stop (see the photo at left on the facing page). Use a felt-tip pen to mark where to cut the supply tube — at a point about ¼ in. below the bottom of the threaded sleeve for the compression nut on the angle stop.

Unthread the supply from the faucet connection, then use a tubing cutter (see p. 9) to cut the tube to length. With the tube positioned between the rollers and the cutting wheel, rotate the cutter one complete turn. Then reverse the direction for another complete turn. Tighten the cutter handle and repeat the process until the supply is severed.

With the tubing cut, you can install the supply permanently. Slide the brass compression nut and ferrule up the supply, and then insert the bottom of the supply tubing into the threaded sleeve of the angle stop. Thread the compression nut onto the sleeve, being careful not to cross-thread the fine threads. Next, insert the acorn head into the faucet connection as perfectly vertical as possible, put some pipe dope on the slip-nut threads and Teflon tape on the threaded connection, and hand-tighten the nut. Now go back and snug up the compression nut on the angle stop with an adjustable wrench, and finish by tightening the faucet slip nut with a basin wrench.

On most installations the angle stops are located more or less directly under the faucet connections, and any bends you have to make in the supply tubes are easily done by hand. When the angle stops are offset from the faucet, however, you may need to use a tubing bender to make tight-radius bends (see p. 9). It can be difficult to bend a short supply to get it inserted in both the faucet connection and the angle-stop connection without kinking, so sometimes I'll use a longer supply and position the angle-stop supply connections pointing down (see the bottom photo at right on the facing page). With the longer supply and two 90° bends, it's easier to run the

With the chromed-brass supply tube bent to the outside of the angle stop, mark the cutting point just below the bottom of the threaded sleeve.

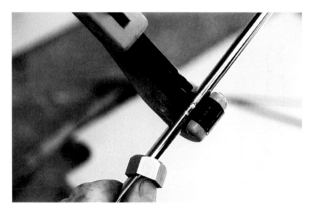

Cut the supply by rotating a tubing cutter in alternate directions around the tube.

If the angle stops are not located directly below the faucet connections, it's often easier to use longer supply tubes and connect them under the angle stop.

tubing straight up into the connections. Also, I think it looks better than running the supplies out of the top of the angle stops on a diagonal.

Before leaving the topic of acorn-head supplies, I'd like to offer a couple of words of warning. If you're installing a cheap faucet that comes with plastic supply nuts, don't use them with the Speedway or Speedflex supplies. These plastic nuts don't provide enough compression force to make the acorn head conform properly to the bevel in the faucet's threaded connection. Find brass replacements for the plastic supply nuts. Also, if you're installing a plastic-bodied faucet (which I wouldn't recommend unless you have very poor water quality), don't try to use the acorn-head supplies. The plastic-threaded faucet connections are too soft to allow the supplies to seal the way they are designed to. Instead, use braided stainless-steel supplies or flush-cut supplies with rubber cone washers at the faucet connections (see below). One final warning: If you're replacing a faucet, don't try to reuse the same supplies on the new faucet. Once the acorn head has been compressed to the faucet connection, it probably won't conform to a different connection and a leak will develop.

INSTALLING FLUSH-CUT SUPPLIES Chromed-brass supplies with flush-cut ends and rubber cone washers aren't used much these days, but I'll give you a few tips on installing them in case you do choose to work with them. The tubing material for these supplies is commonly sold in 5-ft. lengths, which should be enough for two supplies. Once you've cut the sup-

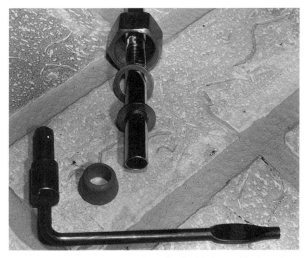

Flush-cut supply tubes are installed with brass friction rings and a rubber cone washer. The tool in the foreground is a beading tool used to form a raised bead around the circumference of the tube. (Photo by Bill Dane)

plies to length, you need to use a beading tool to form a raised welt, or bead, running around the circumference of the tube. Often these supplies are installed without the bead, which is one of the main reasons they fail.

Slide the faucet slip nut down the supply tube, followed by a brass friction ring. Then bead the tubing the depth of the rubber washer from the end of the tubing. As a safety measure, slide on another friction ring and then the rubber cone washer. The bead and first friction ring prevent the end of the supply from backing out of the faucet connection. The second friction ring keeps the cone washer supported at its bottom surface. Other than the faucet connection, the rest of the installation process is the same as for acorn-head supplies.

CORRUGATED SUPPLIES   One other type of chromed-brass supply has a smooth bottom section that can be used with brass ferrule and compression nut connections and a flexible, corrugated center section made for easy bending. The top end of this supply can be found with either the acorn-head or rubber-cone-washer design. These corrugated supplies are quite popular, but I don't like to use them because the grooves of the corrugated section invariably spring a leak a few years after installation.

There's also a one-piece angle stop/supply tube that has a corrugated brass supply soldered to the angle stop. This design is definitely one to avoid.

BRAIDED STAINLESS-STEEL SUPPLIES

Braided stainless-steel supply tubes are relative new-comers to the market, but they've proven very popular because of their ease of installation. These supplies have captive nuts on each end that also serve as unions. There are two particular brands that I like to work with. The Aquaflo brand has ground-metal seals (with no rubber), and can safely be used on high-pressure systems without need for a pressure regulator. Fluidmaster's "No-Burst" supplies do have rubber seals, but can be used on systems regulated to around 50 psi to 60 psi.

Braided stainless-steel supplies come in various lengths but, unlike chromed-brass supplies, cannot be trimmed. If they're long, you just let them bend inward or outward; if they are considerably too long, you can loop them. They are installed in a fraction of the time of rigid supplies and require no tools other than a basin wrench (for the faucet connection) and a small adjustable wrench (for the angle-stop connection). My decision to use braided supplies hinges upon visibility: I think they're fine under a cabinet-mounted sink, but feel they look unsightly for a wall-hung or pedestal sink.

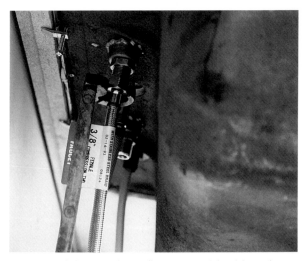

Braided stainless-steel supplies are considerably easier to install than rigid supplies. Here, the supply nut is being threaded to the faucet connection using a basin wrench.

PLASTIC SUPPLIES

Plastic is used extensively for plumbing materials these days, so it's no surprise that you can now get supply tubes made of plastic. There are two types. One is a ⅜-in. diameter polybutylene (PB) plastic supply tube that has a head configuration similar to the acorn head. This type is often used with plastic-pipe systems and plastic angle stops, though it can also be installed on the ⅜-in. compression connections of a brass angle stop. Moen Faucet Co. ships this supply with its bathroom "Riser" lavatory faucet. I try to avoid plastic components as much as possible when hooking up faucets, but concede that PB supplies might be a logical choice for plastic faucets serving very poor quality drinking water, where brass would corrode or react in other ways with the water's content. Where I live, the water quality is excellent, so I don't risk the plastic, either for the faucet or the supply. If you do decide to use plastic supplies (or faucets), make certain that you have a pressure regulator on the main water line that limits the house pressure to 50 psi (see p. 26).

The other type of plastic supply tube, which I recommend you avoid at all costs, is a reinforced PB supply with swaged union nuts on each end. This kind of supply is responsible for untold damage to structures — I've had to remove several (installed by others) that have failed and flooded buildings. It's not the plastic itself that fails in this type, but the joint where the metal connections attach to the plastic.

COPPER-TUBING SUPPLIES

You won't find copper-tubing supplies in your local plumbing-supply store, but they are something you can easily assemble yourself. I use ⅜-in. coiled copper refrigeration tubing for supplies if the distance between the faucet and the angle stop is greater than can be spanned by commercially available supplies.

To use copper tubing for supplies, you first need to attach a ½-in. FIP to ⅜-in. compression adapter to each faucet connection. (This is the same adapter that is used to convert ½-in. IPS angle-stop connections to ⅜-in. compression — see p. 20.) Wrap Teflon tape on the faucet connections and apply pipe dope to the adapters first. With the adapters attached to the faucet, you can slide the cut-to-length copper tubing up into the faucet connection (sometimes several inches) and then lower the bottom of the tubing

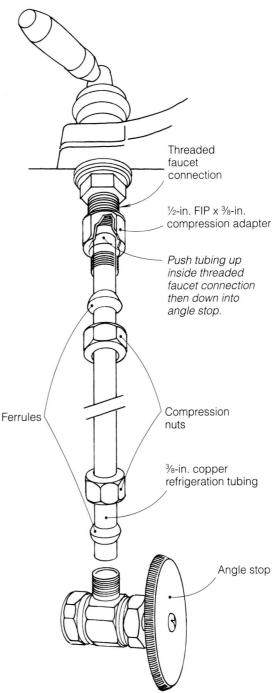

USING COPPER TUBING FOR SUPPLIES

Threaded faucet connection

½-in. FIP x ⅜-in. compression adapter

Push tubing up inside threaded faucet connection then down into angle stop.

Ferrules

Compression nuts

⅜-in. copper refrigeration tubing

Angle stop

into the male threaded connection of the angle stop. Both the upper and lower connections use a brass ferrule and compression nut, so the copper tubing cannot pull out of the fitting.

SINK WASTES AND TRAPS

Once a sink is installed and the faucets are hooked up to the water supply, it's time to make the connections that will allow waste water to drain away from the fixture. This drainage system under the sink is comprised of two parts: the waste and the trap. By the term "waste," I mean the fitting that is set in the hole in the sink bottom, as well as the connecting piping that attaches the fitting to the trap. The "trap" is the piping with two 90° bends (J-bend) and an arm (trap arm) that carries the waste water to the drain line and creates a water seal to prevent sewer gases from backing up into the house. Most traps used today are P-traps, which drain into the wall by way of a 90° trap arm (see the bottom photo on the facing page). On existing installations you might also find S-traps, which drain into the floor via a 180° trap arm. These old-style S-traps are no longer allowed by code in many areas.

Whereas the water-supply system is essentially the same for sinks whether they are in the bathroom or the kitchen, the waste system is somewhat different. Lavatory basins, which have a smaller-diameter drain hole, are typically installed with a pop-up waste. Kitchen sinks (and bar sinks), on the other hand, have a basket strainer. I'll explain how to install both

kinds in this chapter. The trap assembly is essentially the same regardless of sink type, except that lavatory-basin traps are required by code to have a minimum diameter of 1¼ in., whereas kitchen-sink traps must have a minimum diameter of 1½ in.

Installing the waste and trap is fairly simple in terms of pipe joinery, but it can be a challenge conceptually, especially if you're hooking up a continuous waste system to connect two or more sinks (see pp. 119-123). To help visualize the completed system, I advise you always to dry-fit the components together first. This way you can take them apart and make the necessary modifications until you see the path you need to take to get to the wall. Dry-fitting the components also frees up one or both hands so you can "eyeball" or measure connecting pipe for a more accurate installation.

As in previous chapters, you'll see that I voice my preferences for certain materials and warn against others. I've always advocated buying and installing top-quality sinks, but if you slack off on the design and execution of the waste installation you won't fully enjoy the benefits of choosing that quality fixture.

MATERIALS

Waste and trap systems are generally either of ABS or PVC plastic or, less frequently these days, chrome-plated tubular brass. Unless the waste piping will be highly visible (as on a wall-hung sink), I prefer to work with plastic piping since it is less prone to leaks. One other choice for sink wastes is DWV copper. This material is extremely sturdy and durable, but it is more expensive and harder to work with (requiring soldering). DWV copper is very rarely used for sink waste systems, except on million-dollar homes, and I won't discuss its installation here.

ABS AND PVC

Schedule 40 ABS or PVC pipe and fittings, cut to length and cemented together, are a good, economical choice for lavatory and kitchen-sink waste systems. This pipe is the same heavy-duty material that I explained how to install for traps under bathtubs on a slab floor (see pp. 49-52). For that application, where the trap is inaccessible after the tub is down, *all* the joints are cemented. Under a sink, one of the joints (the one between the trap-arm elbow and the J-bend) should be a union so that the trap can be taken apart easily.

In recent years, plastic sink traps have become available in much thinner-walled material, made to the same outside diameter as tubular brass. I recommend that you stay away from this type of trap. Not only is the plastic much flimsier than Schedule 40 pipe (necessitating more frequent repair or replacement), but also all the connections between the trap parts are made with slip nuts and slip washers, which are more likely to leak than cemented joints. If you install the tubular-sized waste system on a stainless-steel (or enameled-steel) kitchen sink that hosts a garbage disposer, the slip-nut joints can work loose over time. The cemented Schedule 40 ABS or PVC waste system will remain watertight in spite of all the vibrations and gyrations caused by the disposer.

Not all communities allow the use of ABS or PVC piping for drainage systems, so always check your local code before installing a sink waste system. In some parts of the country you may be able to use plastic for the in-the-wall DWV piping, but not for

Choices of material for waste systems include ABS plastic (top), DWV copper (left) and tubular brass (right). The wastes and traps shown are for double-bowl sinks.

Tubular-brass trap systems (left) are assembled with slip nuts and washers. Schedule 40 ABS traps (right) have cemented joints, except for the union nut at the J-bend to trap-arm connection.

the outside-the-wall piping under a sink (primarily because ABS and PVC are perceived by some authorities as fire hazards). In this case, your trap and any additional waste piping will have to be tubular brass (or soldered DWV copper).

TUBULAR BRASS

Chrome-plated tubular-brass traps are thinner walled than plastic traps, and the inside diameter is also less (i.e., nominal 1½-in. tubular brass is slightly smaller in diameter than true 1½-in. Schedule 40 ABS or PVC). If you are installing a tubular-brass trap system, I recommend you use only a 17-gauge trap, which is more durable than the thinner 20- to 22-gauge tubular brass. You can also get heavy, cast-brass traps, though they are seldom used in residential construction because of their expense.

Tubular-brass traps and waste piping are assembled with slip nuts and washers, which cannot grip the pipe as securely as cemented ABS or PVC fittings on plastic pipe. On kitchen sinks, tubular-brass traps are prone to vibratory leaks from disposals and subject to deterioration by dishwasher detergents, which do not bother ABS or PVC plastic. Over time, the slip-nut washers lose their elasticity, crack and cause leaks. With the failure of the slip-nut washers, the joined tubular-brass trap components also have the potential to separate, again causing leaks.

INSTALLING A POP-UP WASTE

A pop-up waste is the assembly that is installed in the drain hole in the bottom of a lavatory basin. On old-style lavatory installations, the waste was simply a seat flange that threaded into a pipe below the lavatory basin. The drain opening was closed by a rubber stopper. These rubber-stopper wastes are still available (though their material quality is usually poor), but much more common nowadays are wastes with an integral stopper that is raised or lowered by a lift rod that passes through the faucet body.

Pop-up wastes come with the lavatory faucet, though you usually have the option of buying the faucet without the pop-up. Cheap faucets are often shipped with all-plastic pop-up wastes, which I don't use, nor do I recommend that you use. There are several designs of brass pop-ups, most of which nowadays have a one-piece body, with a separate seat flange and tailpiece that install at top and bottom,

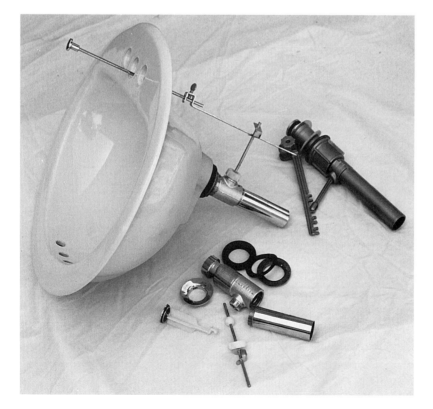

Pop-up wastes are installed in lavatory drain holes and actuated by a lift rod and arm. Shown here are a brass pop-up (installed in the sink and disassembled) and a plastic pop-up (at right).

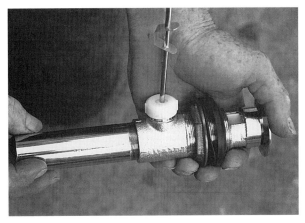

Threading the tailpiece into the pop-up waste body (shown here before installation in the sink) can take time and patience.

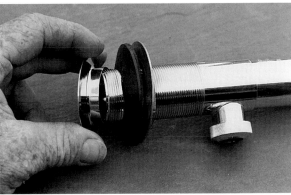

Brass pop-up wastes are available with a seat flange that threads into the waste body (top) or over the waste body (above). (Photos by Bill Dane)

respectively. On some brass pop-ups, the seat flange threads into the waste body, as shown in the top photo above. I prefer the design with a seat flange that threads over the waste body (see the photo above), which leaves a larger drain passage. A less common, though satisfactory, design is a brass pop-up waste with an extended seat flange that fully penetrates the thickness of the bowl and threads onto a coupling below the sink containing the pop-up arm threads. Regardless of the design, brass pop-up wastes will have a large, flat, plated-steel and/or fiber washer, a beveled gasket and a flat lock mounting nut that is usually dull natural brass or dull chrome-plated brass. As ever, if the mounting nut on your waste is die-cast, try to find a brass replacement (or buy a waste that does have a brass nut).

INSTALLING THE POP-UP BODY

Begin the installation by wrapping a ½-in. diameter putty snake under the lip of the pop-up seat flange (see the drawing on p. 108). If the flange is female threaded, apply pipe dope to the threads; if the flange is male threaded, brush pipe dope on the female threads of the pop-up body. Then thread the lock mounting nut down to the last thread on the pop-up body, followed by the flat friction washer and the beveled waste gasket (bevel up). Lift the waste up through the hole in the basin from below and thread the flange to the waste as far as it will go. Next use a 10-in. slide-jaw pliers to thread the lock mounting nut up the pop-up body, carrying with it the washer and rubber gasket. Wrap another putty snake on top of the beveled gasket before it contacts the bottom of the sink, then tighten up the lock nut really snug. Make sure that the hole in the waste body for the actuator arm (or the arm itself if it is already loosely threaded in place) is pointing straight back, away from the front of the bowl.

Once the pop-up body is secured to the bowl, apply pipe dope to the female threads inside the bottom of the body and carefully thread in the tailpiece. (If you're installing a tubular-brass trap, you'll probably have to use an extension tailpiece since the factory-supplied tailpiece is invariably too short to reach the trap opening.) Getting the fine male threads of the tailpiece started into the pop-up body

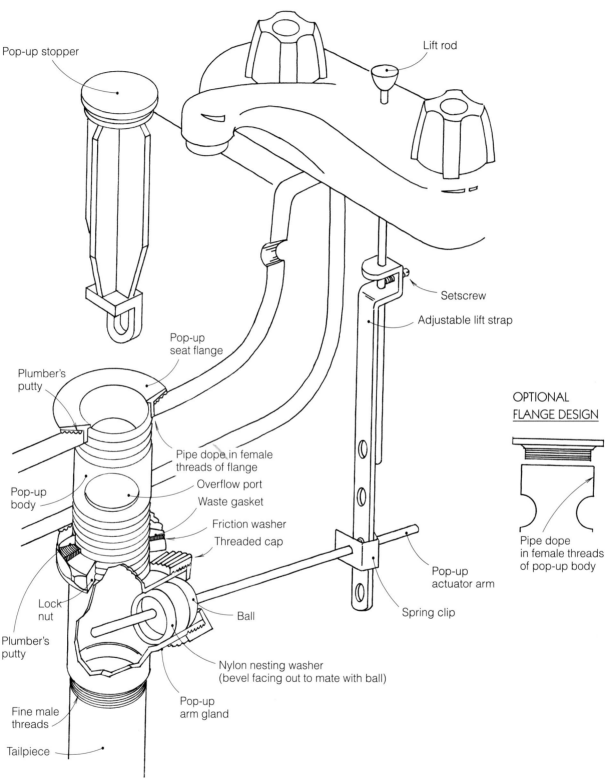

Pop-up stopper

Lift rod

Setscrew

Adjustable lift strap

Pop-up
seat flange

Plumber's
putty

OPTIONAL
FLANGE DESIGN

Pipe dope in female
threads of flange

Overflow port

Waste gasket

Pop-up
body

Friction washer

Threaded cap

Pipe dope
in female threads
of pop-up body

Pop-up
actuator arm

Lock
nut

Ball

Spring clip

Plumber's
putty

Nylon nesting washer
(bevel facing out to mate with ball)

Fine male
threads

Pop-up
arm gland

Tailpiece

without cross-threading can require great patience, so take your time here. And tighten the tailpiece with your hands only (no tools).

INSTALLING THE POP-UP ARM AND LIFT STRAP

Now you're ready to install the arm that raises and lowers the pop-up stopper. First, drop the stopper into the waste and rotate it so that any offset in its lower leg is closest to the pop-up arm opening, as shown in the drawing on the facing page. There should be a small nylon washer that goes into the pop-up arm recess on the back of the waste. Put pipe dope in the recess before inserting the washer. Next wrap Teflon tape on the male threads of the pop-up arm gland and insert the ball end of the arm into the opening and through the hole in the bottom of the stopper. Move the arm up and down to make sure that you have hit the target (the stopper will move up and down), then thread the gland nut finger-tight onto the male threads.

The final stage in the pop-up installation is to connect the arm to the lift rod by way of an adjustable lift strap. Drop the lift rod down the hole in the faucet (see p. 98), and pull it down all the way from underneath until the knob contacts the top of the faucet spout or body. Now pull down on the pop-up arm, sending the stopper to the top of its travel, as shown in the drawing at right. Hold the strap between the lift rod and the arm and eyeball the hole for the arm that will pull the stopper back down into the flange (making sure that the top of the strap won't hit the underside of the sink). Mark the hole with a pencil or awl.

Now slide one leg of the spring clip onto the pop-up arm, followed by the lift strap and the other leg of the spring clip. Pull the pop-up arm back down to the bottom of its travel and insert the lift rod through the two holes at the top of the strap. Pull the lift rod all the way down and secure by tightening the setscrew (or thumbscrew) at the top of the strap. You might later need to trim the lift strap to prevent it from interfering with the trap arm (see the photo at right).

With the pop-up waste installed, the next stage is to install the trap between the bottom of the tailpiece and the sanitary tee at the wall (see pp. 113-119). But first I'll explain how to set the waste — in this case a basket strainer — in a kitchen sink.

INSTALLING THE LIFT STRAP

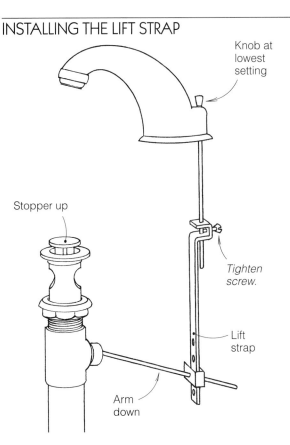

Knob at lowest setting

Stopper up

Tighten screw.

Lift strap

Arm down

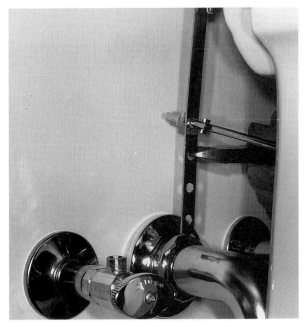

Sometimes you need to trim the lift strap after the trap is installed.

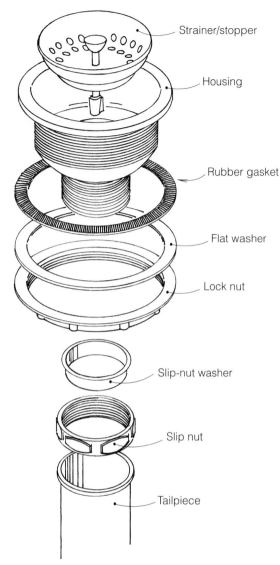

Strainer/stopper

Housing

Rubber gasket

Flat washer

Lock nut

Slip-nut washer

Slip nut

Tailpiece

INSTALLING A BASKET STRAINER

Installing a basket strainer in a kitchen sink is a considerably simpler task than installing a lavatory pop-up waste since there's no movable arm, strap or lift rod to fiddle with. The seal in the drain hole is provided by the basket nesting inside the strainer housing. In my experience, choosing a good-quality basket strainer for the kitchen sink can make a big difference in the level of customer satisfaction with the finish job (for some advice on choosing a basket strainer, see the sidebar on p. 112). Unfortunately, you probably won't be able to find a top-quality basket strainer at a hardware store or even at a building-supply outlet. This is one item you'll probably have to look for at a plumbing-supply house.

To install the basket strainer, first wrap a putty snake about ½ in. in diameter under the lip of the strainer housing, then set the housing in the sink drain hole (see the top photo at left on the facing page). Next, working underneath the sink, butter up the bottom edge of the sink hole with pipe dope. Slide the rubber gasket over the housing, followed by the flat fiber or plastic washer, then thread the brass lock nut up until it contacts the bottom of the sink. You'll have to hold the strainer still in the sink with a strainer wrench as you thread on the lock nut. To snug up the nut, hold the strainer wrench with an adjustable wrench and use a large pair of slide-jaw pliers on the nut, as shown in the bottom photo on the facing page. I wait about ten minutes and then tighten the nut one last time, since the rubber gasket will give a little after it has been compressed initially. If there's an etched manufacturer's name or trademark in the lip of the strainer (as on the Kohler strainer that I like to install), I make sure to set the name at the twelve o'clock position.

The Kohler basket strainer comes with a heavy-duty 17-gauge tailpiece and a solid-brass slip nut. I use the rubber slip-nut washer provided, sliding it up the tailpiece to rest on the underside of the tailpiece lip. Having the washer on the outside of the tailpiece leaves a large opening for drainage — some of the cheaper strainers have a flat-brimmed nylon washer that partially covers the opening. Then I wrap Teflon

Run a putty snake under the lip of the strainer housing and set the strainer into the drain hole (top left). While holding the strainer still in the sink with a strainer wrench (top right), use a pair of slide-jaw pliers to tighten up the brass lock nut (above).

BASKET STRAINERS

If you've read this far, it will probably come as no great surprise to learn that there is a wide variation in the quality of basket strainers, as there is with most plumbing supplies.

Top-quality basket strainers have housings made of cast brass, with a wide, accurately tapered lip and well-cut upper and lower threads. They are shipped with a thick rubber gasket, a solid-brass flat washer (or good-quality plastic flat washer) and a solid-brass nut. The lift-out basket strainer is solid brass, and the stopper on the underside is also brass and seals to the housing without the use of any rubber. The only U.S. company I am aware of that makes a basket strainer to these standards is Kohler.

At the other end of the scale, cheap basket strainers are made with a stainless-steel, plastic-covered steel or even all-plastic housing, often with a narrow lip and poorly cut, rolled threads. They are shipped with a thin rubber gasket, a paper or plastic flat washer and a die-cast or plastic nut, or other fasteners that quickly corrode and jump threads. The basket strainer may also be plastic or stainless steel and have a flimsy stopper. Most have a rub-

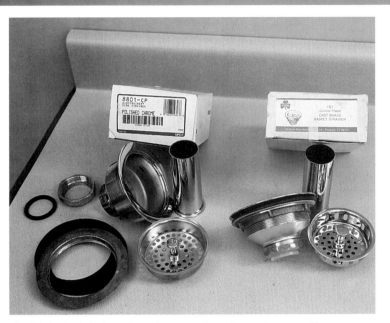

Quality basket strainers have brass parts and superior mounting hardware. Shown here are the Kohler Duostrainer and the McGuire import.

ber seal on the bottom of the stopper with a cheap plastic lift knob. My objection to cheap strainers is not just that they look unattractive and function poorly, but even more that they ruin cabinets by leaking.

In between these two extremes you can find basket strainers with a wrought-brass housing and strainer, but still usually with a rubber stopper and substandard nuts and washers. My advice is to go with the top of the line

strainer. Granted, a quality Kohler strainer can cost as much as the cheapest stainless-steel sink, but with anything less you're selling your customer (or yourself) short. If you're not prepared to pay $30 or so for a Kohler strainer, the McGuire Manufacturing Company (see the Sources of Supply on pp. 178-179) imports a pretty good cast-brass strainer that sells for about half the price.

Secure the tailpiece to the strainer housing with the slip nut and washer that come with the strainer.

INSTALLING THE TRAP

With the waste installed, the final stage in hooking up the sink is to run the trap system from the waste's tailpiece down and over to the sanitary tee in the wall. Installing the trap can be a challenging and time-consuming exercise since you have to make measurements between pieces that are not fixed in position and often have to assemble and disassemble the parts a couple of times before you get it right. If you're working within the tight confines of a small under-sink cabinet, the job can be doubly frustrating.

In this section, I'll first explain how to install a Schedule 40 ABS or PVC P-trap with union, which is what I'd recommend you use if plastic pipe is allowed by code where you live. Then I'll walk you through the installation of a tubular-brass P-trap, which is the most practical second choice if you're not allowed to use ABS or PVC under the sink.

The process of installing a sink trap is essentially the same whether you are trapping a lavatory basin, a kitchen sink or a bar sink. The only difference is that the lavatory basin has a 1¼-in. diameter tailpiece and the kitchen sink (and bar sink) a 1½-in. tailpiece. If you go by the code minimums, you could run pipe of the same diameter to the wall (i.e., a 1¼-in. trap in the bathroom and a 1½-in. trap in the kitchen). However, where possible I prefer to use larger-diameter pipe, which allows for better drainage flow and reduces the risk of stoppages.

ABS OR PVC TRAPS

In the following exercise, I'm going to explain how to install a 2-in. P-trap for a lavatory basin or kitchen sink. Because the tailpiece of either fixture is smaller in diameter than the trap, you have to use adapters to step up to the larger pipe size (and in the case of the lavatory basin, a reducing rubber slip-nut washer to fit the smaller-diameter tailpiece).

ESTIMATING RISER LENGTH   Begin dry-fitting the assembly at the tailpiece end. The first piece onto the tailpiece is a 1½-in. ABS (or PVC) trap adapter, which is available in female ("hub by slip") and male ("spigot by slip") designs. I usually use the female adapter, but the male comes in handy on tight installations where vertical space (altitude) is limited. Slide the

tape on the male threads of the strainer housing, put pipe dope inside the slip nut and thread the nut to the strainer.

If you are installing a bar sink, which has a narrower drain opening than a kitchen sink (typically 2½ in. vs. 3½ in.), the waste is usually a mini-basket strainer or a grid strainer. The mini-strainer has the same number of parts as the standard kitchen-sink basket strainer and is installed in the same way. The basket typically has a bail handle for easy removal from the strainer housing. The grid strainer is a simple one-piece waste without any stopper and a permanent strainer cover of chromed brass with a grid design of punched-out holes. It is installed with a beveled rubber waste gasket, a poly or plated-steel flat washer and a lock mounting nut (which is brass on the better models and die-cast on others).

ABS/PVC TRAP CONNECTIONS

2-IN. TRAP SYSTEM

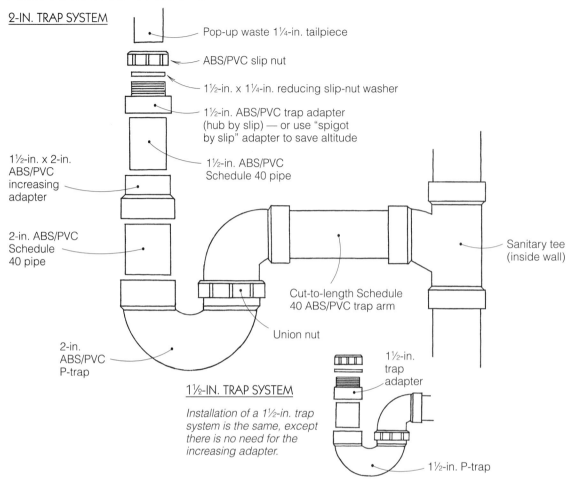

Pop-up waste 1¼-in. tailpiece

ABS/PVC slip nut

1½-in. x 1¼-in. reducing slip-nut washer

1½-in. ABS/PVC trap adapter (hub by slip) — or use "spigot by slip" adapter to save altitude

1½-in. ABS/PVC Schedule 40 pipe

1½-in. x 2-in. ABS/PVC increasing adapter

2-in. ABS/PVC Schedule 40 pipe

2-in. ABS/PVC P-trap

Union nut

Cut-to-length Schedule 40 ABS/PVC trap arm

Sanitary tee (inside wall)

1½-in. trap adapter

1½-IN. TRAP SYSTEM

Installation of a 1½-in. trap system is the same, except there is no need for the increasing adapter.

1½-in. P-trap

1½-in. slip nut from the trap adapter up the tailpiece almost to the top, followed by a 1½-in. slip-nut washer. If you're working on a lavatory basin, you'll need to use a 1½-in. by 1¼-in. reducing slip-nut washer (available in nylon or rubber — use the rubber one for this application). This washer has the same outside diameter as the 1½-in. slip-nut washer, but the hole in the center is reduced to fit the 1¼-in. tailpiece. The washer will hold the slip nut on the tailpiece so you can work with both hands free.

Next, cut a piece of 1½-in. diameter Schedule 40 pipe about 2 in. long and cement one end into the opening in the bottom of the trap adapter. Then cement the other end into the 1½-in. side of a 1½-in. by 2-in. ABS (or PVC) increasing adapter. Thread this

two-adapter assembly to the slip nut at the top of the tailpiece. Now you're ready to measure for the height of the riser that goes into the P-trap opening.

Hold the trap under the waste's tailpiece as plumb as you can judge and at the correct height (see the photo at left on the facing page). Now measure the distance between the stop in the 2-in. side of the adapter and the bottom of the opening in the P-trap's J-bend. Subtract about ¼ in. and cut a piece of 2-in. pipe this length, then dry-fit the three parts.

ESTIMATING TRAP-ARM LENGTH   With the P-trap and connecting piping dangling from the tailpiece, the next step is to measure for the length of the trap arm. With plastic DWV piping, there'll be a short stub of ABS (or PVC) pipe at the wall that was fitted

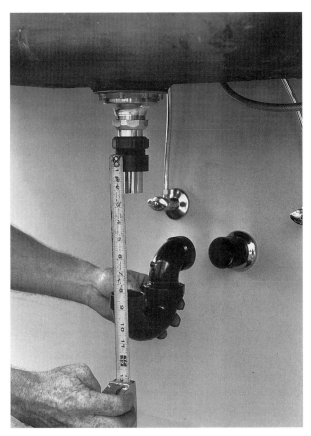

Hold the P-trap in position under the tailpiece and measure for the length of the riser.

With the P-trap and riser dry-assembled, measure for the length of the trap arm.

LINING UP THE TRAP WITH THE WASTE

<u>TOP VIEW</u>

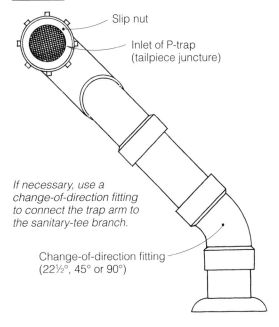

Slip nut

Inlet of P-trap (tailpiece juncture)

If necessary, use a change-of-direction fitting to connect the trap arm to the sanitary-tee branch.

Change-of-direction fitting (22½°, 45° or 90°)

into the 2-in. sanitary-tee branch when the house was plumbed. Attach a Schedule 40 coupling to this stub, and measure the distance from the inside of the coupling to the outlet of the P-trap. This distance (again, less about ¼ in.) will give you the length of the trap arm (see the photo at right above). Cut a piece of Schedule 40 pipe to length and dry-fit the trap arm. Your local code may or may not require you to install an escutcheon over the pipe at the wall; I always like to use one because it makes the job look so much more finished.

On a single-bowl installation, you can usually swing the P-trap far enough to one side or the other so that the pieces will align without having to use a change-of-direction fitting. But if the drain opening in the sink is offset significantly from the connection at the wall, use a 22½°, 45° or 90° fitting on the trap arm so that the arm will enter the sanitary tee on a straight line (see the drawing at right).

After dry-fitting the trap temporarily, take the parts down, cement the joints and hang the assembly from the tailpiece.

FINAL ASSEMBLY Once all the parts have been dry-assembled, you may find that you need to trim the riser or trap arm slightly to get everything to align perfectly. When you're satisfied with the fit of the trap, take all the parts down and prepare for final assembly. As with the dry fit, work from the tailpiece down. Unthread the top slip nut holding the trap adapter and reducing adapter in place and cement this assembly to the riser pipe. Then cement the P-trap to the riser, and the trap arm to the sanitary-tee branch. Wrap Teflon tape on the male threads of the trap adapter and lift it into final position on the tailpiece, threading the union nut on the trap together and the slip nut onto the trap adapter. Once the trap is permanently assembled, test the system for leaks (see p. 119).

If you're working with the smaller 1½-in. P-trap instead of a 2-in. P-trap, the installation is the same, except that you don't need the increasing pipe adapter and the riser and trap arm will be 1½-in. pipe. (The photos on p. 115 and above show the installation of a 1½-in. trap.) For lavatory-basin installations, you can buy a 1¼-in. by 1½-in. trap adapter that uses a 1¼-in. slip nut and washer instead of a reducing washer and the oversize trap adapter. But I prefer to use the larger adapter even with 1½-in. pipe: I don't like the weakness of the smaller-diameter slip-nut washer, and the oversized trap adapter with reducing slip-nut washer allows for a little misalignment in the piece of cut pipe between the adapter and P-trap.

If you use 2-in. pipe, you'll almost never get a stoppage in the drainage system, but on 1½-in. pipe you'll sometimes get a clog right at the sanitary tee's branch. So, if I'm using 1½-in. pipe, I sometimes intentionally cut the trap-arm piping and add a rubber (Mission type) coupling several inches off the escutcheon at the wall. In this way if there is ever a need to get into the drain line above the cleanout tee, which is usually just below the sanitary tee, I can do so without having to send a snake up into the trap-arm elbow, which could possibly damage the inside taper seal of the elbow.

TUBULAR-BRASS TRAPS

Whereas ABS and PVC trap systems are installed with cemented joints (and a union), tubular-brass traps use slip nuts and slip-nut washers. The method of connection may be different, but you still need to test-assemble the parts first to determine the length of the riser pipe (in this case a tailpiece extension) and the trap arm.

You do not have the option of using a 2-in. diameter trap, since this larger size is not readily available in tubular brass. However, you can improve the drainage of lavatory basins by installing a 1¼-in. by 1½-in. trap. This trap is 1½ in. diameter from the trap-arm outlet through the curve of the J-bend, but necks down to 1¼ in. as it nears the top of the tailpiece leg. If the trap is for a cabinet-mounted sink (and will be out of view), I'll even use a straight 1½-in. by 1½-in. trap with a reducing slip-nut washer at the tailpiece connection, as we did for the ABS or PVC trap. I prefer to install this trap because the 1½-in. by 1¼-in. reducing washer makes a much better seal than the smaller 1¼-in. washer used on the necked-down trap. However, there is something awkward looking about the 1¼-in. tailpiece penetrating the 1½-in. trap, so if the sink is wall hung and the trap is in full view, I'll use the smaller trap. In this case, instead of the standard 1¼-in. rubber or nylon slip-nut washer, I use an O-ring made for tubular brass (part number PSMC#W-315D available from Kirkhill, see the Sources of Supply on pp. 178-179). The O-ring is much more resilient and requires very little torque on the slip nut to make a superior seal.

TUBULAR-BRASS TRAP CONNECTIONS

12-in. x 1¼ in.
tailpiece extension,
trimmed to fit for
lavatory...

...or 12-in. x 1½-in.
tailpiece extension cut
to fit for kitchen-sink basket
strainer to J-bend of P-trap

Pop-up waste

Trap arm attached to
threaded nipple, with
slip-nut washer and slip
nut...

17-gauge tubular
brass P-trap
(1¼ in. x 1½ in.)

...or Mission coupling,
either 2-in. or 1½-in.
copper, plastic, steel to
1½-in. bath waste

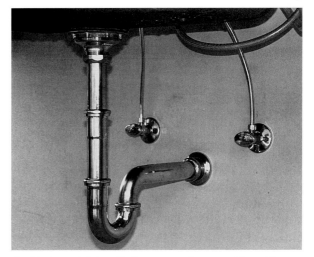

On kitchen-sink installations, you often need to add a
tailpiece extension to reach the inlet of the J-bend.

ESTABLISHING TAILPIECE LENGTH   As with an ABS or
PVC trap, the critical dimensions that you need to establish are the length of the riser pipe (or tailpiece extension) from the trap to the waste and the length of
the trap arm. To measure for the former, first temporarily install the trap arm at the wall. The connection at the sanitary-tee branch might be a threaded
nipple, which the trap arm connects to with a slip
nut and washer, or a trap adapter. I prefer to work
with the nipple (which should be brass, of course),
because the trap arm can usually slide down inside it
at least 1½ in., which provides a lot of support for the
arm. Alternatively, you might have a short stub of
pipe (ABS, PVC or DWV copper) in the sanitary tee,

which the trap arm attaches to by way of a rubber
(Mission type) coupling. Whatever the connection,
slide the trap arm in until the opening in the J-bend
aligns under the tailpiece. If the trap arm sticks out
too far, you'll have to pull it out of the wall and trim
it to length with a tubing cutter or mini-hacksaw.

Now you'll be able to determine whether the
factory-supplied tailpiece is long enough to reach the
trap opening (it should penetrate the trap at least
1 in.). The J-bend on some traps has a higher reach
on the tailpiece leg than others ("high-inlet" traps).
On lavatory-basin installations, this higher leg sometimes means that you can attach the trap directly to
the short factory tailpiece. If the existing tailpiece is
too short, you'll have to replace it with a tailpiece extension. These 1¼-in. diameter extensions (available
in 6-in., 8-in. and 12-in. lengths) are threaded at both
ends. (The threaded ends are prone to dents and
dings during shipping, so inspect the ends carefully
before you buy.) Trim the tailpiece to the necessary
length and then thread it into the waste, being careful not to cross-thread the fine threads.

Alternatively, you can slide a "slip-joint" tailpiece
extension over the factory tailpiece to reach the inlet
leg of the J-bend. This type of extension has a belled
opening and uses a slip-nut washer and slip nut to
grip the existing tailpiece (see the photo above). I prefer the threaded tailpiece extension because it is more

rigid once installed, is more streamlined in appearance and has no rubber slip-nut washer to crack and leak with age.

On kitchen and bar-sink installations, you'll also probably need to replace the factory tailpiece with an extension tailpiece to make it all the way down to the inlet side of the P-trap's J-bend. These 1½-in. diameter "direct connect" extensions are not threaded, but have a flat lip at the top that attaches to the basket strainer with a slip nut and washer. As with lavatory basins, you can also use the slip-joint extension over the factory tailpiece. Whichever type of tailpiece extension you use, try to find one that is 17 gauge rather than the thinner 20 or 22 gauge.

FINAL ASSEMBLY   Once the tailpiece and trap arm are cut to the appropriate lengths, you can install the trap permanently. If you have a threaded sanitary-tee branch at the wall (either a brass nipple or male trap adapter) slide the trap arm into the fitting and seal with a slip nut and nylon slip-nut washer. The nuts that come with your tubular brass P-trap will invariably be die-cast — as I've stressed repeatedly, replace these with solid-brass nuts. And don't forget to use an escutcheon at the wall (either a flat escutcheon, or a box escutcheon if the nipple or adapter protrudes an inch or more from the wall).

If you have a stubbed-off sanitary tee, secure the rubber (Mission type) coupling to the pipe stub and the tubular-brass trap arm. Since the outside of the coupling is polished stainless steel, I feel that it looks good enough to leave in plain view, especially with a flat escutcheon at the wall under a cabinet (and even on a pedestal-sink installation if done with care).

Next slide a slip nut and washer up the tailpiece or tailpiece extension. Wrap Teflon tape around both threaded ends of the J-bend, then lift the high side of the trap onto the tailpiece. Hand-tighten the slip nut. Now swing the other side of the J-bend under the trap arm, mate the two parts and snug up the slip nut. The three basic designs of trap arm to J-bend connections are shown in the drawing at right. I prefer the under-lip design because the male trap arm penetrates farther into the J-bend's female opening,

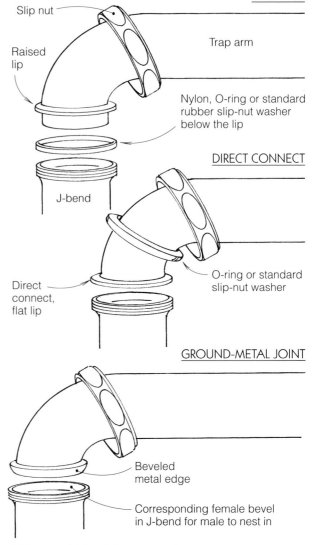

TRAP ARM TO J-BEND CONNECTIONS

UNDER LIP

Slip nut

Raised lip

Trap arm

Nylon, O-ring or standard rubber slip-nut washer below the lip

J-bend

DIRECT CONNECT

Direct connect, flat lip

O-ring or standard slip-nut washer

GROUND-METAL JOINT

Beveled metal edge

Corresponding female bevel in J-bend for male to nest in

This type of J-bend does not work satisfactorily with rubber washers.

leaving fewer chances for leaks. I don't recommend the ground-metal joint since it requires very precise alignment and is prone to leaks.

Once the trap is assembled, tighten the slip nut at the tailpiece side of the J-bend. Then you can test the waste and trap system for leaks.

TESTING FOR LEAKS

If you're working with ABS or PVC traps and were conscientious in the cementing of joints, the only possible waste leaks for lavatory basins or kitchen sinks will be at the slip nut gripping the waste tailpiece (or garbage-disposer elbow) and at the union nut on the P-trap. For tubular-brass traps, each of the slip nuts is a possible leak spot. Of course, you may also have leaks in the water-supply connections and at the waste fitting in the drain hole.

To test the entire system, first remove the aerator from the faucet spout and spread a towel in the bowl (the towel will collect any pipe dope that flows out with the water). With the faucet's hot and cold valves turned off, open the angle stops slowly. If there's a drip at the faucet-supply connections or angle-stop compression-nut connections, tighten the respective nuts a quarter-turn at a time until the drip stops. Then open one valve at a time with the pop-up stopper off the seat (or basket strainer open), and check the tailpiece and slip-nut connections. Again, if you encounter any drips, snug the slip nuts up a quarter-turn at a time.

After you have run each valve and the bowl is draining without drips or leaks, remove the towel and close the pop-up stopper (or basket strainer). For a lavatory sink, fill the bowl until the water begins flowing into the overflow hole(s), and then check the waste to make sure that the water is not leaking out past the beveled rubber waste gasket. For a kitchen sink, simply fill the bowl and check for leaks at the rubber gasket.

JOINING THE WASTES FROM TWO BOWLS

If you are installing side-by-side lavatory basins in the bathroom or a double-bowl kitchen sink, you have the option of running separate traps to each bowl (as long as you have prepared for this in the rough-plumbing stage) or using a "continuous waste" to connect the under-sink drain system to a single trap.

In the bathroom, I prefer to install individual traps and drains and back-vent the vents together (for an extensive discussion of venting, see *Plumbing a House*,

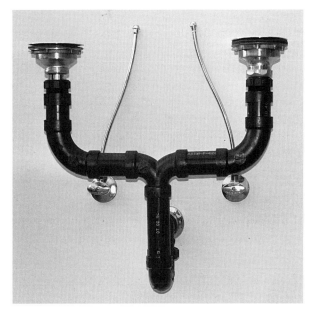

To drain two bowls into a single trap, you need to connect the wastes to the trap with a continuous waste and an outlet tee. Shown here is a continuous-waste system in ABS pipe for a double-bowl kitchen sink.

the companion volume to this book). Lavatory basins have too little water running through them for the materials they are trying to convey to the building drain (such as hair, lard-based soaps and toothpaste). If the bowls are connected to a single drain line, a layer of crud will build up inside the pipe fairly quickly. However, your bathroom-wall design may sometimes prevent you from trapping the basins individually (for example, there may be a heat duct in the way), so you may occasionally have to jam two bowls together on one trap.

Continuous wastes are more commonly used on double-bowl kitchen sinks. For this application, there is usually a greater volume of water pushing waste material into the drain line, so I'm not so concerned about the problem of flow with two bowls on a single trap. Additionally, the two bowls are invariably closer together than two adjacent lavatory basins.

Whereas the waste and trap system for a single bowl is a relatively simple installation, running a continuous waste to join two (or more) bowls can be a real brain-teaser, even for an experienced plumber. In addition to the difficulties of visualizing and assembling the completed system, there are also more code issues to consider. When trapping a single basin, as long as you use the correct, code-sanctioned materials, there is very little for a building inspector to find wrong with the installation. With double bowls, however, you need to keep in mind the maximum distance allowed from the bowl to the sanitary tee (where I live, 3 ft. 6 in. for 1½-in. diameter trap arms and 5 ft. for 2-in. trap arms). You may also be limited in the number of change-of-direction fittings you can use on the trap arm (my code allows no more than two 45° fittings or one 90° fitting on the trap arm, without the use of a cleanout). Some codes require that the outlet tee used to connect the continuous-waste piping have a baffle (the baffle prevents cross flow). Always find out what your local code requires before buying any materials.

The choice of materials for continuous wastes is the same as for wastes for a single bowl: ABS or PVC, tubular brass or DWV copper. Again, Schedule 40 ABS or PVC is definitely better in terms of faster drainage and less joint leakage, but you may not be allowed to use it where you live. The tubular-brass system is universally acceptable, and I'll describe it first.

TUBULAR-BRASS CONTINUOUS WASTES

To join the wastes of two bowls you have to employ a tee to connect the continuous-waste piping to the P-trap. There are two types of tees: end-outlet tees, which are used in a vertical plane, and center-outlet tees, which are used horizontally. These tees are sold either with a factory-installed tailpiece or with a separate tailpiece that is attached with a slip nut or threaded in (see the drawing at right). Both types of tees are available in cast brass or lighter-weight tubular brass. The cast-brass tees are available with baffles, while the tubular tees generally are not. Tees without baffles drain faster, but your code may require the baffled design.

Whether to use the end-outlet tee or the center-outlet tee is determined by the location of the drain in relation to the bowls. If the drain is roughly equidistant between the bowls, you should use the center-outlet tee with two continuous-waste arms (known as "tube 90s") attached to the tailpieces of the basket strainers (kitchen sinks) or pop-up wastes

TEES FOR CONTINUOUS WASTES

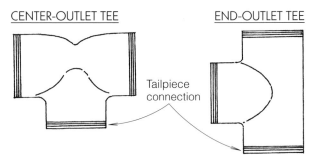

CENTER-OUTLET TEE   END-OUTLET TEE

Tailpiece connection

Tailpiece connection is either slip nut, male threaded or factory-joined.

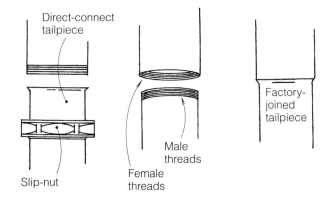

Direct-connect tailpiece

Slip-nut

Female threads

Male threads

Factory-joined tailpiece

(lavatory basins). If the drain is close to one of the bowls, you're better off using the end-outlet tee on one tailpiece with a tube 90 over to the tailpiece of the second sink. If you are installing a garbage disposer, your code may demand that the disposer discharge straight down into the inlet leg of the trap and not into a tube 90. In this case you would have to use an end-outlet tee (for more on garbage-disposer installation, see pp. 131-133). Always consult your code when selecting a pattern to use.

CENTER-OUTLET CONTINUOUS WASTE   If you've determined that you are going to use a center-outlet continuous waste, you first need to estimate the length of the two tube 90s. Measure the distance between each sink tailpiece and the intended location of the center-outlet tee (which will be directly above the inlet leg of the P-trap), and buy two 1½-in. slip-

CENTER-OUTLET CONTINUOUS WASTE (TUBULAR BRASS)

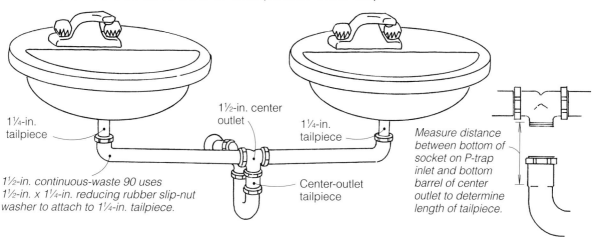

1¼-in. tailpiece

1½-in. center outlet

1¼-in. tailpiece

Measure distance between bottom of socket on P-trap inlet and bottom barrel of center outlet to determine length of tailpiece.

1½-in. continuous-waste 90 uses 1½-in. x 1¼-in. reducing rubber slip-nut washer to attach to 1¼-in. tailpiece.

Center-outlet tailpiece

nut tube 90s the closest length to this measurement. They're generally available in lengths from 7 in. up to 26 in. If you're connecting two lavatory basins, you'll also need two 1½-in. by 1¼-in. reducing rubber slip-nut washers since the tube 90s will be attached to the 1¼-in. lavatory tailpieces.

Next, you need to determine the length of the tailpiece that extends from the bottom of the tee to the inlet of the P-trap. Hang the tube 90s on the tailpieces temporarily, then tape them together if they are long enough to overlap. (If they don't quite reach each other by the width of the tee, tape a pencil against the two arms so that they are held level.) Measure the distance from the bottom edge of the tube 90s to the bottom of the bell in the tailpiece leg of the J-bend. This distance will determine whether you can use a center-outlet tee that has a short (usually no longer than 3½ in. to 4½ in.), factory-installed tailpiece or a tee with a separate tailpiece that you'll cut to length.

If you have to use a separate tailpiece extension, you can buy either a center outlet with a slip-nut connection at the tailpiece or one with a threaded connection. I prefer the slip-nut connection. The 1½-in. diameter tailpiece has a flat lip on the top ("direct connect"), and once the slip nut is threaded to the bottom outlet of the tee the tailpiece cannot be pulled back out. I use a flat, cord-reinforced rubber washer on top of the lip. You could also use a rubber slip-nut washer or an O-ring under the lip, or a clear plastic washer with a downturned lip that slips into the top of the tailpiece, but I find that the reinforced washer provides the best rigidity and longevity.

Now that you have all the components, hold up the center outlet and measure to the full depth of the branch socket to determine the length of the tube 90s. Trim the tube 90s to final length and connect them to the center outlet. Then measure and cut the tailpiece to length.

Now you can go on to determine the trap-arm length. Hang the J-bend temporarily (no Teflon tape or pipe dope for now) to the outlet's tailpiece, then attach the trap arm to the J-bend, again just hand-tight for now. Does the trap arm reach the sanitary tee at the wall straight on, and if so, will it penetrate deeply enough for a good seal? Sometimes you can swing the J-bend and pivot the trap arm to help create an offset that allows a straight-on approach to the sanitary tee. If not, add a tubular change-of-direction fitting to get the trap arm straight into the sanitary tee. If the trap arm is too short to reach the wall, you can purchase a separate, one-piece trap-arm extension at a good hardware store.

Once all the pieces have been cut to length and dry-assembled, take the entire system down and reassemble in the same sequence with Teflon tape and pipe dope at the connections.

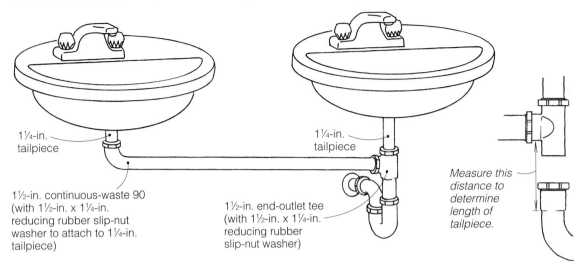

1¼-in.
tailpiece

1¼-in.
tailpiece

1½-in. continuous-waste 90
(with 1½-in. x 1¼-in.
reducing rubber slip-nut
washer to attach to 1¼-in.
tailpiece)

1½-in. end-outlet tee
(with 1½-in. x 1¼-in.
reducing rubber
slip-nut washer)

*Measure this
distance to
determine
length of
tailpiece.*

END-OUTLET CONTINUOUS WASTE   The procedure for installing the end-outlet waste is much the same as for the center-outlet pattern, except that in this case you need to install only one tube 90. The end-outlet tee is available with the same options as the center-outlet tee — that is, with either a factory-installed tailpiece, female threads for a threaded tailpiece or all-slip-nut connections. Again, your choice of outlet design will depend on the distance between the bottom of the end outlet and the top of the P-trap.

Begin by installing the end-outlet tee to the tailpiece on the bowl nearest the drain. (You'll need the 1½-in. by 1¼-in. reducing rubber slip-nut washer again for the connection at a lavatory basin's tailpiece.) Measure over to the tailpiece of the other sink to determine what length tube 90 you need. Install the tube 90 on the far tailpiece and into the end-outlet tee on the near tailpiece, then measure for the length of the outlet tailpiece. Fit the P-trap and trap arm as explained for the center-outlet pattern.

TESTING FOR LEAKS   Test the continuous-waste drainage piping by first running water from one faucet and then adding the stream of the other. If no leaks appear, fill one basin to the overflow level and let it drain. If you still have no leaks, fill both basins to the overflow and drain both simultaneously. If you have no leaks when both bowls are draining, you

need not test any further, unless you're working with a double-bowl kitchen sink with a garbage disposer. Then fill both bowls and run the disposer. Many times the vibrations caused by a disposer will cause leaks that do not show up when draining the bowls without the disposer running.

If there are leaks, loosen up the slip nuts and make sure that the washers are in good shape. Then reapply Teflon tape to the male threads and pipe dope to the female threads, reassemble and try again. If you still get a drip at the tube 90s' slip-nut threads, look closely at the joint where the male threads have been soldered to tubular brass. On low-quality tube 90s, this threaded ring may be loose or poorly soldered (in which case you'll have to replace the tube 90).

ABS AND PVC CONTINUOUS WASTES

If you are installing an ABS or PVC continuous waste, the configuration of the system is the same as for tubular brass but the components are different. Instead of the brass center-outlet fitting, you'd use a double quarter bend (also known as a "double 90"); and instead of an end-outlet tee, a standard sanitary tee. These two plastic fittings are difficult to find with baffles, so check with your local code to see whether baffles are required.

CENTER-OUTLET CONTINUOUS WASTE (ABS/PVC)

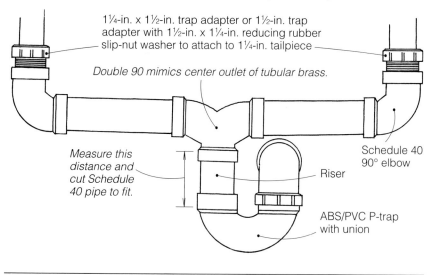

1¼-in. x 1½-in. trap adapter or 1½-in. trap adapter with 1½-in. x 1¼-in. reducing rubber slip-nut washer to attach to 1¼-in. tailpiece

Double 90 mimics center outlet of tubular brass.

Measure this distance and cut Schedule 40 pipe to fit.

Schedule 40 90° elbow

Riser

ABS/PVC P-trap with union

END-OUTLET CONTINUOUS WASTE (ABS/PVC)

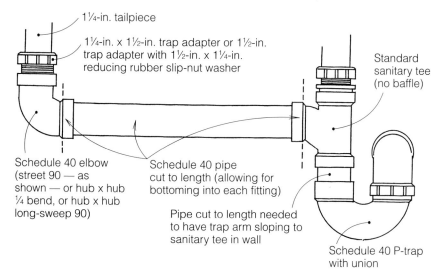

1¼-in. tailpiece

1¼-in. x 1½-in. trap adapter or 1½-in. trap adapter with 1½-in. x 1¼-in. reducing rubber slip-nut washer

Standard sanitary tee (no baffle)

Schedule 40 elbow (street 90 — as shown — or hub x hub ¼ bend, or hub x hub long-sweep 90)

Schedule 40 pipe cut to length (allowing for bottoming into each fitting)

Pipe cut to length needed to have trap arm sloping to sanitary tee in wall

Schedule 40 P-trap with union

Cut-to-length sections of Schedule 40 pipe with a quarter bend (90° elbow) take the place of the tube 90s used for the tubular-brass system. And Schedule 40 pipe is also used for the riser pipe that fits in the inlet leg of the P-trap. As with an ABS or PVC waste system for a single bowl, cement all the connections, except for the union at the P-trap and the slip nuts at the fixture tailpieces.

The process of determining pipe lengths between fittings for an ABS or PVC continuous-waste system is much the same as explained for tubular brass. The drawings above show the center-outlet and end-outlet patterns in 1½-in. pipe. If you ran a 2-in. drain line, you could use a 2-in. by 1½-in. double fixture tee instead of a double quarter bend and have a cleanout in the top barrel (check that this is allowed by code first). If there's enough altitude under the sink, I like to use "long sweep 90s" rather than the standard quarter bends. The longer the sweep of the 90s, the faster the bowls will drain. And if I'm joining the wastes of two lavatory basins, I try to use the shortest possible 1¼-in. tailpieces, so that there'll be more larger-diameter Schedule 40 pipe in the system.

The narrowness of the slot in the back of the pedestal can make it difficult to get tools in to tighten the upper slip nut on the J-bend and the lock nut for the pop-up waste. (Photo by Bill Dane)

INSTALLING A PEDESTAL SINK

I've covered a lot of ground in these three chapters on sink installation, but one topic I've pretty much steered clear of is installing a pedestal sink. This is one of the trickiest tasks in finish plumbing, which is the main reason I've left it until last. Additionally, it will provide a useful review of many of the points I've discussed earlier.

One of the major difficulties in installing a pedestal sink is that the waste and trap assembly is partially concealed within the pedestal, which makes it awkward (and sometimes well-nigh impossible) to get tools in to tighten and loosen the connections.

The degree of difficulty depends on the size of the opening in the back of the pedestal (see the photo at left). On some antique sinks, which tend to be larger than their modern counterparts, even the J-bend to trap-arm slip nut may be completely concealed within the pedestal.

Another problem with modern pedestal sinks is that the bowl doesn't always rest stably on the pedestal. Today's porcelain sinks tend to be more fluid and elliptical in styling, with narrower pedestals than the old-style cast-iron sinks and a considerably smaller contact area between the bowl and the pedestal. A lot of pedestal-sink bowls are now designed to be anchored to the wall to compensate for their inherent design instability. A related problem is that pedestal sinks can be difficult to level. A cabinet created to house a sink can be leveled with little visible evidence, but this isn't the case with a pedestal. If the floor is badly out of level, the installation will be difficult and the final result won't look good.

Many pedestal sinks come with hardware (bolts, washers and nuts) to secure the bowl to the pedestal. Unfortunately, this hardware can be very difficult to install. Many times it's impossible to install the hardware after the waste is hooked up. And if you install the hardware first, then installing the waste can be extremely tedious to next to impossible (depending on the width of the slot in the pedestal). Because of these limitations, I choose to install pedestal sinks without the hardware. Instead, I run a bead of silicone caulk along the top edge of the pedestal to hold the bowl in position (see p. 127).

POSITIONING THE SINK

The first thing I do on a pedestal-sink installation is to stand the pedestal in its intended location, centered between the angle stops at the wall, and check that the trap will clear the bottom of the slot in the back of the pedestal. (You'll have to eyeball this for now, of course, as the trap is not yet installed.) When you roughed in the drains and water supply, you would have worked from the sink manufacturer's rough-in schematic or taken measurements from the actual sink. The trap's J-bend has to be far enough off the floor so that the bottom of the bend clears the bottom of the slot.

PEDESTAL-SINK INSTALLATION

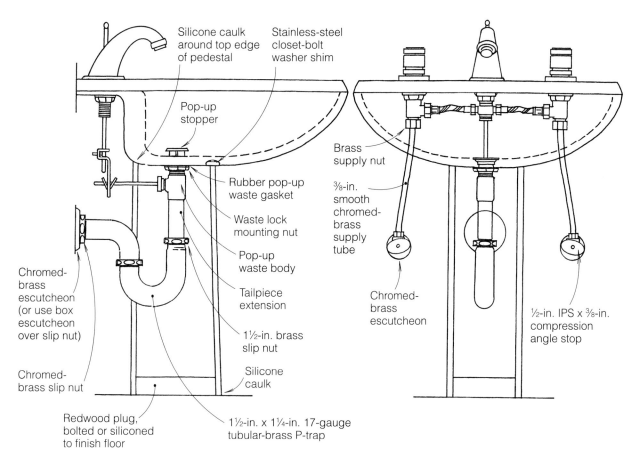

Silicone caulk around top edge of pedestal

Stainless-steel closet-bolt washer shim

Pop-up stopper

Rubber pop-up waste gasket

Waste lock mounting nut

Pop-up waste body

Tailpiece extension

1½-in. brass slip nut

Silicone caulk

Chromed-brass escutcheon (or use box escutcheon over slip nut)

Chromed-brass slip nut

Redwood plug, bolted or siliconed to finish floor

1½-in. x 1¼-in. 17-gauge tubular-brass P-trap

Brass supply nut

⅜-in. smooth chromed-brass supply tube

Chromed-brass escutcheon

½-in. IPS x ⅜-in. compression angle stop

Once you've determined that the trap height is okay, install the faucet and pop-up waste on the bowl (see pp. 97-98 and 106-109). Hook up the linkage between the pop-up and the faucet, but leave the tailpiece off for now. Next, carefully set the bowl onto the pedestal, making sure that the top of the pedestal is nested in the recess in the bowl's underside. Now slide the pedestal and bowl as a unit to their final location (a helper can come in handy here). If the bowl has a straight back, you'll probably want to have the back flush against the wall. On some designs — such as those with an oval bowl — you'll need to set the bowl slightly away from the wall.

Once the sink is in position, check that the bowl is level. If the bowl needs leveling, I use stainless-steel closet-bolt washers as shims on the top edge of the pedestal. You may also need to add shims between the pedestal and the floor. Now use masking tape to outline the perimeter of the pedestal on the floor and the top and side edges of the bowl on the wall.

If your pedestal has webbing near the bottom with a hole or slot in it, then you can mark the hole's position on the floor and go ahead and sink a long draw bolt into the floor for fastening the pedestal down. (I use a bolt only if I'm working on a wood or linoleum floor, not on tile.) Some new pedestal sinks that I've set lately did not have any webbing in the base. For these sinks, the manufacturer recommends that you cut out a piece of redwood or pressure-treated wood to fit snugly in the bottom of the pedestal, and then anchor this wooden "plug" to the floor and press the pedestal over it.

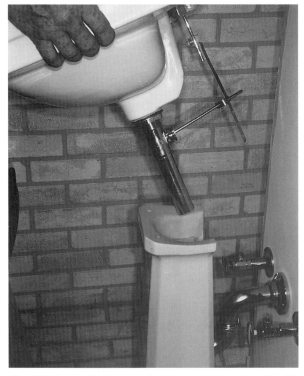

Carefully lower the bowl onto the pedestal to test the fit of the tailpiece in the P-trap. (Photo by Bill Dane)

FITTING THE SUPPLIES AND TRAP

With the sink level and in its exact location, cut and fit the supply tubes between the faucet connections and the angle stops. (I use ⅜-in. smooth chromed-brass supplies for this application — see pp. 99-101). You'll have to rock the sink gently to get the supplies bottomed out in the angle stops and/or the acorn heads nested in the faucet connections. Keep a check on the levelness of the bowl during this process. Just hand-tighten the nuts for now since you'll be disconnecting the supplies shortly.

Once you've got the supplies installed temporarily, you can move on to the trap. For pedestal sinks, I use a 1¼-in. by 1½-in. 17-gauge, polished-chrome-brass trap (see p. 116), with an O-ring slip-nut washer at the J-bend's inlet connection. The J-bend's smaller-diameter 1¼-in. slip nut sometimes makes all the difference in getting it loosened up later if the waste needs working on. Existing installations might have

a 1¼-in. trap (the code minimum), but on new construction I always run larger-diameter drainage so I can use the more effective trap size.

Start by trimming the trap arm down, little by little, until the attached J-bend can be positioned under the waste as best you can determine (remember the tailpiece is still missing at this point). The trap arm should penetrate at least 1½ in. into the nipple or trap adapter at the wall (with at least 1 in. to spare so that you can push the trap arm farther into the wall when later making the permanent connection with the J-bend). Now with a folding rule you can measure the length of the 1¼-in. tailpiece needed. If the factory-supplied tailpiece on the pop-up waste is too short, buy a 12-in. extension with male threads on each end (see p. 117) and trim it to length.

Next unthread the faucet's supply nuts and lift the bowl off the pedestal. Install the cut-to-length tailpiece in the pop-up waste. Now remove the slip nut and washer from the top, tailpiece-inlet leg of the J-bend and carefully lower the bowl back onto the pedestal, inserting the tailpiece into the J-bend (see the photo at left). If you can let go of the bowl and not apply undue pressure to the trap, the tailpiece was trimmed to the right length. If it pushes down on the trap arm, you'll have to cut the tailpiece down farther. I like to put a piece of masking tape on the tailpiece about ½ in. above the height of the J-bend's exposed male threads so I'll know how high up the tailpiece to apply the pipe dope. Check the bowl for level again, then put another piece of masking tape on the trap arm to mark its present penetration into the wall nipple or trap adapter. Wrap Teflon tape on the faucet connections, and lift the bowl off the pedestal for the last time. Set the bowl upside-down on a felt- or carpet-covered work table.

Now put pipe dope in the female threads of the 1¼-in. solid-brass slip nut, and slide the nut down the tailpiece until it comes to rest on the waste housing. Slide the O-ring down until it is fairly close to the nut, then butter up the tailpiece with pipe dope up to the masking tape. Next, undo the J-bend from the trap arm and wrap Teflon tape on both male threads of the bend. Slide the J-bend onto the tailpiece and tighten up the slip nut firmly, just by hand. We're almost ready for the final assault. Push the trap arm into the nipple or trap adapter for now. If there's no hardware holding the pedestal to the floor, pick up the pedestal and move it off the tape marks. (Don't lose any shims and make sure their position and number are marked.)

SETTING THE PEDESTAL

Make sure that the floor is absolutely dry where the pedestal will sit, then run a bead of clear silicone sealant all the way around the bottom edge of the pedestal. Set the pedestal in position (on top of the wooden plug if you're using one) and gently press down. Reposition any shims on the top edge of the pedestal, then run another bead of silicone all around the rim, going right over the shims.

FINAL INSTALLATION

Now lower the bowl onto the pedestal permanently and hook up the supplies. You'll find that it helps greatly to have two extra hands to guide the supplies into the angle stops. Put pipe dope on the angle stop's male compression threads and around the brass ferrule. By gently applying orbital pressure to the supply with one hand, start the compression nuts with the thumb and forefinger of your other hand. Don't use a wrench until you are sure the supply is going in straight, or you'll cross-thread the nuts.

Depending upon the temperature of the room, you've got about 15 to 20 minutes before the silicone starts to set up. If you move the bowl after that (and you're likely to as you're fiddling with the supplies), the adhesion will be poor. Once you get the supplies in place and the nuts finger-tight, make sure the pedestal is centered and check the bowl for level one last time. Then take a break for an hour or more (preferably overnight) so the silicone can firm up.

The last stage in the installation is to hook up the trap. Slide an escutcheon down the trap arm (either a flat escutcheon or a box escutcheon, depending on how far the nipple or male adapter protrudes from the wall), followed by a solid-brass slip nut, then a beveled nylon slip-nut washer. Put Teflon tape on the male threads of the nipple or trap adapter and pipe dope in the threads of both 1½-in. slip nuts. I swing the dangling J-bend to the far side of the pedestal slot and then work the end of the trap arm into the nipple or trap adapter.

Using a Mission-type coupling on the trap arm can make it easier to install the trap. (Photo by Bill Dane)

Now it's a matter of pushing, pulling and pivoting the J-bend and the trap arm until the two parts mate accurately. (On some installations where there's little room for play between the components, it can be easier to install a rubber, Mission-type coupling on the trap arm, as shown in the photo above.) Sometimes you have to push up slowly and firmly on the J-bend to have the necessary room to slide the trap arm into the pedestal slot and then back into the wall nipple or trap adapter. That is why I recommended that you use an O-ring on the tailpiece and butter up the tailpiece with pipe dope, which allows you to slide the bend up and down with steady pressure. Because the O-ring adheres so well to the metal, the upper slip nut on the J-bend need only be finger-tight — which means that you don't have to struggle with a wrench in the narrow slot.

Once the J-bend and the trap arm nest together, snug up the lower nut on the J-bend and the slip nut at the wall. If you're using a box escutcheon, leave the escutcheon forward until you've checked for leaks (see p. 119). Finish the installation by anchoring the bowl to the wall with the mounting hardware provided (if the sink is of this design).

APPLIANCES

In previous chapters, I've explained how to install the major plumbing fixtures in the kitchen and bathroom. In this chapter, I'll tackle the installation of a variety of routine appliances (such as a dishwasher and water heater) and optional accessories (such as a hot-water dispenser and garbage disposer). I'll discuss the appliances in the sequence I would install them in a new house.

Most appliances come with manufacturers' installation instructions. Here, I'll give you some general guidelines for installation of each appliance, with some tips on avoiding common pitfalls. As ever, it pays to buy quality appliances and use quality hardware and supplies to hook them up.

Many of these appliances require gas and/or electrical connections in addition to standard plumbing connections. Plumbers do not routinely do electrical work, and in some areas plumbers are not permitted to do much gas work. So it's important that you understand the restrictions that apply in your area and that you not try to perform potentially dangerous work that you are not trained for.

HOT-WATER DISPENSER

A hot-water dispenser is a small appliance mounted below the sink or countertop that delivers instant hot water at the touch of a faucet. I'm not a great fan of these appliances since they tend to have a high failure rate and seldom last more than a couple of years before needing repair or replacement. However, if the idea of having instant hot water for your coffee or tea without the need to boil water on the stove appeals, a hot-water dispenser is easy to install.

If you're installing a dispenser in a new kitchen, it makes sense to hook it up before you connect any continuous waste and garbage disposer because you'll have more room under the sink to work. The water intake for the dispenser attaches to the cold-water supply. On new construction, I usually stub out a separate nipple for a separate cold-supply angle stop for the dispenser. If you decide to install a dispenser after the rough pipes have been run, you can add a brass tee to the existing nipple so that you can install two angle stops to the cold supply (see pp. 22-23 and the photo on p. 135). The angle stop for the hot-water dispenser should be ½-in. FIP to ¼-in. compression.

HOT-WATER DISPENSER

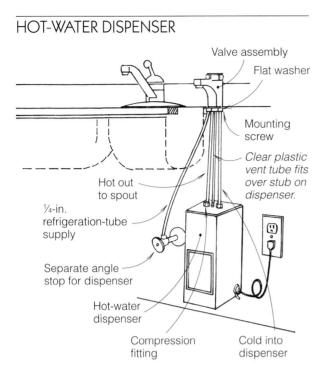

Valve assembly

Flat washer

Mounting screw

Clear plastic vent tube fits over stub on dispenser.

Hot out to spout

¼-in. refrigeration-tube supply

Separate angle stop for dispenser

Hot-water dispenser

Compression fitting

Cold into dispenser

Locate hot-water dispenser close enough to its cold-water supply angle stop so ¼-in. factory-supplied tubing doesn't need lengthening.

INSTALLATION

Begin the installation by mounting the valve assembly to the sink. Most sinks are available with a precut hole for a hot-water dispenser, though you can also punch your own hole if the sink is stainless steel (see p. 99). Alternatively, you can mount the dispenser to the countertop after drilling a 1¼-in. diameter hole. Depending on the design, the dispenser might attach to the sink or countertop with a mounting plate and screws, or a threaded shank and lock nut.

On the simplest designs (which I prefer to install), the tank hangs from the valve assembly and there is just one water line from the angle stop to the tank. More common is the design with a separate tank, which mounts to the wall, and three water lines (as shown in the drawing above). Cold water is piped from the angle stop to the valve assembly, then down to the tank, where the water is heated. When the valve is opened, hot water travels from the tank to the spout. If you didn't purge the angle stop of debris when you installed it, do so now before hooking up the dispenser (see pp. 68-69).

The dispenser's intake and output tubing is usually ¼-in. copper refrigeration tubing. The unit will probably come with short stubs of ¼-in. tubing protruding from the case, or it could have compression fittings on the case that you attach the tubing to. If your dispenser has stubs, I suggest that you use copper couplings and make soldered connections instead of using compression unions to join the additional tubing required. In addition to the copper intake and output tubing, most dispensers will also have a plastic vent tube, which fits over a stub on the top of the tank.

GARBAGE DISPOSER

A garbage disposer (sometimes referred to as a "garbage disposal" and, more politely, as a "food-waste disposer") mounts in the drain hole of a kitchen sink and drains into a P-trap, or into a continuous waste on double-bowl installations. These appliances are popular on new construction, but in my experience they are often more problematic than helpful — indeed, over the years I've probably taken out more garbage disposers than I've installed. Here, I'll tell you what to look for if you're thinking of buying a disposer and explain how to install the appliance. In Chapter 10, I'll suggest some solutions for common garbage-disposer problems.

CHOOSING A DISPOSER

As with most plumbing fixtures and appliances, it makes sense to buy a top-quality model. The initial price difference between a top-quality disposer and an economy model can be considerable, but the former should last at least ten years, whereas an economy model will probably wear out after only a year or two. Also, if you have to replace a disposer, you may have to modify or even discard the entire continuous waste design of both bowls to accommodate the new disposer, which can be time-consuming (and expensive if you have a plumber do it for you).

Desirable features of a garbage disposer include a stainless-steel grinding chamber and stainless-steel cutters, a reversing motor (preferably ¾ hp) that starts up in the opposite direction each time the disposer is activated, and an insulated shell to cut down on noise. Two other important features that aren't likely

GARBAGE DISPOSER

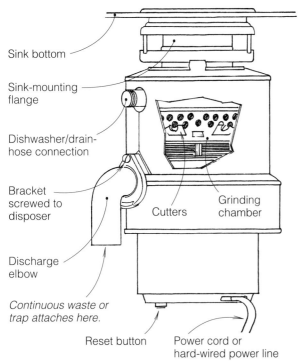

- Sink bottom
- Sink-mounting flange
- Dishwasher/drain-hose connection
- Bracket screwed to disposer
- Cutters
- Grinding chamber
- Discharge elbow

Continuous waste or trap attaches here.

- Reset button
- Power cord or hard-wired power line

A discharge-elbow connection that is an integral part of the disposer body is prone to premature corrosion.

to be mentioned in the advertising literature are the connection for the dishwasher drain hose and the discharge elbow.

The dishwasher drain-hose connection is the stub near the top of the disposer case onto which you attach the hose from a dishwasher air gap (the drawing on p. 138 shows a typical installation for a garbage disposer and dishwasher). This hose connection should be a rubber or preferably stainless-steel stub, not merely an integral cast part of the housing. If the connection is part of the housing (which is invariably an aluminum/magnesium alloy), the highly caustic detergents used with automatic dishwashers will quickly eat away the metal. I've had to replace many disposers that were leaking badly because the hose connection was corroded (there's no way to repair this condition).

The discharge-elbow connection, which is the point at which you attach the trap or continuous waste, is just below the dishwasher drain-hose connection. On most units, the discharge elbow is a separate piece that attaches to the housing with a bracket and screw. This method of attachment works fine,

but I recommend you avoid disposers with elbows that attach with a slip nut and rubber washer to another cast, integral part of the case. As with similar dishwasher drain-hose connections, the integral stub will corrode long before the mechanical innards fail (see the photo above).

You should also consider the way in which the disposer mounts in the sink hole. Almost every disposer that I am familiar with has a lipped, stainless-steel flange that nests in the sink's drain hole, with three screws and a plate to fasten the flange in the drain hole. The disposer is attached to the bottom of the flange by various means, usually with a rubber seal between the grinding chamber and the bottom of the flange. Depending on the type of sink you're working with (stainless or enameled steel, porcelain, cast iron or acrylic), one design of sleeve and plate may mount more easily than another. The thickness of the sink bottom and the slope around the drain hole are the determining factors. On stainless-steel sinks, you might need to stack an additional, thick rubber gasket under the sink hole so you can tighten the screws sufficiently to hold the flange in the sink securely.

INSTALLATION

Installing a garbage disposer is a three-step process: installing the mounting assembly in the sink's drain hole, hanging the dispenser from the mounting assembly, and hooking up the waste.

INSTALLING THE MOUNTING ASSEMBLY   Begin by setting the disposer flange in the sink opening. Roll a ½-in. diameter putty snake around the underside lip of the flange, then press the flange into the sink opening, making sure to center any manufacturer's name stamped in the lip (this is the same procedure as for installing the housing for a kitchen-sink basket strainer, as discussed on p. 110). Now, working from below the sink, slide the mounting-assembly hardware over the sleeve of the flange.

If you're working with the standard "split-ring" mounting assembly (see the drawing at left below), slip the flat cardboard or fiber washer over the sleeve first, followed by the steel pressure plate. If this triangular plate has a rolled edge, install it with the lip pointing down. Next slide the screw plate over the sleeve, then spread open the steel split ring to fit in the groove that runs around the circumference of the sleeve. This split ring holds the mounting assembly in position while you tighten the three screws to secure the assembly to the sink. The screws drive the pressure plate up and the screw plate down.

A less common, but easier to install mounting assembly has pressed-out lugs in the side of the flange sleeve (see the drawing at right below). The pressure plate and screw plate have corresponding notches on

GARBAGE-DISPOSER MOUNTING ASSEMBLY

SPLIT-RING DESIGN

LUG DESIGN

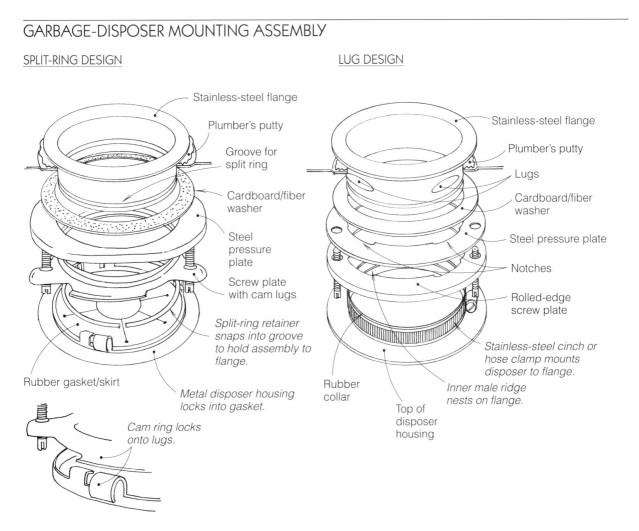

Stainless-steel flange

Plumber's putty

Groove for split ring

Cardboard/fiber washer

Steel pressure plate

Screw plate with cam lugs

Split-ring retainer snaps into groove to hold assembly to flange.

Rubber gasket/skirt

Metal disposer housing locks into gasket.

Cam ring locks onto lugs.

Stainless-steel flange

Plumber's putty

Lugs

Cardboard/fiber washer

Steel pressure plate

Notches

Rolled-edge screw plate

Stainless-steel cinch or hose clamp mounts disposer to flange.

Inner male ridge nests on flange.

Rubber collar

Top of disposer housing

their inside edge. If your disposer has this design, slide the plates up the sleeve, then turn them slightly so that the lugs hold the washer and plates in position as you tighten the screws. The beauty of this design is that you don't have to fuss with the split ring, which can be tricky to install. On cast-iron sinks that have thick bottoms and long radiuses in the drain hole, it can be almost impossible to get the split ring snapped into place (unless you have a helper to push down on the flange from above while you are lying on your back in the cabinet).

One other style of mounting assembly that you might occasionally find is one with a threaded flange. This design uses neither a split ring nor lugs, but has fine threads on the flange sleeve onto which you thread a large lock nut similar to the one used on a kitchen-sink basket strainer.

HANGING THE DISPOSER   Once the mounting assembly is secure in the sink opening, the next step is to hang the disposer from the mounting. If you're working with the split-ring design, the cam ring on the top of the disposer body locks onto the lugs on the side of the screw plate (as shown in the drawing on p. 131). A rubber gasket on the inside edge of the cam ring forms a watertight seal against the bottom edge of the flange sleeve.

On the lug design, the disposer attaches directly to the flange sleeve. A ridge around the inside opening at the top of the disposer nests over a recess in the bottom of the sleeve. The disposer is secured to the flange by tightening the stainless-steel hose clamp around the rubber gasket.

Regardless of the design, position the disposer so that the discharge elbow aligns with the drainage stub at the wall. (Note that if you are going to drain a dishwasher into your garbage disposer, you have to remove the knockout from the dishwasher drain-hose connection before you hang the disposer. Lay the disposer on the floor and use a dowel or a punch to tap in the knockout, then turn the disposer over to shake the small plug out.)

For a garbage disposer in a single bowl, the waste piping (here ABS) connects to the disposer's discharge elbow.

HOOKING UP THE WASTE   With the disposer in place, you're ready to hook up the waste. If you're working in a single bowl, the installation should be straightforward. For an ABS or PVC waste, attach a 1½-in. trap adapter to the disposer's discharge elbow and then measure a piece of Schedule 40 pipe to fit between it and the open leg of the P-trap's J-bend. Hold the P-trap below the adapter, eyeballed for level with the sanitary-tee branch. Position the trap adapter about halfway up the disposer's discharge elbow, so you'll be able to slide it up or down to compensate for a not-so-perfect eyeball estimate. If you're installing a 2-in. Schedule 40 P-trap, you can either cement a flush bushing into the J-bend's inlet socket and then glue in the 1½-in. pipe stub with a trap adapter on the top (see the drawing on the facing page), or you can use a 1½-in. by 2-in. increasing adapter that has a solvent-weld socket on each end (see p. 114). The increasing adapter takes up more altitude but makes for a better-looking finished job.

HOOKING UP THE DISPOSER WASTE

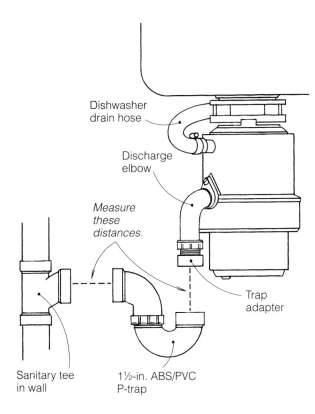

Dishwasher drain hose

Discharge elbow

Measure these distances.

Trap adapter

Sanitary tee in wall

1½-in. ABS/PVC P-trap

INSTALLATION WITH 2-IN. P-TRAP

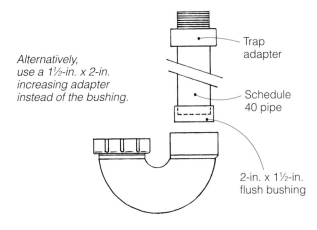

Alternatively, use a 1½-in. x 2-in. increasing adapter instead of the bushing.

Trap adapter

Schedule 40 pipe

2-in. x 1½-in. flush bushing

If you have to use tubular brass for the waste system in your part of the country, you'll probably need to add a tailpiece extension to the discharge elbow to reach the opening in the J-bend of the 1½-in. tubular-brass trap. The tailpiece extension attaches to the el-

bow with a slip nut and washer. Whether you're using tubular brass, ABS or PVC, the connection from the trap-arm outlet of the P-trap to the sanitary-tee branch is the same as for a kitchen sink (see pp. 114-116). As with the standard kitchen-sink waste installation, you might need a change-of-direction fitting on the trap arm to run the pipe straight into the sanitary tee.

If the garbage disposer is to be installed in a double-bowl sink, I like to run a continuous waste off the disposer's discharge elbow and the basket strainer's 1½-in. tailpiece (a typical installation is shown in the drawing on p. 138). Some local codes require that the end outlet be used at the disposer's discharge elbow, so that the disposer drains straight down into the trap rather than traveling horizontally before dropping. Other local authorities have no such requirement, and you can use either the end-outlet or the center-outlet waste pattern (see pp. 120-123). The disposer can be installed in either bowl, though it is usually easier to install it in the bowl that is closer to the sanitary-tee branch (especially if you are required to use the end outlet). As always, check with your local authority before doing any work, and find out which fittings in which pattern you are allowed to use.

Depending upon where you buy the disposer, it may come with an electrical cord and plug already installed. As a rule, economy models purchased at building-supply stores usually do have a factory-installed power cord, whereas top-quality disposers from plumbing suppliers do not. If you don't feel comfortable wiring the disposer yourself, call a licensed electrician.

To test the disposer for leaks, first fill the sink bowl with water (just running water from the faucet is not as effective a test). Turn on the disposer and check for leaks at the mounting assembly, the discharge-elbow connection and all the connections in the waste and trap system.

One final point: On the disposer body, there should be a label with the appliance's model and serial numbers. Once you've installed the disposer this label may well be out of sight, so make a note of the numbers (either in plain view on the case or on a separate piece of paper) in case you need to call the manufacturer for service, repair or warranty information.

ICE-MAKER SUPPLY LINE

When I started out in the plumbing business over 20 years ago, running a supply line for an automatic ice maker was not that common an installation, but now it's something I do on most new kitchens. The ¼-in. copper water line runs from an angle stop under the sink to a stub, or "barb," on the back of the refrigerator. On a routine finish job on new construction there's a good chance that the refrigerator won't yet have been delivered when I plumb the kitchen, but I go ahead and attach the supply line to the angle stop now.

Most plumbing suppliers and hardware stores sell an ice-maker kit. It usually consists of a length of ¼-in. poly tubing, a self-piercing saddle valve (which taps into the cold-water supply) and some little brass inserts for the tubing that are supposed to work with brass ferrules and compression nuts. For a few years, I confess that I did use this type of plastic ice-maker supply line, but I was never really satisfied with the safety of the seal that I got with the poly tubing, or with the quality of the hardware. Now I'm back to running coiled copper tubing with separate angle stops, and I can sleep at night.

INSTALLATION

As when plumbing a hot-water dispenser (see pp. 128-129), you can either stub out a separate nipple for the ice-maker angle stop or run two angle stops from the existing nipple. You can buy a double-handle angle stop with two outlets, but I prefer to install a brass tee on the nipple and individual angle stops (see the photo on the facing page).

Begin by connecting the copper refrigeration tube to the ½-in. FIP by ¼-in. compression angle stop (after first purging the angle stop of debris, as explained on pp. 68-69). If the refrigerator is located across the room from the kitchen sink, then you'll have to run the ¼-in. copper line under the floor, through the walls or over the ceiling to reach it. If the refrigerator sits just to one side of the sink counter, all you have to do is bore a small hole at floor level in the side wall of the cabinet and fish the tubing through. I like to leave three or four loops (about 7 ft.) of copper tubing at the wall so that the refrigerator can be rolled in and out for access behind the appliance.

The supply line connects to the stub at the back of the refrigerator with a brass "female hose by compression adapter." This adapter has female hose threads on one side, which attach to the male plastic threads

ICE-MAKER SUPPLY LINE

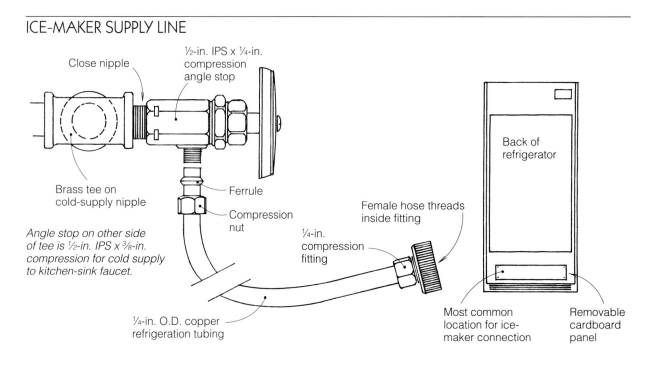

Close nipple

½-in. IPS x ¼-in. compression angle stop

Brass tee on cold-supply nipple

Angle stop on other side of tee is ½-in. IPS x ⅜-in. compression for cold supply to kitchen-sink faucet.

Ferrule

Compression nut

¼-in. compression fitting

¼-in. O.D. copper refrigeration tubing

Female hose threads inside fitting

Back of refrigerator

Most common location for ice-maker connection

Removable cardboard panel

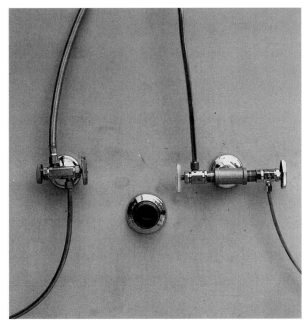

A double-handled angle stop (left) allows dedicated water supply to the sink and the refrigerator but is prone to leaks. A better alternative is to install a brass tee to the nipple and then connect individual angle stops (right).

DISHWASHER

Installing a dishwasher is usually the last job I do in the kitchen on new construction. Hooking up the water supply and waste lines under the kitchen sink is fairly straightforward. The hard part is routing the lines through the dishwasher chassis and cabinet wall — you invariably have to slide the appliance in and out a couple of times to get everything lined up.

The water line for the dishwasher is run from the hot supply. As with the hot-water dispenser and ice-maker supply line, I like to install a brass tee with two individual angle stops on the nipple at the wall (one to serve the dishwasher, the other to supply the kitchen-sink faucet). The drainage pattern for the dishwasher can vary, depending on code and whether or not a garbage disposer is installed under the sink. Where I live, for years it was permissible to drain a dishwasher into its own trap, which was usually behind it in the wall or in the floor. However, my local code now requires use of an air gap in the draining process and draining the dishwasher into the kitchen sink's trap (or into the garbage disposer). Air gaps, which are installed near the faucet on the back edge of the sink, prevent waste water from the sink drain or garbage disposer from back-siphoning into the dishwasher (for more on dishwasher air gaps, see the sidebar on p. 136).

LOCATING THE DISHWASHER

Because the dishwasher is usually required to drain into the kitchen sink, it makes sense to work the floor plan so that the appliance is on the same wall as the kitchen sink, preferably right next to it. Since most people are right-handed, dishwasher manufacturers usually build machines with frames and pumps that are more easily plumbed for right-side-of-sink installation. Dishwashers can be installed to the left of the sink, but the job usually takes a little longer. You can also position the appliance at 90° to the sink, but the drain hose then has to go a much greater distance to reach the air gap, which makes the pump work harder. A 90° installation also means that you have to bore a passageway through cabinets.

on the solenoid valve at the back of the refrigerator, and a ¼-in. compression fitting on the other, which attaches to the copper supply line with a ferrule and compression nut (as at the angle stop). The adapter may have a built-in union to allow you to tighten it onto the male stub without twisting the small-diameter copper line. Keep an eye out for water on the floor for the first few days after installation, since this is when any leaks are most likely to occur.

On earlier models, the connection on the refrigerator was merely a short stub of ¼-in. copper tube. If you have an appliance with this older-style copper stub, you can use a ¼-in. by ¼-in. compression union to connect the supply line. However, these unions are prone to leaking, so it's better to solder the copper tubing to the stub with a ¼-in. copper-refrigeration tube coupling.

An air gap is a "break" in the waste line that prevents waste water from back-siphoning into a dishwasher. If your local code requires you to drain the appliance through an air gap, I recommend you install one made of copper or brass, not plastic. I've found that the Eastman CD-3 all-copper air gap (available from U.S. Brass, see the Sources of Supply on pp. 178-179) works better than any of the other brands I've tried.

The discharge from the dishwasher — hot, soapy wash water carrying lots of food particles — is pumped into the air gap under pressure. When the discharge reaches the top of the air gap, it rolls back down under gravity into the larger hose taking it to the garbage disposer or side-inlet tailpiece (see the drawing on p. 139). A top-quality air gap like the Eastman CD-3 has generously sized internal passageways, which reduce the risk of stoppages and leaks. In addition, because this air gap is made of heat-retaining copper, the heat of the discharge water helps keep fats and soaps from layering in the passageways.

The Eastman CD-3 has a hemispherical cap that's easy to unscrew for cleaning, and a good-quality chrome finish on the slotted vent cover. In my mind, the little extra I have to pay for this air gap is worth every cent in reduced annoyance and water damage.

A dishwasher air gap mounts from below in a hole at the back of the sink. The portion of the air gap that protrudes above the sink is covered with a chrome cap (shown to the left of the hole). (Photo by Charles Miller)

At the other end of the scale, plastic air gaps have narrow internal passageways with tight turns in which the discharge must travel before it can drain into the garbage disposer or tailpiece. The smaller-diameter passageways not only make it more likely that the air gap will get clogged but also mean that the dishwasher's pump has to work harder.

Some plastic air gaps have a 180° return bend at the top to direct the discharge back downhill, which can further increase the risk of stoppages (on a quality air gap, the discharge simply shoots up into the cap and then cascades back downhill). If the drain line gets clogged, the discharge will overpower the air gap and take the path of least resistance — out the vent holes in the air gap, or even out the appliance door past the rubber seal. One other problem with plastic air gaps is that the under-sink portion can break off when you attach the drain hoses.

MOUNTING THE AIR GAP

Most sinks come with a hole predrilled for the air gap, which is usually just to the right of the faucet holes on the back edge of the sink. Sometimes I prefer to put the air gap on the side of the sink farthest from the dishwasher, because this position may allow me a better path for the $7/8$-in. drain hose to the waste inlet (garbage disposer or side-inlet tailpiece).

If you have a stainless-steel kitchen sink, you can punch an additional $1\frac{1}{4}$-in. hole with a chassis punch (a tool made for cutting large-diameter holes in sheet metal). Don't be tempted to mount the air gap on a countertop — if the air gap clogs, water will pour out of the vent holes onto the counter.

If your local code allows you to drain a dishwasher into its own trap, without an air gap, then it doesn't matter so much where you place the appliance (though the farther from the hot-water nipple, the greater the length of water-supply line you'll need). All you need to do is loop the drain hose to prevent back siphonage. For this installation, I buy 180° copper returns or copper straps to attach the discharge hose to the back of the cabinet.

I strongly recommend that you place the dishwasher in a pan, with a drain if the appliance is over a crawl space. Most dishwasher leaks are slow, continuous drips that can damage floors over time, and even a holding pan can save you some headaches because the accumulated water usually has a chance to dry up before it ever overflows.

INSTALLING THE DISHWASHER

Begin the installation by positioning the dishwasher in front of the rough opening, which should be about ½ in. wider than the appliance (most dishwashers are 24 in. wide). As recommended in Chapter 4, the finish floor should have been run right into and across the entire opening. If the floor of the opening is lower than the finish floor, you can have difficulty getting the appliance in and out of the enclosure. I use a piece of carpet, fuzzy side down, to protect the finish floor as I slide the appliance in and out to mark and cut the hole(s) for the water supply and drain hose.

With the appliance slid up to the rough opening, inspect the side of the dishwasher that will be next to the sink cabinet. You're looking for gaps between the dishwasher components and chassis that will afford a route for the supply line and drain hose (and the power cord if you're wiring the appliance yourself). The supply line attaches to the solenoid valve, which regulates water intake into the dishwasher and is usually located at the front left side of the appliance (behind the lower front panel). The drain hose is attached to the pump at the bottom center of the dishwasher (see the drawing on p. 138).

Take measurements to ascertain where you can route the lines through the chassis to a hole that you will bore in the cabinet wall. On most dishwashers there is enough space at the rear of the chassis, but sometimes an inopportunely positioned dryer motor will make for a tight fit or the floor height of the kitchen-sink cabinet will mean that you have to bore a hole through the cabinet floor as well as the cabinet side. When routing the drain hose, always take the path to the air gap that has the fewest kinks (not always the shortest path), since any kinks in the hose can cause stoppages.

Once you've marked the hole in the cabinet wall, bore a ¼-in. pilot hole at this location. Now slide in the appliance and, with the lower front panel removed, look to see whether the hole aligns with the gap at the back of the chassis. (If the floor level in the enclosure is very uneven, you should level the dishwasher now. If it's not too far off level, you can wait until the appliance is in its final position, as discussed below.) Slide the appliance back out of the enclosure and use a hole saw to drill a larger hole in the cabinet wall (after making any necessary adjustment to the position of the hole). I like to bore a 1½-in. diameter hole in the cabinet wall, which is large enough for both the drain hose and the water supply. However, if it's not feasible to bore a large-diameter hole, you can drill two smaller holes.

With the hole cut in the cabinet wall and the dishwasher out of the enclosure, start feeding the ⅝-in. drain hose and ⅜-in. copper supply line through the hole (also thread the power cord through this hole if it has already been installed). Now inch the appliance into the enclosure (still atop the carpet) while simultaneously pulling the drain hose and supply line out the front.

Once the dishwasher is all the way in, pull out the carpet, then level the appliance. Most machines have adjustable feet at each corner that screw up and down, with a nut that allows you to lock the feet at the desired setting. Unless your arms are the diameter of broomsticks, it can be almost impossible to reach the back feet when the appliance is all the way in (which is why I recommended getting the dishwasher close to level before this final slide-in). If you still need to adjust the back feet now, you'll probably have no choice but to pull the dishwasher out of the opening once again to make the adjustment.

HOOKING UP THE WASTE   Now you're ready to hook up the drain hose and the supply line. Most dishwashers are shipped with a ⅝-in. corrugated-plastic drain hose (usually about 5 ft. long) preinstalled to

DISHWASHER INSTALLATION

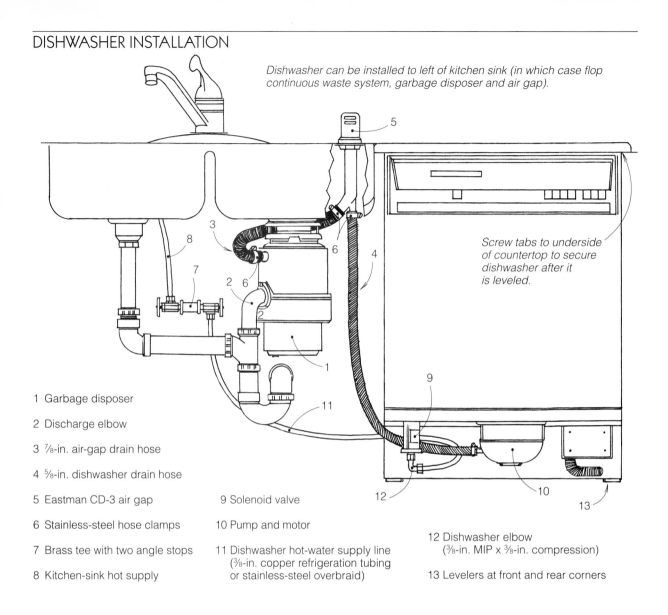

Dishwasher can be installed to left of kitchen sink (in which case flop continuous waste system, garbage disposer and air gap).

Screw tabs to underside of countertop to secure dishwasher after it is leveled.

1 Garbage disposer

2 Discharge elbow

3 ⁷⁄₈-in. air-gap drain hose

4 ⁵⁄₈-in. dishwasher drain hose

5 Eastman CD-3 air gap

6 Stainless-steel hose clamps

7 Brass tee with two angle stops

8 Kitchen-sink hot supply

9 Solenoid valve

10 Pump and motor

11 Dishwasher hot-water supply line
 (⅜-in. copper refrigeration tubing
 or stainless-steel overbraid)

12 Dishwasher elbow
 (⅜-in. MIP x ⅜-in. compression)

13 Levelers at front and rear corners

the hose barb at the front or side of the pump. With this type of hose, check that the hose clamp is tight. If your dishwasher has a separate ⁵⁄₈-in. rubber drain hose (or the preinstalled plastic hose is too short), connect the rubber hose to the barb with a stainless-steel hose clamp. On most dishwashers, the barb is sized to fit ⁵⁄₈-in. drain hose (the industry standard), but I have installed some models that have a smaller hose barb on the pump. With these models, you need to add a rubber adapter between the barb and the drain hose, which means another hose clamp and a greater risk of leaks.

Next, connect the other end of the drain hose to the air gap, as shown in the drawing above. The air gap has two legs, one ¾ in. in diameter and the other ½ in. Slip the ⁵⁄₈-in. drain hose over the ½-in. leg, and secure it with another stainless-steel hose clamp. Now attach a shorter length of ⁷⁄₈-in. drain hose (usually 3 ft.) to the ¾-in. diameter leg of the air gap. If you have a garbage disposer, this ⁷⁄₈-in. hose attaches to the inlet on the side of the disposer (check to make sure you've removed the knockout in the inlet, as explained on p. 132). Route the hose in the most direct, downhill path — the hose evacuates by gravity, so you don't want any kinks in it.

DISHWASHER DRAINAGE OPTIONS

DRAINAGE INTO GARBAGE DISPOSER   **DRAINAGE INTO SINK TRAP**   **DRAINAGE WITHOUT AIR GAP**

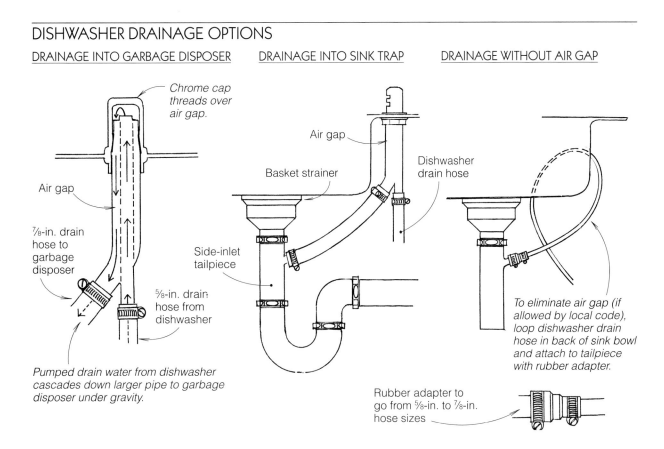

Chrome cap threads over air gap.

Air gap

⅞-in. drain hose to garbage disposer

⅝-in. drain hose from dishwasher

Pumped drain water from dishwasher cascades down larger pipe to garbage disposer under gravity.

Air gap

Basket strainer

Side-inlet tailpiece

Dishwasher drain hose

To eliminate air gap (if allowed by local code), loop dishwasher drain hose in back of sink bowl and attach to tailpiece with rubber adapter.

Rubber adapter to go from ⅝-in. to ⅞-in. hose sizes

If you don't have a garbage disposer, you should still route the ⅝-in. discharge hose to the air gap and then drop down with the ⅞-in. gravity drain hose to a side-inlet tailpiece, which attaches to the basket strainer of your choice. The side-inlet tailpiece has a branch sized for the ⅞-in. drain hose.

You can install the air gap in the hole in the sink first and then hook up the two drain hoses from below. However, I find it much easier to shove the hoses onto the air gap, tighten the hose clamps and then push the air gap through the sink hole from below. If you work the other way, not only is it very awkward to secure the hoses but there's also the risk that the entire bottom of a plastic air gap will break off flush with the nut that holds it to the sink (which is one of the reasons I suggest you use a copper or brass air gap).

HOOKING UP THE SUPPLY   Before you can hook up the water supply, you need to install a "dishwasher elbow" into the threads of the solenoid valve at the bottom of the appliance (see the photograph on p. 140). The opening on the solenoid is usually pointing straight out (sometimes down), and the elbow gets the connection onto a horizontal plane. Almost all dishwasher manufacturers use ⅜-in. diameter threads in the solenoid valve, which accepts a ⅜-in. IPS by ⅜-in. compression elbow. If your dishwasher has ½-in. threads in the solenoid valve, you can buy a ½-in. MIP by ⅜-in. compression dishwasher elbow.

At this point, the ⅜-in. copper refrigeration tubing should be sticking out the front of the appliance. (Note that you can also use a flexible stainless-steel braided supply for the water connection, but I prefer to use copper tubing for a real clean-looking installation.) Now use a tubing bender to make the 90° bend needed to align the supply tube with the dishwasher

The dishwasher elbow connects the hot-water supply line at the solenoid valve. (Photo by Bill Dane)

elbow. Make sure to leave at least 1 in. of straight tubing at the end so that the brass ferrule in the compression fitting will make a tight seal. Wrap the elbow's threads with Teflon tape before you thread on the compression nut. Follow this same procedure to hook up the supply line to the hot-water angle stop under the sink.

Once you've made all the plumbing connections, drive a screw through each mounting tab at the top of the machine to secure the dishwasher to the underside of the countertop. A word of caution: If you have a thin ⅜-in. particleboard countertop base with a laminate-finish surface, the mounting-tab screws might be long enough to go right through the laminate. For thin countertops, I keep the dishwasher down lower and glue a ¼-in. thick by 1-in. wide strip of wood to the underside of the counter above the mounting tabs.

TESTING FOR LEAKS

Now you're ready to give the dishwasher a trial run. Slowly turn on the angle stop until you hear the water start to flow. I leave the lower panel off for the rest of the day as I go about other tasks, coming back into the kitchen to check on the supply connections for drips, which have a way of showing up hours to days later. If you discover a leak, shut off the valve and slightly tighten the compression connections, taking care not to overtighten the nuts.

Many times on new construction the water heater has yet to be installed, but you can still have "live" pressure on the hot piping if the cold is coupled to the hot via the water heater's supply and discharge piping. However, the cold-water test isn't a true test of the dishwasher's supply connections, since the connections do not expand and contract as they do when 140°F hot water is coursing through the machine. So, if the water heater has yet to be installed, do it now so you can truly test the efficacy of the dishwasher's supply connections. When the water heater is making hot water and you have run the dishwasher through several full cycles without leaks, you can go ahead and replace the front panel.

WATER HEATER

On new construction, I usually leave the installation of the water heater until I have finished plumbing the kitchen (though sometimes a contractor will ask me to hook it up sooner). A water heater is a large, cumbersome appliance and it can be tricky to maneuver into position, but otherwise the installation is relatively simple. If the water heater is gas, I'll hook up the gas and the water. If it's an electric water heater, I'll make the water connections but leave the wiring for an electrician.

Gas-fired water heaters require venting to carry combustion gases safely out of the building. During the rough-plumbing stage, I install a gas-vent system with double-wall "Type B" pipe, either through the ceiling, through an interior wall or up the exterior wall (for detailed instructions on running the vent system, see *Plumbing a House,* this book's companion volume). When I come back to do the finish plumbing, I set the water heater in position and install a single-wall vent connector, or "flue," between the storm collar on the top of heater and the vent. (If you're installing a water heater that's fired by fuel oil, coal or wood, you'll also need to vent it — probably with triple-wall chimney pipe. Check with your local authority first.)

Also during rough plumbing, I would have run ¾-in. copper water lines (or 1-in. lines for large-capacity heaters) to the intended location of the heater, and left them looped together for the water test (see the photo at left on p. 142). To begin the finish installation, I turn off the water supply, break the loop and install escutcheons at the wall followed by

WATER HEATER

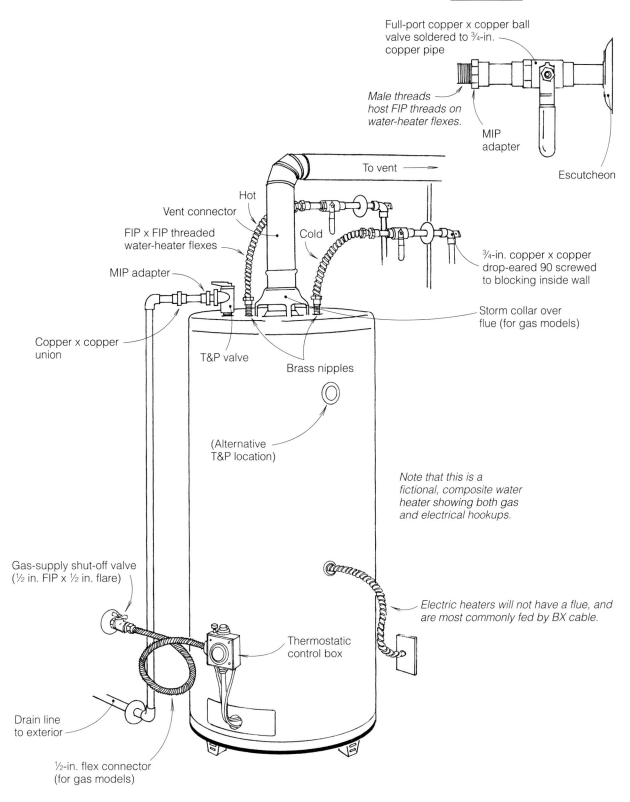

Full-port copper x copper ball valve soldered to ¾-in. copper pipe

Male threads host FIP threads on water-heater flexes.

MIP adapter

Escutcheon

To vent

Hot

Vent connector

Cold

FIP x FIP threaded water-heater flexes

MIP adapter

¾-in. copper x copper drop-eared 90 screwed to blocking inside wall

Storm collar over flue (for gas models)

Copper x copper union

T&P valve

Brass nipples

(Alternative T&P location)

Note that this is a fictional, composite water heater showing both gas and electrical hookups.

Gas-supply shut-off valve (½ in. FIP x ½ in. flare)

Electric heaters will not have a flue, and are most commonly fed by BX cable.

Thermostatic control box

Drain line to exterior

½-in. flex connector (for gas models)

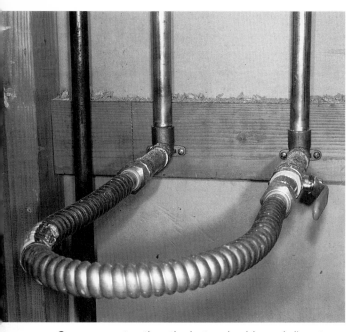

On new construction, the hot and cold supply lines to the water heater are looped together during rough plumbing. To hook up the water heater, you have to turn off the water and unthread the loop.

Use a crimping tool to shape the end of cut-to-length vent-connector pipe.

a full-port ball valve (or valves). Most homes have a valve on only the cold supply to the water heater, but it's worth considering a valve on the hot supply too. When it comes time to replace a thermostatic control box, an element or the entire heater, you'll have to drain down the entire system if you have just the cold valve. While draining the system is no big deal for a small structure, it can take considerably longer for a large one. If you have a valve on the hot side too, you can leave all the water in the structure's piping and merely drain the heater itself.

INSTALLING THE VENT CONNECTOR

Once the valves are installed, you can turn the water back on and get the heater in place under the valves. If the water heater is on a finished floor, it's a good idea to set it in a pan to catch any drips.

The next step is to run the vent connector. You want to establish the most direct path for this light-gauge galvanized pipe with the fewest number of change-of-direction fittings possible, so it's best to install it before the water-supply lines are in the way.

I buy most of my vent-connector pipe in 10-ft. lengths, with a few short (1-ft.) pieces of button-seamed pipe (the type that snaps together). One end of the connector pipe is crimped so it will slip into the open end of another piece of pipe or fitting (allow about 1½ in. extra at each joint when measuring the vent-connector pieces). Cut pieces of pipe to length with a hacksaw and shape the ends with a crimping tool, as shown in the photo above. Vent-connector pipe is very inexpensive so don't get too concerned if you ruin one or two pieces.

When you've finished assembling the vent connector, secure each joint with three self-drilling sheet-metal screws. Also screw the starting length to the storm collar (sometimes known as a "draft hood"), and the collar to the top of the heater. Some storm collars come with screws in their feet for attachment to the heater; others require securing with plumber's tape and screws. With the vent connector hooked up, it's back to the water connections.

CONNECTING THE WATER

Where I live, most authorities require the use of flexible connectors for the heater's water connections (regardless of whether the heater is gas-fired or electric). I suspect that this code requirement is because of seismic concerns, though ¾-in. flexible connectors are pretty much standard in all areas of the country now. Water-heater flexes come in various lengths up to 24 in. The two types that I like to use are the standard corrugated copper flex, and the less common, all-stainless-steel flex (see the sidebar on p. 144 for more on water-heater connectors).

I solder a short stub of copper pipe (about 2 in. to 3 in. long) onto the ball valves at the wall above the heater, and then solder on copper by MIP adapters (see the detail drawing on p. 141). One end of the copper water-heater flex then threads onto the end of the copper stub. I use flexes with a captive solid-brass FIP connection nut at each end (see the top photo at right). Some plumbers use copper flexes that have a belled female socket at one end that can be soldered directly onto the copper stub at the wall. However, if these flexes need replacing they have to be cut and resoldered. With male pipe threads on the stubs, you merely unthread the old connections and thread on new ones.

Next, I install a Teflon-taped ¾-in. brass nipple (about 3 in. to 4 in. long) into each opening on the top of the heater (after first running a ¾-in. pipe tap into each female-threaded hole to make sure they are true and clean). The copper flexes thread onto these nipples. (If you're using stainless-steel flexes with captive male adapters, you don't need the nipples.) I like the nipples to stick up past the belled edge of the storm collar so that I don't have to remove the collar to make the water connections. Positioning the connections above the collar, away from the exhaust heat, also prolongs the life of the rubber washer inside the female nut and the plastic dielectric sleeve sticking out the top.

You won't always be able to run the water connectors in a straight line from the supply line to the heater because the vent connector doesn't always go up in an absolutely vertical path. But with the flexible connectors, you'll be able to bend them around the vent connector.

The author prefers to use flexible copper water-heater connectors with FIP connections at each end.

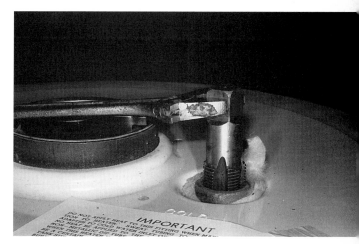

Run a pipe tap into the threaded holes on top of the heater before installing the nipples.

INSTALLING THE TEMPERATURE AND PRESSURE RELIEF VALVE

Once the water connectors are hooked up, you can thread the temperature and pressure (T&P) relief valve into the heater. This valve, which is required by code on all storage-tank water heaters, is designed to open if temperature or pressure levels within the tank become dangerously high. As with the nipples on top of the heater, run a pipe tap into the opening first, and wrap the T&P threads with Teflon tape. The threaded hole for the T&P valve is either on top of the heater or on the side. I prefer working with the

WATER-HEATER CONNECTORS

I like to use either copper or stainless-steel flex connectors to make the water connections at the top of the water heater. The quality of the copper water-heater flexes varies considerably from manufacturer to manufacturer. Better-quality flexes have solid-brass connection nuts, not plated steel, and are more flexible. The flexibility of the connectors is determined by the shape of the corrugations: The spiral corrugations on good copper flexes have a rounded bottom, which allows you to make tighter bends, while on lower-grade flexes the corrugations are merely sharp creases at the bottom, which kink as soon as you try to bend them in anything but the most gradual of wide radiuses (see the drawing at right).

The best, most versatile water-heater flexes that I have ever used are stainless steel. The corrugations on these flexes are round bottomed and very close together so that you can bend them freely without kinking. One of the great features of these stainless-steel flexes is that they have a built-in male iron pipe (MIP) adapter on one end, which eliminates the need for a brass nipple at the top of the heater. These flexes are

Top-quality flex bends well because of full radius at bottom of groove.

Lower-grade flex kinks very easily because of sharp crease at bottom of groove.

made in Japan (by Stainless Steel Flex Industries), and unfortunately they are not always easy to find where I live. When my supplier can get them, he sells them for the same price as the top-quality copper flexes.

Run the drain line from the temperature and pressure relief valve to the edge of the heater and then down and out the building.

T&P valve on top because it's generally more accessible. If possible, I install the valve so that its opening is pointing toward the front of the heater, so that I can run pipe to the edge of the heater and then down and out of the building.

For a top-mounted T&P valve, measure the distance from the valve opening to the edge of the heater and cut a stub of ¾-in. copper pipe to length. Now solder an MIP adapter to this short stub and thread it into the valve temporarily. Make a mark on the stub about 3 in. in from the edge of the heater, then unthread the stub and cut at the mark. Next, solder on a ¾-in. copper-to-copper brass union. Put pipe dope on the female threads in the T&P valve and Teflon tape on the MIP and thread the adapter into the valve tightly. Hold a copper 90° elbow in position near the edge of the heater, with one leg pointing down to the floor, far enough out from the heater to keep the drop clear of obstructions. Measure the distance into the full socket depths of the elbow and the union and cut ¾-in. copper pipe to length. Solder this stub into the union. Add the 90° elbow and then solder another cut-to-length piece of ¾-in. copper into the lower leg of the 90°. This drain line should run down the side of the heater, then turn horizontally to go out the wall within 6 in. of the ground outside.

CONNECTING THE GAS LINE

With the vent connector hooked up and the flexes and T&P valve installed, all that remains is to connect the gas line (or to run the cable from the power source for electric water heaters). The gas line was installed during the rough-plumbing stage, and somewhere close to the gas heater there should be a capped ½-in. galvanized nipple (it might be a ¾-in. or even a 1-in. nipple if you're installing a large-capacity water heater). Now you need to attach an end-line gas valve to this nipple, then run a flexible supply to the thermostat control box on the heater (see the drawing on p. 141).

To install the valve, first turn the gas off to the building. If the nipple protrudes from a wall, slide on an escutcheon before attaching the valve. I like to use a spring-loaded ½-in. FIP to ½-in. male-flare type valve, which has a short, easy-to-turn actuating handle (see the top photo at right). The ½-in. gas flex connector threads right onto the end of the valve, without the need for another nipple or adapter. At the water-heater end of the flex I use a ½-in. male-flare by MIP adapter, which threads into the female iron pipe threads of the thermostat control box. I put pipe dope in the captive flare nuts on the flex before installing it.

In the past, gas connectors for water heaters were epoxy-coated brass tubing. This material is still available, but I prefer to use the more durable stainless-steel connectors. For most residential water-heater installations, a 24-in. or 36-in. long gas flex will make the connection between the shut-off valve and the thermostat control box without being stretched or overlong. However, your local code might designate a shorter maximum length of connector, in which case you may have to rotate the heater toward the gas shut-off valve so you can use a shorter flex.

If you live anywhere near earthquake country, you may want and/or be required to provide some stabilization for the water heater in the event of an earthquake. Some suppliers sell a lightweight, manufactured bracket that is slid down over the nipples on

A gas-supply shut-off valve for a water heater attaches to the gas line at the wall.

Some local codes recommend that water heaters be chained to the wall for seismic protection.

top of the heater and then nailed to bracing or structural members behind the heater. If the heater is in an alcove or closet, you can wrap the heater with galvanized plumber's tape at two or three levels, and anchor the ends to wood members in the side walls with 3-in. drive or drywall screws (with flat washers under the heads of the screws). Some plumbers bolt lengths of chain around the heater in a similar fashion.

Once the gas line is connected, open the ball valves above the appliance and fill the heater slowly. When the heater is fully pressurized, light the pilot (assuming you have gas service to the house). Then turn the control on and wait until the heater shuts off automatically at the 140°F setting. (If the water heater is electric, flip the breaker on and wait until it reaches full temperature.) If you have any drips at the water connections, just turn the control to pilot, tighten the connections in quarter-turn increments until the drip stops and then turn the burner back on and proceed. Don't be tempted to lift the handle on the T&P valve (as some people recommend). If you get one speck of dirt in the seat of the valve, it will leak continuously.

GAS COOKTOP/RANGE

On new construction, after I've installed the water heater I go back into the kitchen to hook up any gas cooktop or freestanding range. For either of these appliances, there will be a capped line that was installed during rough plumbing: ½-in. for a cooktop, and ¾-in. for a range. On the finish, it's simply a matter of making the connection between the gas line and the appliance.

INSTALLING A GAS COOKTOP

A gas cooktop drops into an opening in the countertop, usually on top of a storage cabinet. This appliance almost always come with a separate in-line gas regulator that has to be installed along with a flexible gas connector and valve (on most freestanding ranges, this regulator is factory installed). Invariably, the regulator won't fit inside the cooktop, but you want to keep it as close to the appliance as possible so that you won't bang into it with pots and pans and other items as you move them in and out of the cabinet. The gas-intake connection is usually at the bottom of the appliance, though the exact location varies from model to model.

For fire-safety reasons, many local authorities require that the gas shut-off valve for the cooktop be in a prominent, easy-to-reach location. You may also be required to install a pull-down door on the front of the cabinet for access to the valve. Before proceed-

ing with the installation, check with your local authority to see if there are any codes governing the position of the shut-off valve.

If you are installing the cooktop on a cabinet that's against a wall, the rigid-pipe gas line is probably protruding through the back wall of the cabinet (on island cabinets, the line might be coming up through the floor of the cabinet). Add a brass 90° elbow to bring the pipe parallel to the front of the cooktop, then thread in a ½-in. brass nipple, followed by the regulator (see the drawing on the facing page). I use superior-sealing brass nipples and fittings rather than galvanized on this appliance, because of the proximity of the piping to in-cabinet traffic. On all threaded gas connections, I wrap the male threads with Teflon tape and apply pipe dope to the female threads.

I like to keep the regulator within about 2 in. of the bottom of the cooktop, unless there is a warning accompanying the appliance recommending otherwise. Look for the arrow on the regulator, which is usually cast as part of the aluminum housing, and make sure that it is pointing in the direction of the gas flow. Next thread another brass nipple into the outlet of the regulator, then install a spring-loaded brass FIP to male-flare gas valve (the same valve that I recommended for the gas water heater, see p. 145)

The gas connection on the cooktop itself is usually a ½-in. FIP tapped hole flush with the bottom of the appliance box. Thread a street 90° fitting (which has one end male-threaded and the other end female-threaded) or a close nipple and elbow into this hole, followed by an MIP to flare adapter. Then attach a ½-in. gas flex connector of the appropriate length to reach the shut-off valve. As with a gas water heater, I prefer to use stainless-steel connectors rather than the epoxy-coated brass tubing for this application. Inspectors take a good look at the cooktop's gas hookup, so make sure you know what your code allows. My code states that the connector should be no longer than 3 ft. and that no part of the flex connector should be concealed within or extended through any wall, floor or partition (including the cabinet wall, floor or partition).

VENTED COOKTOPS   In addition to the standard unvented drop-in models, cooktops are also available with powered, out-of-the-bottom ventilation. In my experience, these high-tech models can be a real

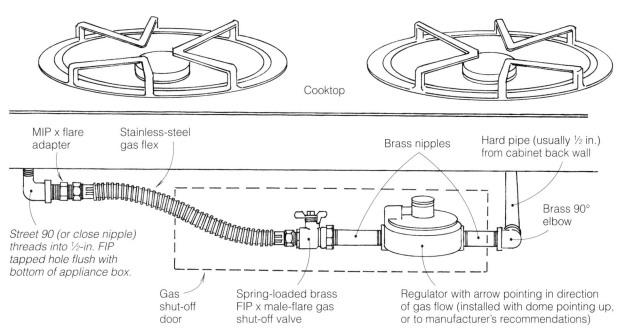

Cooktop

MIP x flare adapter

Stainless-steel gas flex

Brass nipples

Hard pipe (usually ½ in.) from cabinet back wall

Brass 90° elbow

Street 90 (or close nipple) threads into ½-in. FIP tapped hole flush with bottom of appliance box.

Gas shut-off door

Spring-loaded brass FIP x male-flare gas shut-off valve

Regulator with arrow pointing in direction of gas flow (installed with dome pointing up, or to manufacturer's recommendations)

headache to install. The trim overlap that supports these larger appliances is usually very narrow, and it's all too easy to scratch the counter surface if you're installing them on tile or dark, textured laminate. If you do decide to install this type yourself, I recommend that you run wide tape around the opening in the counter and then use a sharp utility knife to trim off the exposed portion of the tape after the installation is complete. Mating the below-floor vent to the vent stub on the bottom of the appliance while at the same time getting the cooktop set back at full depth in the cabinet many times requires several attempts. If you're short on patience, don't even think about doing it yourself. Instead, have it installed by the appliance dealer's subcontractor, who will be aware of the idiosyncrasies of each model and be more adept at installing the cooktop.

INSTALLING A FREESTANDING GAS RANGE

Although I usually install gas cooktops on new construction these days, there is still some demand for freestanding household ranges, especially in custom-built homes. These appliances are more expensive than drop-in cooktops, but they are easier to install because you don't have to work inside the cabinet — the valve and flex connections are made behind the range at the wall.

Begin the installation by moving the range to its intended location and checking for level. I check for level by moving a pan of water from burner to burner. Sometimes inaccurately cast burner grates will not be level on top of the leveled range cabinet, but it's more important to have the actual cooking surfaces level than the cabinet itself. If the range is badly out of level, I'll make the necessary adjustment now (if it's not far off level, I'll wait until I've hooked up the gas). Most ranges have threaded, flat-footed leveling bolts similar to those used on dishwashers (see p. 137).

Household ranges usually come with a gas regulator already installed, typically mounted inside the top left or right side of the appliance. (If the regulator is not already in place, make sure you install it with the arrow on the housing pointing in the direction of the flow of gas. Check the accompanying literature for any restrictions on regulator position.) From this regulator, you need to run rigid pipe through the interior of the burner compartment and out the back of the range. Thread a ¾-in. nipple into the regulator outlet, followed by a coupling and a long enough

FREESTANDING GAS RANGE

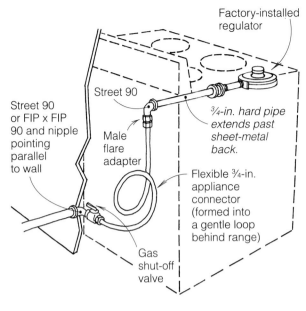

Factory-installed regulator

Street 90

Street 90 or FIP x FIP 90 and nipple pointing parallel to wall

Male flare adapter

¾-in. hard pipe extends past sheet-metal back.

Flexible ¾-in. appliance connector (formed into a gentle loop behind range)

Gas shut-off valve

piece of ¾-in. pipe to extend past the sheet-metal back of the appliance. Next install a street 90° fitting (or an FIP to FIP 90° elbow and nipple) and male flare adapter pointing down toward the floor, as shown in the drawing above.

Most local authorities will allow you to position the shut-off valve for the freestanding range out of sight behind the appliance, and allow you to use flexible appliance connectors (either stainless steel or epoxy-coated brass) to make the gas hook-up. As always, check your code first. You'll need to use longer flex connectors than on a gas cooktop (and ¾-in. diameter flexes rather than ½ in.), because you want to be able to slide the range all the way out of any gap between cabinets so that you can walk behind it and turn off the valve. My local code allows the use of appliance connectors up to 6 ft. long behind a range, which gives more than enough slack to pull the appliance out.

The flexible connector should be formed into a loop behind the range, so that when you pull the range out and shove it back in again, the connector goes from loop to helix and back again. What you want to avoid are kinks in the connector. I find that installing the shut-off valve parallel to the wall helps the flex connector take a natural course in forming the loop (adding the 90° elbow at the back of the

range also helps). To bring the valve parallel to the wall, you first need to install a 90° elbow horizontally to the rigid piping at the wall (as shown in the drawing at left).

With the gas shut-off valve installed parallel to the wall, it's important to make sure that you can turn the valve from the full-on to the full-off position without hitting the wall. Clearing the wall usually isn't a concern with the newer spring-loaded valves, but you can run into trouble with old-style tapered core valves with lever handles (which are still manufactured). I recommend that you stay away from this archaic valve design.

Most freestanding ranges (and cooktops) are now manufactured with electronic ignitions rather than pilot lights. These ignition systems have a tendency to fail within a few weeks to months of installation. Usually it requires only one visit by the service technician (on warranty) to get everything ironed out, and after that the appliance should operate without problems for many years. If you are installing a freestanding range or cooktop, make sure to mail in any warranty papers and keep point-of-sale receipts handy for the first several months.

GAS DRYER

Not all plumbers install laundry machines, but if there's a gas dryer to hook up on new construction I'll usually do it. Once I get the building's gas supply shut down to install the valves for any gas-fired water heater and gas-fired cooktop or range, it makes sense to install the gas valve for any gas dryer. If I leave this job for the appliance installer, it means another interruption in the gas supply later.

INSTALLATION

Installing a gas dryer is much the same procedure as hooking up a freestanding range. I run the gas valve parallel to the wall and use a flexible connector to the appliance, but the diameter of the connector and fittings is smaller than on a range. Most individual-unit, residential gas dryers have a ⅜-in. MIP stub sticking out of a recess down low on the back of the appliance. I don't like to use ⅜-in. valves and flexes, mainly because it's inconvenient for me to carry two more parts around that cannot be used on any other appli-

GAS-DRYER CONNECTION

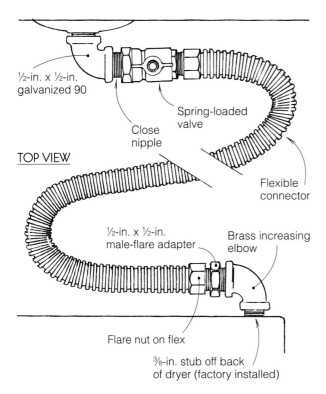

½-in. x ½-in.
galvanized 90

Close
nipple

Spring-loaded
valve

TOP VIEW

Flexible
connector

½-in. x ½-in.
male-flare adapter

Brass increasing
elbow

Flare nut on flex

⅜-in. stub off back
of dryer (factory installed)

ance. So, I use an increasing elbow on the appliance stub, which allows me to run a ½-in. flex connector (see below).

I begin the installation by replacing the galvanized test nipple at the wall with a shorter, permanent galvanized nipple (it's okay to use galvanized rather than brass here since the nipple is behind the appliance and isn't as likely to get hit). This new nipple should be just long enough to have its tapered pipe threads protruding past the outside surface of the escutcheon that I slide to the wall. Then I install a standard ½-in. by ½-in. galvanized 90° elbow onto the nipple, followed by a close galvanized nipple. Onto the end of the close nipple I install a ½-in. FIP by ½-in. male-flare spring-loaded gas valve (preferably brass, not plated steel). On all these connections, I wrap the male threads with Teflon tape and apply pipe dope to the female threads.

Next, I thread a ⅜-in. by ½-in. increasing brass 90° elbow onto the Teflon-taped ⅜-in. MIP stub on the back of the appliance. I leave the elbow in a horizontal plane, pointing the opposite direction to that of

the gas valve, parallel to the wall. Into the ½-in. FIP threads of the 90° elbow, I thread a ½-in. MIP by ½-in. male-flare adapter (also preferably brass rather than plated steel).

Most codes allow only a 3-ft. connector behind the dryer, which can make it difficult to pull the appliance out far enough for access to the gas valve (or for cleaning behind the dryer). I'd prefer to use a longer connector here for the same reason that I use the accepted 6-ft. connector on the freestanding range, but that's the code. The flexible connector, with pipe-doped female-flare nuts, threads onto the male flares of the valve and adapter in the dryer's 90° elbow, making a loop that will allow you to slide the appliance in and out without kinking the connector. As with the freestanding range, running the gas valve parallel to the wall helps send the flexible appliance connector into the proper path for forming the loop. A gas valve parallel to the wall also allows an extra inch or so of clearance, which is often needed in tight locations. Once the gas supply is hooked up, you can connect the flexible vent duct to the vent hole that was cut in the wall during rough plumbing.

WASHER/DRYER COMBINATION

In laundry rooms where there's no room to position a washing machine and a dryer side by side, some people choose to install a stackable washer/dryer combination. This appliance is offered by some very reputable manufacturers, but it's not an installation that I recommend. You need to work closely to the manufacturer's schematic when roughing in the water lines and gas service (or electrical service for an electric dryer) as well as the through-the-wall vent fitting — it seems that no two models have the connections in the same place.

The toughest part about installing a stackable washer/dryer is making sure that the dryer vent fitting in the wall is accurately placed. While you can be slightly off with the gas location, there's very little room for error with the vent. (Unlike standard gas dryers, most combination washer/dryers use rigid metal ducting rather than a flexible vent connector.) If the floor where the appliance is going to rest is not close to level, you'll have a very frustrating time trying to level the appliance to match the through-the-wall vent rough-in.

DIRECT-VENT HEATER

Small, wall-mounted direct-vent heaters are a popular alternative to stand-up gas furnaces, because they don't require a costly and labor-intensive Type B double-wall vent run to above the roof height. Instead, they are vented directly outside through a doughnut-shaped vent cap that doubles as a combustion air intake. Low-profile heaters start at about 11,000 Btu, while the top-of-the-line models range up to about 65,000 Btu.

The biggest problem with a direct-vent heater is finding an appropriate exterior wall on which to mount it. Code-imposed restrictions on venting systems limit your choices (as might the location of studs and diagonal bracing). My code specifies that the vents must terminate at least 1 ft. above, 4 ft. below or 4 ft. horizontally from any door, window, or gravity-air inlet into the building. Further, vents must terminate at least 3 ft. above any forced air-inlet located within 10 ft. or at least 4 ft. from any property line except a public way. If you manage to satisfy these requirements, your local code may impose additional limitations. A chat with your local authority in the early planning stages of the project is the best defense against problems later.

Because the exhaust pipe and intake pipe of these heaters slide together, they can accommodate different wall thicknesses. However, if your exterior walls are extra thick, you'd better check with the distributor before making a purchase to make sure that the heater can be adapted to your wall. There are two brands that I particularly like: Williams's Debonair series, which adapts to walls from 5 in. to 9 in. thick, and Perfection's Super-Tite series, which adapts to walls 5 in. to 13 in. thick (see Sources of Supply on pp. 178-179). The Super-Tite is available with an extension Vent Tube Kit that adapts to walls up to 20 in. thick. Williams also manufactures direct-vent stand-up wall furnaces of 40,000, 55,000 and 65,000 Btu, which adapt to walls up to 12 in. thick.

Direct-vent heaters mount on the wall and are vented to the outside through an exhaust/intake pipe. (Photo by Bill Dane)

INSTALLATION

The toughest part of installing a direct-vent heater is making the rough-in hole through the wall. Sometimes you run into a stud or diagonal bracing, or you may have to blast through old 1-in. thick stucco over expanded metal lath. Small direct-vent heaters sometimes fit between standard 16-in. on-center studs, reducing the distance that the cabinet trim must protrude from the wall. Large models usually mount to the surface of the finish wall, with cabinet trim protruding several inches farther into the room.

When you purchase a direct-vent heater, you get a rough-in template for laying out the rough openings you must make in the wall (one for the exhaust/intake, one for the gas supply). The holes on the interior wall must correspond with the holes on the exterior wall, and getting the two to line up can be tricky. Using a long pilot drill, I make small holes all the way through the wall in the center of the rough openings for the exhaust/intake and the gas supply, and then lay out the openings from those holes with a compass on both sides of the wall.

DIRECT-VENT HEATER

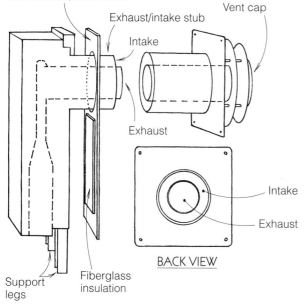

Optional heat shield slides over exhaust/intake stub.

Exhaust/intake stub

Vent cap

Intake

Intake

Exhaust

Exhaust

Support legs

Fiberglass insulation

BACK VIEW

Screw appliance to wall after exhaust/intake hole has been cut and gas line installed.

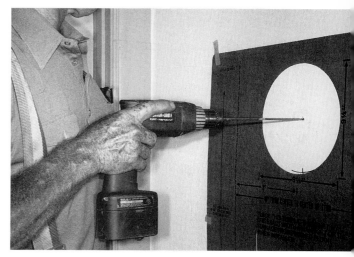

With the template in position, drill a hole through the center of the rough opening for the exhaust/intake vent. (Photo by Bill Dane)

The exhaust/intake vent passes through the rough opening in the wall. (Photo by Bill Dane)

Once the holes are cut, the gas lines can be brought in and the heater can be screwed to the wall, following the manufacturer's instructions. On the back side of the heater you will usually find a pair of support members or legs, which are merely lightweight sheet-metal channels spot-welded to the unit. The legs will have screw holes near the top and bottom. There may also be a heat shield that fits between the appliance and the wall; the shield slips over the exhaust/intake pipe before installation.

Factory-installed to the heater itself will be the exhaust/intake vent stub that will pass through the rough opening in the wall. The accompanying vent-cap/intake duct has a stub on the back that consists of two sheet-metal pipes. The inner pipe is the exhaust pipe; the outer pipe is the intake pipe. The vent cap slides over the exhaust/intake stub on the heater box. Depending upon the wall thickness, the length of the vent-cap stub will vary. If the stub is too long for your wall, you will need to trim it down with a pair of aviation snips.

CHAPTER
10

TROUBLESHOOTING

If you buy quality fixtures and appliances and install them as I've described in this book, you can expect to get a good, long life out of them. But sooner or later you'll inevitably need to make some repairs. Troubleshooting can involve nothing more than tightening a nut or replacing a washer; at other times it may require replacement of the fixture, or calling in a professional to clear an inaccessible clog.

The key to troubleshooting is early detection — identifying the problem before it becomes more serious and more expensive to fix. Some problems are easy to diagnose: If you have a stopped-up sink, for example, you can be sure that there is a blockage somewhere in the waste or drain line. Other problems are harder to pin down: If there's water on the floor around the toilet, it might have come from under the bowl, from the tank or from the connection between the angle stop and supply tube. In this chapter, I'll go through all the plumbing fixtures and major appliances, identify potential problems and tell you how to fix them. And remember, a true repair is made only when the problem goes away and stays away.

PLUMBING PROBLEMS

In my experience, the most common plumbing complaint is a clogged drain, followed by leaks and then mechanical failures.

CLOGS

Clogs vary from a complete blockage, where no water will drain away from the fixture, to cases where water drains slowly. There are various tools and strategies for dealing with clogs. The first line of offense is the plunger, or force cup (see p. 12 and the top photo on the facing page), which is used to force the blockage out of the trap or drain. Other tools, such as the closet auger and mechanical fingers, can be used to retrieve objects from the trap. If these tools prove ineffective you can sometimes disassemble the trap to remove the clog (or simply unthread the cleanout on the bottom of the trap, if there is one). If the problem is serious — all the drains are backing up into the tub and/or shower, for example — you'll need to call in a professional drain-cleaning service to have the blockage removed with a powered mechanical snake.

A plunger with pliable sides and a fold-out skirt is an effective tool for clearing clogs in toilets and sink traps.

A stoppage in the main building-drain line requires use of a powered mechanical snake. This professional drain-cleaning tool can also be used inside the house to unclog individual fixture drains.

LEAKS

Leaks can be classified as either pressure leaks or gravity leaks. When diagnosing plumbing problems, it helps to know the difference between the two.

Each plumbing fixture in the home has water piped to it under constant pressure, either from a well pump on the property or from a municipal utility line brought to the property. Pressure leaks occur when there is a failure in one of the connections, typically caused by a worn-out washer or a loose nut. Sink faucets and tub and shower valves that drip from spouts, from shower heads and around stems

represent the most noticeable examples of pressure leaks. Pressure leaks can also occur at supply-to-valve and supply-to-angle-stop connections.

Once the water leaves the valve or valves of a fixture, it is carried away by a gravity drainage system. If the water escapes the drainage system, it is classified as a gravity leak. Included here are leaks in the waste, trap and trap arm, as well as splash-water leaks under the rim of a cabinet-mounted sink.

MECHANICAL BREAKDOWNS

Whereas clogs and leaks are the most common problems with plumbing fixtures, appliances such as dishwashers and garbage disposers are more prone to mechanical malfunctions. I'll suggest some repairs for these appliances at the end of this chapter, though you'll often have to call in a service person to tackle the problem. Toilets also have mechanical components that can fail, though these failures often show up as pressure leaks.

TOILETS

"The toilet's plugged up. The tank won't fill. The toilet runs and runs. When I flush the toilet, water comes out from underneath the bowl." These are just a sample of the calls I commonly get about toilets, which have more potential trouble spots than any other plumbing fixture. Although there are many things that can go wrong with a toilet, most of the repairs are not that difficult to make yourself. In this section, I'll tell you how to deal with clogs, leaks and the mechanical failure of toilet components.

CLOGS

A toilet bowl becomes clogged when fecal matter or other articles fail to pass all the way through the internal trap, or, if they do pass through the trap, become caught in the drain line. To remove a blockage in the internal trap, first try the plunger.

Fold out the little skirt on the bottom of the cup, which allows the plunger to form itself into the bottom of the bowl's funnel, and then make four or five rapid, strong, full strokes. Don't be timid here — push down firmly as though you were trying to shove the plunger right through the toilet. Some water will

TOILET CLOGS

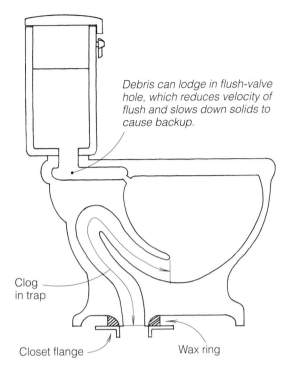

Debris can lodge in flush-valve hole, which reduces velocity of flush and slows down solids to cause backup.

Clog in trap

Closet flange

Wax ring

If you flush one of these down the toilet, it usually doesn't get all the way through the trap, which is actually a blessing in disguise — it's much cheaper to retrieve it out of the bowl than from the building sewer line 30 ft. to 50 ft. away. The important thing to remember if you flush a cloth diaper is not to flush the toilet again, thinking you might be able to send it on its way to the main building drain. Instead, snake the closet auger down into the trap to try and snare the diaper and pull it out.

Facial tissue and paper towels can also cause clogs in the trap — unlike toilet tissue, these papers do not decompose in water. Get what you can first with the auger and then try the plunger. Sanitary napkins are the foremost toilet-drain-line stopper. They usually make it through the smooth fixture passage itself but can become snagged at pipe joints, in change-of-direction fittings or at branch fittings in the building drain or building sewer. If sanitary napkins are blocking the drain line, no amount of plunging will get you out of this predicament — it's time for the mechanical snake and its experienced operator.

Believe it or not, dental floss can also cause a clog in a toilet. The floss can catch on rough edges in the drain line or embed in "line slime" and then flail around like seaweed in undersea currents, generally slowing down the flow of matter until the toilet gets blocked. Dental floss is very difficult to get rid of and usually has to be cut out with a powered snake (again, plunging is ineffectual).

Other household items that can get flushed inadvertently and wedged in the trap include combs, toothbrushes and small cosmetic containers. Plunging may straighten out the object temporarily, but unless you remove it you're likely to get a blockage again at some later date. You stand a fair chance of extricating a comb or a toothbrush with a closet auger, but it won't help you with small, solid objects. To remove these items, you'll need to lift the fixture and try gently rolling it this way and that until the object comes out.

One other cause of toilet clogs that I've encountered is cat litter. Don't be tempted to flush cat feces from the litter tray down the toilet! The clay gravel will settle in the bottom of the trap and may build up enough to cause a blockage, which is usually too heavy to be moved by a plunger. You'll have to lift the toilet and hose it out outside to dislodge the clay.

slosh out of the bowl, so make sure you take appropriate steps to protect the finish floor (I wrap towels around the base of the bowl). Repeat the series of strokes, then rest and observe. Try it a dozen times before giving up. If you should force all the water out of the bowl, lift the flush valve in the tank by hand and let the bowl refill, being prepared to shove the valve closed if the bowl gets close to overfilling before all the water in the tank is gone. Then repeat your plunging maneuvers. When you're ready to try a full-flush cycle, just keep your hand near the flush valve so that you can close it manually if you have to.

If the plunger fails to move the blockage, next try a closet auger (see p. 14). To operate this tool, turn the handle as you introduce the end of the auger into the bowl's passageway, and continue to turn the handle as you push the rod all the way down. About a dozen turns in rapid succession should be enough to break up the blockage.

You can also use a closet auger to retrieve objects that have been flushed down the toilet unintentionally. One of the chief offenders here is cloth diapers.

Alternatively, if you don't mind getting wet, you can snake a soft garden hose with the metal end removed into the trap and have a helper turn the hose on while you flush the toilet at the same time.

In addition to clogs in the trap, another potential clog zone is at the tank-to-bowl connection (see the drawing on the facing page). This blockage most commonly occurs when a piece of worn-out flush ball gets lodged in the flush-valve hole. To clear the blockage, drain and remove the tank and then use mechanical fingers (see p. 161) to remove the debris.

LEAKS

If you find water on the floor around the toilet, you can be fairly certain that the fixture is leaking. The hard part is finding where the water is coming from (see the drawing below). The source of the leak might be a failed seal between the tank and the bowl or between the bowl and the closet flange (both gravity leaks). Alternatively, it could be a pressure leak at the angle-stop or fill-valve connection. It might also be the result of a pressure leak within the tank. In this section, I'll explain how to repair all these leaks, beginning with gravity leaks.

GRAVITY LEAKS   In my experience, the most common gravity leak for toilets is water seeping out from under the toilet bowl, which is usually caused by a failed bowl wax (see p. 156). If you see water around the base of the bowl, however, don't immediately jump to the conclusion that you need to lift the toilet and replace the wax — it might be a leak requiring an easier fix.

On a close-coupled toilet, the tank sits on a shelf on the back edge of the bowl. If the gasket between the tank and the bowl fails, water will pool up on the shelf and then run down the back of the bowl to the floor. Flush the toilet and look for a rivulet of water running down the back of the bowl, or any water dripping off the tank bolts. The leak might be caused

TOILET LEAKS

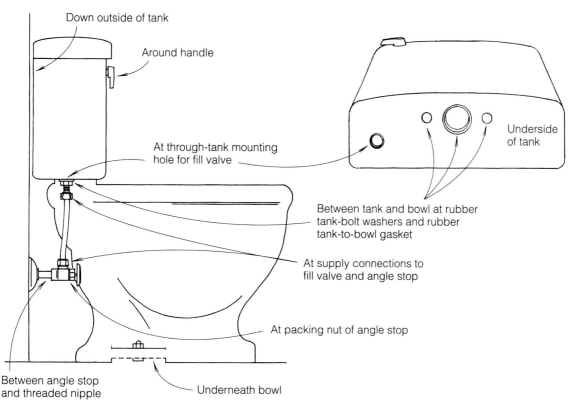

Down outside of tank

Around handle

At through-tank mounting hole for fill valve

Underside of tank

Between tank and bowl at rubber tank-bolt washers and rubber tank-to-bowl gasket

At supply connections to fill valve and angle stop

At packing nut of angle stop

Between angle stop and threaded nipple

Underneath bowl

by a poor tank-to-bowl gasket seal, by failure of the rubber washers under the tank-bolt heads (inside the tank) or by loose tank bolts.

In most cases, you'll need to remove the tank to make the necessary repairs, but sometimes just snugging up the nuts on the bottom of the tank bolts will buy you some time. Take the lid off the toilet tank, and insert the bit of a long, slotted screwdriver into the tank bolt's slotted head. Hold the bolt still with the screwdriver and try tightening up the nut below with a box wrench or a socket wrench. If you can tighten both nuts and the leak remains, or if you cannot tighten the nuts at all, then you'll have to take the tank off the bowl. You may find that the nuts are corroded and won't unthread off the bolts, in which case you'll have to use a hacksaw blade to cut the bolts in half between the tank and the bowl (remove the toilet seat first). Replace the rubber gasket and/or the rubber tank-bolt washers. If you need to replace the tank bolts and nuts, make sure you use solid-brass replacements. (For detailed instructions on installing the tank to the bowl, see pp. 66-68.)

If you have an old-style toilet with a wall-hung tank, the tank does not sit on the bowl but is connected to it by a 90° fitting called a "flush elbow." This elbow is attached to the underside of the tank and the back of the bowl with 2-in. slip nuts and rubber slip-nut washers. If you have a leak at either connection, you can try tightening the slip nuts, but you'll probably have to replace the flush elbow since the slip nuts will invariably be corroded. If there's a leak between the flush valve's lock mounting nut and the tank, you'll also have to replace the flush valve's rubber gasket. These repairs can be time-consuming.

In addition to the leak at the tank-to-bowl connection, another potential location for a gravity leak is at the mounting hole for the fill valve on the bottom of the tank. If there's a leak at this point, drain the tank, remove the fill valve and replace the rubber gasket at the base of the valve. A less common leak is around the flush handle: If water is escaping here, adjust the float rod to lower the water level in the tank (see the drawing on p. 159).

If you still can't find where the water on the floor is coming from, there is one other place to check before you lift the bowl. Remove the tank lid and then flush the toilet. Sometimes you'll see a stream of water spurting out the top of the fill valve. When the water hits the inside of the tank lid it can run down the outside of the tank and onto the floor. In this case, you'll need to replace the ballcock piston seals (see below).

If you determine that the only possible location for the leak is from under the bowl, the most likely cause is a bad seal between the toilet's horn and the closet flange. In this case, you'll have to lift the bowl and replace the failed bowl wax. Use a putty knife to remove the old bowl wax and install a new one with a plastic sleeve, as explained on pp. 65-66. (If the toilet has been down for a long time, it might be set on plaster of Paris and plumber's putty, with no wax seal. Remove this material before installing the bowl wax.)

A leak under the bowl might also be caused by a broken closet bolt(s) or closet flange (replace as necessary), or even a crack in the underside of the bowl (replace the entire toilet). On older installations, the toilet may be set on a lead closet bend (an elbow with no flange) and held to the floor with wood-screw-type closet bolts. Over time, gradual seepage may have rotted the floor around the bolts, which can no longer hold the bowl tight to the floor. In this extreme case, you'll have to replace the rotted flooring (and preferably the lead closet bend too).

PRESSURE LEAKS   Pressure leaks in toilets, which can occur at threaded connections in the supply line or within the tank, are usually easier to diagnose than gravity leaks. If you discover a leak at the supply to angle-stop connection or at the supply to fill-valve connection, simply tighten up the nut (reapplying Teflon tape if necessary). If you have a leak in an old-style toilet supply with a rubber cone washer, it's a good idea to replace the supply with an acorn-head or braided stainless-steel supply (see pp. 69-71). A leak between the angle stop and the threaded nipple may require replacement of the angle stop and/or nipple (see Chapter 2). A leak at the packing nut of the angle stop indicates a loose nut or worn-out packing.

More common than leaks in the supply line are pressure leaks within the tank itself. On a toilet with a conventional brass ballcock, a leak within the tank usually involves the piston. The piston is moved up and down by the float ball on the end of the float rod during the flush and fill cycle. A rubber washer on

the bottom of the piston (or a rubber diaphragm on some models) shuts off the incoming water when the tank is full. If the rubber washer or diaphragm wears out it can no longer stem the incoming water and the tank overfills, with the excess water running down the overflow tube and then through the toilet tank (this is one possible cause of a continuously running toilet, see below).

In addition to the rubber washer on the bottom of the piston, there is also a leather washer (or washers) around the outside of the piston, which seals the ballcock opening. If this seal fails, water squirts out the top of the ballcock during the flush cycle. Usually most of the water remains in the tank, and the leak stops when the tank has completely refilled at the end of the fill cycle. As explained above, however, the water can escape between the lid and the top edge of the tank. To replace either washer, remove the two

A worn leather washer on the side of a ballcock piston will cause a pressure leak inside the tank. (Photo by Bill Dane)

BALLCOCKS
BRASS BALLCOCK

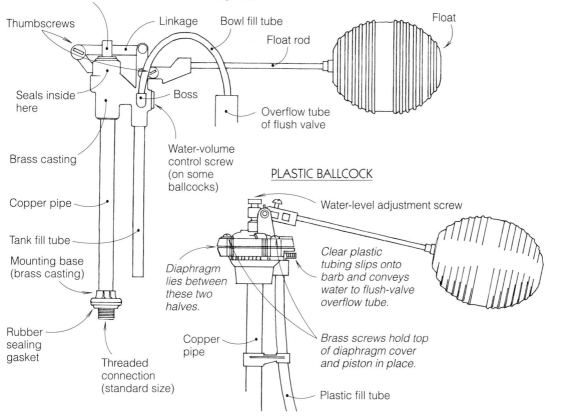

thumbscrews from the linkage and pull the piston up out of the ballcock. Make a mental note of how the linkage goes back together.

Nowadays, most standard close-coupled toilets are shipped with plastic ballcocks. Some of these ballcocks have a rubber washer on the end of the piston and an O-ring around the outside; others use just a diaphragm to control water flow. Plastic ballcocks tend to have fewer leak problems than brass ballcocks, but they are more prone to breakage. Another problem with plastic ballcocks is that they do not handle high water pressure well. The all-plastic water-regulation components can distort under high pressure, causing the tank to overfill. One plastic model that I do like is the Fluidmaster 400A, which is a good-quality aftermarket replacement ballcock for standard close-coupled toilets (it is also factory-installed in some Kohler toilets and other top brands). The Fluidmaster 400A, which has a float on the stem of the fill valve rather than at the end of an arm (see the photos on p. 160), has a very good record against leaks. I have installed literally hundreds with very few rejects.

MECHANICAL PROBLEMS

The standard close-coupled toilet has three basic components: the fill valve (or ballcock), the flush valve and the flush-handle assembly. If these mechanisms fail, the toilet may run continuously, flush inadequately or not flush at all.

FILL VALVE   I've already talked about the problems associated with failed fill-valve seals — the incoming water never shuts off, or water squirts out from the top of the ballcock. Water squirting wildly in the tank can also be caused by a broken or loose fill tube, which attaches to a boss on a brass ballcock and goes over to the overflow tube to refill the bowl on the flush cycle. This ¼-in. copper tube becomes very brittle over the years, and can easily be broken by accident when you try to replace the washers on the piston. Use an Ace nipple back-out (see p. 16) to remove the broken threads from the boss and then install a new copper tube, bending it carefully into the overflow tube. On plastic ballcocks, the clear plastic tubing is often too short and can sometimes blow out of the overflow tube (or off the barb).

FLUSH VALVE   A toilet may run continuously if the flush valve does not seat properly and sufficient water constantly escapes to keep the fill valve adding more water to the tank. There are three basic types of flush valves: lift-wire flush balls, rubber flappers and tilt-backs (see the drawing on the facing page). All three types use rubber to seal on the flush-valve seat. When the valve doesn't seat properly, it can be the result of a worn-out rubber seal (your fingers will turn black when you touch it), or a failure of the rubber to contact the valve seat.

On lift-wire flush balls, if the water is escaping because of a worn-out ball, try installing a new ball (after first shutting off the water supply and flushing the toilet). In most cases, the ball simply unthreads off the wire, though there might be a little square brass lug on the bottom of the wire that you need to remove first. If I'm just replacing the ball, I like to use Chicago Specialty's Pro-Pel #7513C flush ball, which has a propeller on the bottom that helps make a better seal with the valve seat. If the flush ball hangs up in the guide, which is a common problem when the hole in the guide wears and becomes oblong, then you'll have to replace the guide too. This can be a real chore if the screw clamping it to the overflow tube is so corroded that you cannot back it up. In such a case I'd replace the entire lift-wire flush-ball assembly with Fluidmaster's "Flusher Fixer Kit" (#555C).

If you have a flapper-type flush valve, it either slides up and off the overflow tube or peels off two ears at the bottom of the tube. To replace the flapper, unhook the old chain or rubber string from the flush-handle arm, slide a new flapper down (or hang the legs onto the ears) and connect the new chain to the flush arm. I really don't care for this flapper design because there is too much lateral movement in the rubber and a strong jet of water out of the bottom of the ballcock can deflect it off the valve seat.

In my experience, the tilt-back flush valve is the most trouble-free of the three designs. It usually has a rubber pad on the bottom, which is easy to replace either by screwing or snapping it on. One possible problem with the tilt-back design is that the hinge can malfunction, causing the valve to hang up in the open position. If this happens, the entire valve has to be replaced (again, I recommend you use the Fluidmaster #555C).

TOILET MECHANICAL PROBLEMS

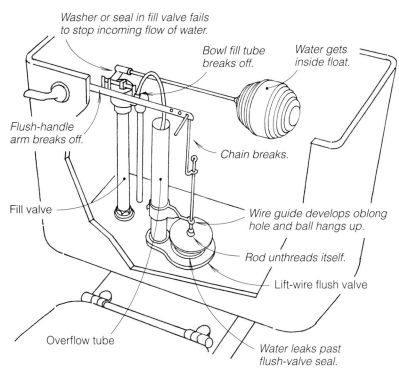

Washer or seal in fill valve fails to stop incoming flow of water.

Bowl fill tube breaks off.

Water gets inside float.

Flush-handle arm breaks off.

Chain breaks.

Fill valve

Wire guide develops oblong hole and ball hangs up.

Rod unthreads itself.

Lift-wire flush valve

Overflow tube

Water leaks past flush-valve seal.

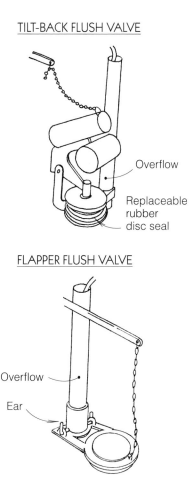

TILT-BACK FLUSH VALVE

Overflow

Replaceable rubber disc seal

FLAPPER FLUSH VALVE

Overflow

Ear

Another possible cause of a continuously running toilet is a waterlogged float. If water gets into the hollow float (either at the crimped joint on two-piece copper floats or at the float to float-rod connection), it loses the necessary buoyancy to regulate the piston and water continues to enter the tank. Unscrew the float, shake it to test for water and replace if necessary. You might also try bending the float rod down to lower the water level in the tank so the ballcock valve shuts off.

FLUSH-HANDLE ASSEMBLY   Now you know what to do if your toilet won't stop running, but what if it won't flush at all? If you push the handle and nothing happens, the chain or rubber string has probably broken and the movement of the arm does not open the flush-valve seal. In this situation you can either be creative and re-establish a link or entire new chain with materials (preferably synthetic) on hand in your junk drawer, or replace the seal portion on your flush valve, which will come with a new chain.

If the flush-handle arm is broken or the retaining nut holding the handle in the tank is missing, you'll need to replace the entire flush-handle assembly. I recommend you install a Price Pfister solid-brass flush handle (available in either a polished-chrome finish — #S15-51BC — or polished brass — #S15-51BP), which fits most standard close-coupled toilets. This attractive, heavy-duty handle should last many years. The flush-arm portion is heavy brass, but bendable, which allows you to center the arm over the flush-valve seal for a straight-up-and-down lifting action. (If the flush arm pulls off to the side, the flush valve will tend to get hung up and wear out sooner.)

Sometimes it's necessary to replace all the tank components — the fill valve, flush-valve assembly and overflow, and flush handle.

On older toilets with failing tank components, it's sometimes best to remove the tank from the bowl and replace all the parts. Once you've gutted the tank, first install an all-brass flush valve with the overflow tube next to the back wall of the tank. To recap my earlier recommendations, you should then install a Price Pfister flush handle, a Fluidmaster 555C flush-valve repair kit and a Fluidmaster 400A fill valve (all come with installation directions). With this combination of tank components, your toilet should be trouble-free for many years to come.

One final note: Many fine old toilets have parts that are no longer made by the original manufacturer (if the manufacturer is even still in business). Often these parts, especially the flush valve, have unique installation hardware and custom-spaced holes that preclude the installation of any modern, generic flush and fill valves. In this case, the only solution may be to replace the entire toilet.

SINKS AND LAVATORIES

The two main problem areas with kitchen sinks and lavatory basins are clogs and gravity leaks. The strategies for removing clogs and fixing leaks are much the same for lavatories and single-bowl kitchen sinks, but there are some differences for double-bowl sinks (with or without a garbage disposer). I'll discuss pressure leaks in the faucets that attach to these fixtures later in this chapter (see pp. 169-172).

LAVATORY-BASIN CLOGS

Soap sludge, hair, dental floss, cosmetic residues and inadequately flushed toothpaste are some of the more common causes of stoppages in lavatory-basin wastes and drains. If your lavatory won't drain, resist the temptation to reach for a chemical drain cleaner (see the sidebar on p. 162); try the plunger first. If the bowl has the standard pop-up stopper waste (see pp. 106-109), it helps greatly to remove the stopper first. You also need to block off the overflow slot or holes; if you don't, the force generated by plunging will merely bounce off the stoppage and come back out the overflow. I use a soaked sponge in a plastic bag to seal off the overflow port as best I can (you may need a helper to hold the bag in place).

LAVATORY-BASIN CLOGS

Overflow port · Overflow passage

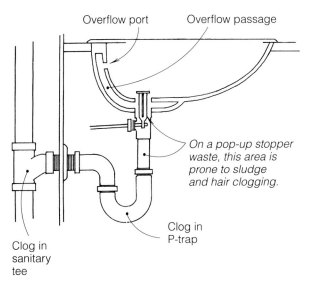

On a pop-up stopper waste, this area is prone to sludge and hair clogging.

Clog in P-trap

Clog in sanitary tee

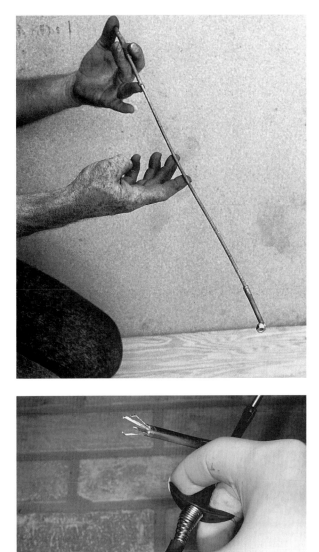

Small objects can be retrieved from sink traps using mechanical fingers, a tool with a long flexible cable and spring-loaded 'fingers' on the bottom end.

Because the drain of the lavatory basin is usually close to the back wall of the bowl, it can be difficult to get the plunger to form a perfect seal — I find it works best to fold up the skirt into the cup. Make sure there's enough water in the bowl to cover the top of the plunger, then start a gentle, slow, up-and-down movement of the handle, pressing firmly on the handle at the bottom of each stroke. Count four or five of the down strokes and then give the plunger a stiff jolt at the bottom of the next downward stroke. (You, the floor and the wall are likely to get wet, so take appropriate precautions.) Try this maneuver four or five times and then change the final stroke from a downward jolt to an abrupt upward lift, pulling the plunger right off the drain. Do this about five times before trying an alternate strategy.

If plunging fails to remove the stoppage, the next step is to take the trap down (on some traps there is a cleanout at the bottom of the bend, which may save you from having to take the trap apart). Set a bowl under the sink to catch the water and any sludge that falls from the trap. If clearing the trap doesn't work, it indicates that the clog is below the sanitary tee, and you'll need to call a professional drain-cleaning service.

Another potential problem with lavatory basins is that objects such as toothbrushes, hairpins, earrings and make-up pencils can fall into the drain and lodge in the trap (this occurs most frequently on sinks with old-style rubber-stopper wastes, because of the open areas in the rubber stopper's strainer). If possible, I remove the trap to retrieve the object. However, with some old sinks the waste and trap may be encrusted with several coats of paint and taking them down can be time-consuming (you also risk cracking a worn, old trap). In the latter case, I try to grab the object by sending mechanical fingers down the waste (see p. 15 and the photos above).

CHEMICAL DRAIN CLEANERS

I would venture a guess that most home owners faced with a stopped-up drain reach first for a chemical drain cleaner. Pouring something from a container may be the least labor-intensive remedy, but it's unlikely to be the most effective — and it can be downright hazardous, both to your health and to the health of your pipes.

Home owners are most likely to choose from the supermarket selection of brand-name liquid drain cleaners, which, on the whole, are not strong enough to clear tough clogs. (In my experience, the most effective drain cleaner commonly available to the home owner is the crystal form of the Drano brand.) More potent solutions, usually containing mixtures of sulfuric and hydrochloric acid, are intended primarily for professional use. These products (which go under such imaginative names as Mule Kick, Clobber and Mad Mother-In-Law) are invariably packaged in plastic, foil-sealed under screw-top bottles. Many suppliers require the purchaser to sign a liability release before buying these professional-strength drain cleaners. I advise you not to use them.

Before using any chemical on a clog, you need to consider the possibility of damage to the plumbing system. Most chemical solutions generate heat when attacking a clog. As a rule, the in-the-wall and under-the-floor drain piping can withstand the heat (though the professional-strength solutions can pose problems with ABS pipe), but fixture wastes are a different matter. By these I mean sink tailpieces, traps and trap arms, as well as tub and shower traps. If the waste is thin, tubular chromed brass of some vintage, drain cleaners can eat right through it.

Chemical drain-cleaning agents can also wreak havoc with garbage disposers, though there is now at least one product that is safe to use — a liquid enzyme flow improver manufactured by Cloroben Corporation that contains no acids, caustics or solvents (see the Sources of Supply on pp. 178-179). Drain cleaners can damage mechanical snakes, so if you have any intention of calling a professional drain-cleaning service if all else fails, don't pour chemicals down your sink.

If you are determined to try a chemical attack on a clog, do so only as a last resort after plunging has failed. When using any drain-cleaning agent, always wear safety goggles and rubber gloves. And never use a plunger after you have introduced chemicals into the drainage system, or you could be burned or blinded in the event of squirt-back.

KITCHEN-SINK CLOGS

Kitchen sinks can become clogged over time with the buildup of food particles, grease and other materials. As with lavatory basins, you should first try to remove a clog by plunging the sink. If that fails you'll have to take down the trap or call a professional.

If you have a single-bowl kitchen sink without a garbage disposer, then plunging the sink is fairly straightforward. The drain in a kitchen sink is usually far enough away from the sink wall to allow you to get the plunger cup directly over the drain; you can also get the fold-down skirt into the basket-strainer housing for a tighter seal. Make sure there's enough water in the bowl to cover the cup — the more water in the sink, the more pressure you can throw at the clog. Most kitchen sinks don't have an overflow that needs plugging, so you can use both hands on the plunger handle. You want to push and then lift on the stoppage, trying to loosen it up so the weight of the sink's standing water will drive the food dam downstream to the building drain. Give it a series of downward jolts and then a series of abrupt lifts. Go for a dozen attempts before giving up.

TALE OF THE DRAIN UNCLOGGER

About ten years ago I was very excited when a new product for clearing clogged drains came onto the market. It was a black rubber drain unclogger that threads onto a garden hose. When installed into a drain line and the water is turned on, the device expands in the pipe and then lets a stream of water (at house pressure) into the pipe and out the far end, taking the clog with it.

I bought a drain unclogger and used it within a few days on a stopped-up kitchen sink. I took down the waste piping and inserted the device into the branch of the sink's sanitary tee. I turned the water on for several minutes, then removed the unclogger and replaced the waste piping. The stoppage was still there. So I took down the waste again and this time left the water on for twenty minutes, figuring that I'd surely blast away the clog. After twenty minutes, my helper went outside and turned off the hose bibb. At that instant, the black rubber clog buster came flying out of the tee, chased by a column of water that shot all the way across the large kitchen, through an open door before touching down in the dining room under an oriental rug.

I found out several days later (after calling a drain-cleaning service) that the stoppage had been caused by a root in the drain line. I've never had the courage to try a drain unclogger again.

If you have a blocked double-bowl sink, then you need to keep the strainer tightly closed in one of the bowls. If you're working by yourself, it's a matter of trying to hold the stopper in place while using the other hand on the plunger. This technique usually doesn't work too well, so try to find someone to hold the stopper in the other sink.

If you have a garbage disposer in your kitchen sink, the unblocking technique is somewhat different. For a single bowl with a disposer, you'll have to plunge through the disposer itself — try first with the disposer turned off and then again with it turned on. Chances are you'll have to take down the trap and clean out the J-bend if it's plugged, and the trap arm too if the clog is in the sanitary-tee branch in the wall. If the trap and sanitary tee are clean, flash a pen light into the tee and see if there's water up to the level of the branch — if there is, the blockage is in the drain line and you'll need to call a drain-cleaning service. If there's no water, remove the discharge elbow from the disposer and shine the light up into the grinding plate. Here's the likely trouble spot if the disposer has seen better days. With the appliance unplugged or circuit breakers thrown, use needle-nose pliers to reach into the grinding chamber and drag out the fiber dam.

KITCHEN-SINK CLOGS

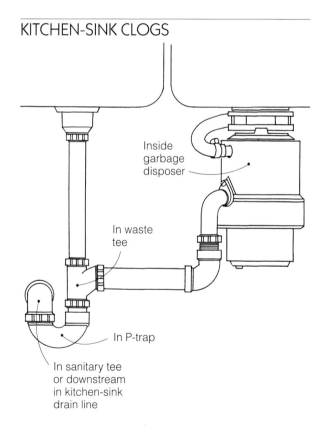

Inside garbage disposer

In waste tee

In P-trap

In sanitary tee or downstream in kitchen-sink drain line

If you have a double-bowl sink with a garbage disposer and both bowls are blocked, then try to get a helper to keep the stopper tightly sealed in the disposer's drain hole while you work the plunger in the other bowl. If you have a double bowl with a disposer in one bowl and the disposer's bowl is the only one stopped up, then you know that the disposer is the villain. (For more on garbage-disposer problems, see p. 172.)

LAUNDRY-SINK CLOGS

If your washing machine drains into a laundry sink, the sink's trap can become clogged fairly frequently. Even modern filtered washing machines allow some lint to pass, which builds up in the trap and drain like a furry lining, sometimes reducing the inside diameter of the pipe by an inch or more. A plunger can sometimes open up the line enough to let you limp on for another few weeks' worth of laundry, but when a laundry drain line starts to back up because of lint choking it's definitely time to think about calling a professional drain cleaner. (If the washing machine drains into a standpipe instead of a laundry sink, you won't be able to use the plunger at all.)

GRAVITY LEAKS

There are three areas of a sink (kitchen or lavatory) that are especially vulnerable to gravity leaks: under the sink edge, under the faucet body and in the waste system. All of these leak sources can be responsible for water damage to the cabinet. The source of a gravity leak is not always obvious, and you may find it only through a process of elimination.

SPLASH WATER UNDER THE SINK EDGE   If you have a self-rimming stainless-steel sink, especially if it's set on tile, the first place to look is along the edges of the sink where it contacts the counter. If possible, lie in the sink cabinet and have a helper shine a bright light around the edge of the sink from above and find the voids where water gets in. Alternatively, you can purposely splash water on the counter and check for drips underneath. If any of the sink hold-down clips are missing, replace them. If water still gets in around the edge, try to get all the clips loose, lift the sink, re-seal with plumber's putty and re-install (see p. 88). You may find that some of the clips are so corroded

LAVATORY-BASIN GRAVITY LEAKS

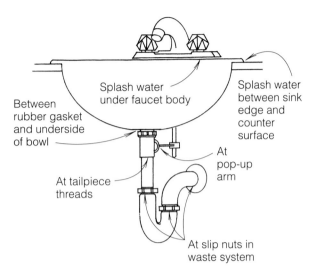

Splash water under faucet body

Splash water between sink edge and counter surface

Between rubber gasket and underside of bowl

At tailpiece threads

At pop-up arm

At slip nuts in waste system

that they won't come free, in which case you'll have to destroy the sink's clip-hanging system and replace the sink.

If you have a sink that mounts with a separate clamp-down rim (see pp. 85-87), look for gaps between the sink edge and the rim, and between the counter edge and rim, and then check for missing mounting clips. Make repairs as explained above for a self-rimming stainless-steel sink (except that you can replace just the mounting rim if the clips are badly corroded, and salvage the existing sink).

If you have a mudded-in sink and water is getting into the cabinet, check for gaps between the grout and the edge of the sink. It can be difficult to test for possible grout leaks, because the mortar bed absorbs the moisture and it takes some time before it shows up in drips. If you find cracks, temporarily fill them with latex caulk (which adheres even with water in or on the joint), then re-grout with an epoxy grout (which must be applied on dry tile). You might want to call a tile setter for the grout repair.

I have had fewest edge-leak problems with heavy, cast-iron self-rimming sinks set on plumber's putty. If you do get an edge leak with this type of sink and the sink was glued down with adhesive caulk, your best bet is to dry the edge thoroughly with an electric blow dryer and then caulk around the outside edge with clear silicone caulk.

KITCHEN-SINK GRAVITY LEAKS

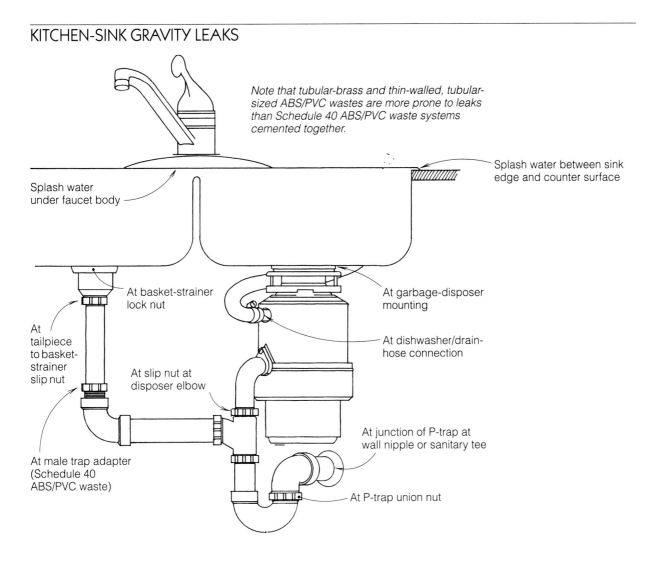

Note that tubular-brass and thin-walled, tubular-sized ABS/PVC wastes are more prone to leaks than Schedule 40 ABS/PVC waste systems cemented together.

Splash water between sink edge and counter surface

Splash water under faucet body

At basket-strainer lock nut

At garbage-disposer mounting

At tailpiece to basket-strainer slip nut

At dishwasher/drain-hose connection

At slip nut at disposer elbow

At junction of P-trap at wall nipple or sanitary tee

At male trap adapter (Schedule 40 ABS/PVC waste)

At P-trap union nut

SPLASH WATER UNDER THE FAUCET BODY   If the sink isn't leaking around the edge of the fixture, next check for splash water getting under the faucet body (or under the spout base and valve trim on wide-spread faucets). Above-deck-mounted faucets that are set on a base strip of rubber or plastic are especially prone to this type of leakage, as are faucets that have a loose-fitting cover or housing. Drop-lead faucets that mount to the sink or counter with threaded studs (see pp. 95-96) can come loose if the mounting hardware rusts, again allowing splash water to get in under the faucet. If you have a problem with leaks around the sink's mounting holes with any of these styles of faucet, I recommend that you replace the faucet with a better-quality brass faucet, remembering to set it on plumber's putty.

Underhung kitchen- and lavatory-sink deck-mounted faucets have escutcheons to cover the valves' upper mounting nuts, main stem or cartridge nuts and packing nuts. If the valves were not installed with plumber's putty under at least the upper mounting washer, then water seeping out around the stem or packing nuts drips down into the cabinet (technically a pressure leak, though the water finds its way into the cabinet under gravity). To eliminate the drips around the sink holes, remove the faucet from the sink, re-install with putty under the valves' top and lower washers (and under the spout base), and then pack the escutcheons with putty.

WASTE-SYSTEM LEAKS   All sinks can spring a leak in the waste system, especially if the waste was installed improperly or with poor-quality parts. Lavatory-basin pop-up or rubber-stopper wastes often leak at the rubber gasket at the underside of the sink. If the mounting nut is not corroded and can be backed up, remove the waste from the sink and re-install with a new waste gasket and plumber's putty under the lip of the flange and also between the new gasket and the bowl. Find a solid-brass replacement for a die-cast mounting nut. If you have a pop-up waste, look closely at the female or male threads where the pop-up arm enters the waste. These nuts often loosen up and allow water to escape. Usually disassembly is not necessary, just a little snugging up on the nut.

Gravity leaks in kitchen sinks are sometimes the result of a poor-quality basket strainer. The rubber gasket under the sink may squirm out at one point, and the escaping water can corrode the threads of the large die-cast mounting nut underneath. The basket starts to slip in the sink's hole, and you cannot re-tighten the frozen nut to stem the leak. The water dribbles down the strainer, then flows onto the waste's slip nuts and maybe all the way down to the trap (the untrained eye may mistakenly believe that these areas are the source of the leak). Removing the basket strainer can be a real chore — I often have to use a mini-hacksaw to cut the strainer's mounting nut, before getting the basket out of the sink hole for a solid-brass replacement.

Baskets with plastic mounting nuts are not a great improvement. To get the basket installed tightly enough in the hole requires stronger threads than the plastic can provide. When you try to snug up on the plastic nut, it jumps its threads and you're never able to get it tightened sufficiently. The only advantage of the plastic nut is that it usually comes loose without the need to saw it into little pieces.

The rest of the sink-waste system, including the trap and trap arm, all the way to the wall, may also develop leaks. (If you have a double-bowl sink with garbage disposer and dishwasher hook-ups, there are several additional potential leak spots — see the drawing on p. 165.) In a tubular-brass waste system, each slip-nut connection is a prime suspect, and the trap arm and J-bend may develop cracks. To find leaks in this portion of the waste, slide the escutcheon on the trap arm back from the wall to expose the slip nut behind it. Then fill the basin to the overflow and open the stopper. With a flashlight underneath, check each slip nut for drips. If you have a leak at a slip nut and the nut is tight, then the washer underneath is probably cracked or deformed. Take down the whole trap system and replace the washers and upgrade any non-brass nuts to solid brass. If you encounter a metal-to-metal-joint trap (see p. 118), you might want to replace it with a slip-washer variety, which is less prone to leaks. If the 1½-in. tubular-brass components break while you are trying to disassemble them, buy new tubular-brass parts in 17 gauge, or convert over to Schedule 40 ABS or PVC, if these materials are allowed in your area.

BATHTUBS AND SHOWERS

Bathtubs and shower stalls are susceptible to the same kind of problems as sinks and lavatories, namely, clogs and gravity leaks, as well as pressure leaks at the valves and at the spout or shower head.

CLOGS

Like lavatory basins, bathtubs (and showers) become stopped up most often with soap sludge and hair. If your tub has a trip-lever waste and overflow, undo the two screws holding the overflow plate at the head of the tub and pull out the linkage. You might find a large hair ball wrapped around the lift bucket, or around the pop-up stopper linkage if your W&O is a pop-up design. If you have an old-style rubber-stopper W&O, a hair snake can form at the metal cross in the strainer and hang out of sight into the W&O's tee. You have a more difficult task in retrieving the hair here. You can sometimes pull out the blockage by twisting a soft copper wire with a tight hook on the end through the strainer, or down the overflow tube from above. Alternatively, try snagging the hair clog with mechanical fingers down the overflow tube.

Plunging a tub can meet with limited to miraculous success. After trying to retrieve any hair from the W&O, block off the overflow with a small, wet sponge in a plastic sandwich bag and fill the tub up to about half depth. With the skirt tucked back up into the cup, place the plunger over the drain and start

TUB CLOGS

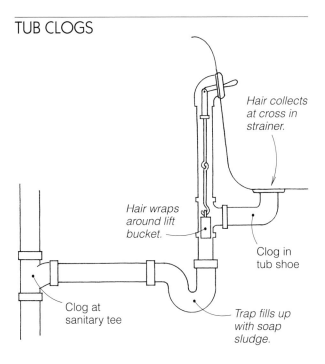

Hair collects at cross in strainer.

Hair wraps around lift bucket.

Clog in tub shoe

Clog at sanitary tee

Trap fills up with soap sludge.

with a slow push and lift, keeping the cup on and over the drain, and the palm of your hand on the sponge to keep it from blowing back out of the overflow. Start out with a slow up-and-down movement, building slowly until your sixth or seventh downward thrust and then briskly yank the cup off the drain. If you start to get "crud" coming back into the tub, you are on the right track. Don't give up until you have plunged for about 20 minutes, and prepare to get wet. If you are going to be successful, it will be by moving the hair and sludge obstruction back and forth far enough until it starts to break up. Then the weight of the water on top of it should send it down the line to a larger, more effectively draining line.

If you have a stopped-up shower, there's no overflow to worry about — just follow the same plunger technique as for a tub. If water is backing up into the tub or shower when you use the lavatory basin, then the stoppage is downstream of a branched fitting on the drain line. If you plunge the fixture, your efforts will be for naught unless you have a helper to plug off the drain and overflow of the lavatory basin with more soft sponges in plastic bags. Your chances of success here, where such a long distance of pipe is involved, are not very good, but do give it a try.

If waste from the toilet is backing up into the tub or shower, the 3-in. or 4-in. drain line accommodating all three fixtures is plugged (maybe with roots, sanitary napkins or other materials). You'll need to call a drain-cleaning service to remove this blockage.

BATHTUB GRAVITY LEAKS

Gravity leaks on tubs occur primarily at the W&O's tub-shoe strainer and at the overflow gasket (see the drawing on p. 168). (On built-in tubs, another potential leak spot is the joint along the wall, which can be repaired by caulking.) If you can get underneath the tub, either by crawling or by cutting drywall or plaster, fill the tub and then release the water and look closely at the rubber gasket sandwiched between the shoe and the tub. If water drips out of this joint, the rubber gasket is no longer sealing adequately. Use a strainer wrench to remove the strainer, then replace the gasket as explained on pp. 45-46. Be careful not to tighten the strainer so tightly that it squashes out the rubber washer below.

Water running down the backside of the tub head is the result of a cracked or worn-out overflow gasket. In most instances, you can replace this gasket from inside the tub. Unscrew the overflow plate, get the old overflow gasket free and then slip a new one in (painted with pipe dope) and resecure the overflow plate. If this doesn't work you'll have to replace the gasket from underneath the tub.

Other possible leaks are at the W&O's slip-nut connections and at the junction of the trap and tailpiece. If tightening these connections doesn't work, the slip-nut washer is probably worn out. Rather than taking down the entire W&O, first try to back up the offending slip nut and wrap Teflon tape on the male threads of the W&O tee. Wrap plumber's string or Teflon string packing in place of the broken slip-nut washer, load up the female threads of the nut with pipe dope and then rethread the nut in place. If this fails to fix the leak, you'll have to disassemble the W&O and reassemble with new washers (or even replace the entire W&O).

W&Os also sometimes leak at the factory-threaded or -cemented joint between the strainer housing and the tub-shoe tubing. To prevent a leak here, I apply a two-part plumber's epoxy around the joint when I install the fixture (see the photo on p. 58).

TUB LEAKS

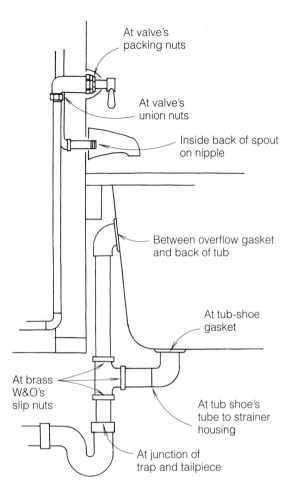

At valve's packing nuts

At valve's union nuts

Inside back of spout on nipple

Between overflow gasket and back of tub

At tub-shoe gasket

At brass W&O's slip nuts

At tub shoe's tube to strainer housing

At junction of trap and tailpiece

SHOWER-STALL LEAKS

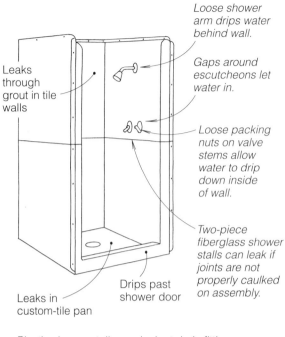

Loose shower arm drips water behind wall.

Gaps around escutcheons let water in.

Leaks through grout in tile walls

Loose packing nuts on valve stems allow water to drip down inside of wall.

Two-piece fiberglass shower stalls can leak if joints are not properly caulked on assembly.

Leaks in custom-tile pan

Drips past shower door

Plastic shower stalls can leak at drain fitting. Loose drive bushings around drain riser can also let water escape under stall.

If water is leaking out around the back of the tub spout, unthread the spout and reapply Teflon tape on the nipple. Replace chrome-plated die-cast or plastic spouts with brass spouts (and galvanized nipples with brass nipples).

SHOWER-STALL GRAVITY LEAKS

When a customer calls me concerning a leak in a ceiling under a shower stall, there are several possible causes but the most obvious has often been overlooked — namely, a poorly closing door (or shower curtain). If the door becomes warped, splash water will quickly find its way out of and then under the enclosure (which is why you should always run the finish floor under the fixture, as discussed on p. 42). Fixing the door is a job for a glazing company.

If the door or curtain is not the culprit, there are several other potential leak spots to check in the enclosure. On ceramic-tile shower stalls, the leak is most likely caused by failure of the grout between the tiles or an improperly formed shower pan. On fiberglass stalls, the problem is usually the result of a loose drain fitting. As discussed in Chapter 4, the best defense against leaks is to install a terrazzo-cement shower pan (with a Casper's brass drain fitting) with cultured-marble walls.

Leaks can be caused by a failure in the shower-valve system. Sometimes the packing nuts on the valve stems come loose and water drips down on the backside of the shower wall; or the valve union inside the stud wall might spring a leak (see the drawing at left above).

TESTING FOR LEAKS A good way to test the valve system is to hook up a garden hose to the shower arm and run the hose out the window. To hook up the hose, remove the shower head and install a ½-in. FIP by union female hose adapter to the end of the shower arm. (If you have a shower arm with a ball on the end, remove the arm completely and install a long, galvanized nipple, then the pipe-to-hose adapter.) Run the water (hot and cold) for ten minutes or more. If the drip still shows up on the ceiling below, you know that the valve is the culprit since the water never got to the walls or floor. Depending on the valve style, tighten the packing nuts, replace stem washers or replace the cartridge. Also make sure that the shower arm is threaded securely into the 90° fitting behind the wall.

If there's no leak when you run the valve-system test, next test the drain line. Remove the strainer from the drain hole and insert the end of the hose into the drain fitting. Turn the water on again, but not so hard that water backs up out of the fitting and gets the shower floor wet. If there is a leak in the trap or drain line, you'll have to cut a hole in the ceiling and make the necessary repairs from below.

If you still haven't discovered the source of the leak, next test the shower pan and the drain fitting. Remove the hose and replace the shower head, then tape polyethylene sheets on all the walls, including the door. Make sure to tape the plastic to the wall securely under the shower arm. If the drip shows up when you run the water, on a tiled shower floor it's probably the result of a cracked pan under the tile or water getting in between the lip of the drain fitting and the pan.

On a fiberglass shower stall the leak can probably be traced to a poorly installed or a poorly designed drain fitting. If the drain fitting is an integral part of the floor, it probably has a rubber drive-bushing type seal. Remove any grid strainer and try pounding the bushing farther into the fitting with a short length of wooden dowel. Then, use a hair dryer to dry up the area around the fitting and apply clear silicone caulk between the top edge of the drain pipe sticking up through the center of the fitting, over the drive bushing and onto the surface of the pan. Let the silicone dry for a day before putting back the strainer and using the fixture. If the fitting was added to the pan separately, you might try to tighten up any compression ring in the fitting that applies sealing force to a rubber seal around the drain pipe. If these measures fail to stop the leak, replace the fitting with a Casper's brass drain fitting.

If you've eliminated all other potential leak spots, the water must be getting through the walls of the shower — test by removing the plastic and using the shower. Tile walls will leak if the grout fails — typically in the corners, along the top edge of the tile or around a tiled-in soap dish. It's best to call a tile setter for these repairs. Two-piece fiberglass stalls can leak at the joints (and be repaired by caulking). On all stalls, gaps around the escutcheons can let water in, so caulk here as necessary.

FAUCETS AND VALVES

After a clogged drain, a constant drip from a faucet spout, tub spout or shower head is probably the most common plumbing complaint. These drips, which are pressure leaks, originate inside the valve and are usually caused by a worn-out stem washer or cartridge (see below). However, leaks at the spout are by no means the only problem areas with faucets; other potential pressure-leak sites are shown in the drawing on p. 170.

If water dribbles out under the base of a center-set faucet every time you turn the faucet on, many times the cause is a casting or assembly defect, and you'll have to replace the faucet. (Often it's difficult to distinguish this type of leak from a splash-water leak under the faucet body — see p. 165.) However, if the faucet has threaded connections that are not a part of the solid casting, the water may be escaping at these connections. In this case, disconnecting the faucet and applying Teflon tape and pipe dope to the threaded connections may stop the leak.

Water may also leak out from underneath the valve handles, indicating that the thin washer under the bonnet nut has cracked or that the seal on the side of the valve has failed. To repair this leak, turn off the water supply and remove the faucet handles (use a faucet-handle puller to avoid marring the finish). If water is leaking out under the washer, replace the washer; if the leak is around the stem, replace the O-ring or packing on the stem. On kitchen-sink faucets with a swing spout (as shown in the drawing on p. 170), a similar leak can develop at the base of the spout and can be repaired by replacing the O-ring. If water escapes from the base of a fixed spout on a 4-in. center set, however, you'll have to replace the faucet.

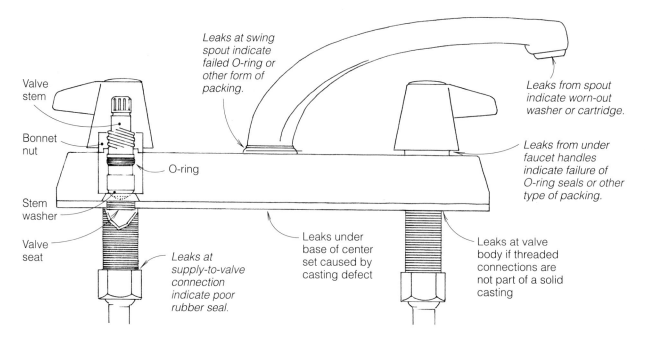

Leaks at swing spout indicate failed O-ring or other form of packing.

Leaks from spout indicate worn-out washer or cartridge.

Valve stem

Bonnet nut

O-ring

Leaks from under faucet handles indicate failure of O-ring seals or other type of packing.

Stem washer

Valve seat

Leaks at supply-to-valve connection indicate poor rubber seal.

Leaks under base of center set caused by casting defect

Leaks at valve body if threaded connections are not part of a solid casting

Under the sink, pressure leaks can occur at the supply-to-valve connections and, on widespread faucets, at the threaded connections between the manifold tubing and the spout and the valves. Leaks at threaded connections can usually be repaired, either by tightening up the nuts, replacing any rubber cone washers, or reapplying Teflon tape and pipe dope. If your house water pressure is high, installing a pressure-reducing valve (see p. 26) may help prevent frequent pressure leaks.

LEAKS FROM THE SPOUT

Now let's get back to that annoying drip from the faucet spout. How you fix this problem depends on the style of valve in your faucet: either the traditional stem-washer valve, or the newer, so-called "washerless" valve (typically some kind of cartridge).

STEM-WASHER VALVES   A spout drip indicates that the stem washer on the bottom of the valve stem is worn and the valve can no longer hold back the water pressure. To replace the washer, first remove the valve stem. While it's usually easy to remove valve stems on conventional sink faucets (simply remove the handle and bonnet nut), it can be tricky with tub

and shower valves. On tiled-in fixtures the holes in the wall where the valve stems protrude are often plugged up with cement, or the tile may be right up against the stem. In this case you can try using a socket wrench to loosen up the bonnet nut or use a cold chisel to chip away the cement. Occasionally you may need to cut a hole in the back of the valve wall and replace the entire valve.

Once a valve stem is out, unscrew the bibb screw on the bottom and replace the stem washer. If you still get a drip from the spout or shower head, you can try using a seat wrench (see p. 15) to replace the seats in the valve body. The seats are replaceable if the hole in the bottom is hexagonal or square (if the hole is round, the seat is an integral part of the faucet and cannot be removed). Sometimes the seat wrench is ineffective and just strips the hole — your only hope then is to use a seat-polishing stone to smooth the surface of the seat (see p. 15).

You can either use the stone by hand (using the crank handle that comes with the stone) or mount the shaft in a small variable-speed drill. To operate the tool by hand, you need to apply steady, even pressure as you rotate the stone. Try going 20 rotations in one direction and then reversing direction for the next

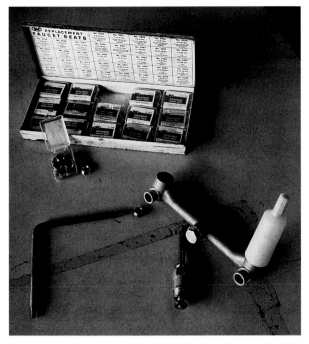

Spout leaks in a tub and shower valve can be repaired by replacing the stem washer on the bottom of the valve stem or the seats in the body of the valve or faucet.

Use a seat wrench to remove the seats from the faucet. (top), or a seat-polishing stone to grind the seat (above).

20, and so on, until you can see a polished face surface on the seat. This process can take a lot of time — half an hour or more per seat, depending on how badly pitted or gashed it is. Using the stone in the drill produces quicker results, but you have to make sure you don't grind away too much material. There is also a seat-cutter tool available, but I find that it's too aggressive to use accurately. If all your efforts fail and you cannot cure a dripping spout or shower head by washer and seat replacement or seat polishing, then it's time to replace the valve itself.

Another possible problem with stem-washer valves is that you hear a loud groaning and rattling when you turn the faucet on. This noise can indicate that the stem washers are loose or malformed, the threads on the valve stems are worn or the water pressure is very high. The edge of the threads should be flat — if they are sharp, they are worn out and you'll need to buy a replacement stem or stems. If the noise persists, attach a water-pressure test gauge to a hose bibb and read the building pressure. If it is over 80 psi, install a pressure-reducing valve. This regulator valve usually corrects the noise problem and also goes a long

way to improving the longevity of all your valves, including the toilet ballcock valve, dishwasher solenoid valve, water-heater T&P valve and refrigerator ice-maker valve.

CARTRIDGE VALVES   Cartridge-type valves have an internal mechanism that regulates water flow. In spite of manufacturers' claims to the contrary, these valves are not necessarily an improvement over stem-washer valves, and they are not necessarily washerless. Most still use rubber as a sealing material, though not in the shape of the traditional stem washer. In my experience, the only time that cartridge valves work well is in new homes with a clean water supply. If you have an older house with galvanized piping (which is often laden with rust and scale), I recommend you stick with stem-washer valves.

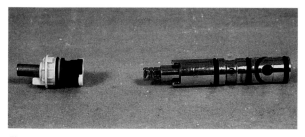

The Delta #RP1740 cartridge for two-handle faucets (left) and the Moen #1200 mixing valve cartridge (right) are two of the better-performing cartridges.

If cartridge valves leak from the spout, you'll have to replace the cartridge. Most cartridges are held in place by a retaining clip and/or a round, faceted nut, which must be removed before you can pull the cartridge out.

Faucet companies seem to be forever changing the design of their cartridge valves, though the Moen company is one exception. Moen has been making its single-handle mixing valve #1200 cartridge, which fits many of its faucets, for almost 30 years. This valve is the most leakproof cartridge I've worked with. Delta makes an excellent cartridge for its two-handle faucets (Delta #RP1740), which employs ceramic and rubber parts. I'm crossing my fingers that this model is kept in production.

GARBAGE DISPOSERS

Garbage disposers can suffer from gravity leaks at the mounting flange and at the discharge elbow and dishwasher-hose connections (see the drawing on p. 165), but more common are clogs and mechanical breakdowns. In fact, these latter two problems are closely related: A disposer can break down if it gets clogged, and if components fail, the disposer is more prone to clogs.

Top-quality garbage disposers tend to run for several years without suffering mechanical glitches. Poorer-quality disposers with plain steel cutters, which dull much faster, tend to overheat and shut down sooner. All models should have a reset button (usually on the bottom of the disposer). If the disposer shuts off in use, wait at least ten minutes to let it cool down before pushing the reset button.

The disposer may also come to a halt if you feed it long, stringy or fibrous food scraps — such as banana peels, artichoke leaves, corn husks, celery, asparagus or fish bones. If the disposer is clogged with any of these materials, pressing the restart button will usually prove futile. The appliance will have to be taken down, the case separated and the food clog removed. In many instances, this can cost as much as a new disposer (taking the case apart is a job for a plumber or an appliance-repair person), so you might think about spending your funds more wisely. (And before you buy another disposer, ask yourself if you really need one at all.)

If your garbage disposer comes to a grinding halt after eating some reasonably benign items and the reset button fails to restart it, I have one final suggestion. With the disposer turned off, stick the end of a wooden-handled broom or mop down through the drain hole into the grinding chamber. Lever the handle against the rim edge of the drain hole, trying to catch it on the cutters in the disposer to make the plate rotate in either a clockwise or counterclockwise direction. If you get the plate turning, quickly remove the broomstick, then flip the on/off switch. If you can't get it going with the broomstick, it's time to replace the disposer.

DISHWASHERS

Dishwashers are prone to two basic types of problems: those that are plumbing-related, such as leaks in the hot-water supply or drainage system, and those that are mechanical, such as the failure of electrical components. While plumbing-related problems are usually simple enough to tackle yourself, mechanical problems often require the services of an electrician or appliance-repair person. When making repairs yourself, always shut off power to the dishwasher first.

LEAKS

If you see water coming out from under the bottom of the dishwasher, first check the water-supply connections. Dishwashers are under constant vibration during their operating cycles, and threaded fittings can work loose. Remove the bottom panel and shine a flashlight on the solenoid valve, which is usually located on the left-hand side. If the leak is at the sup-

DISHWASHER PROBLEMS

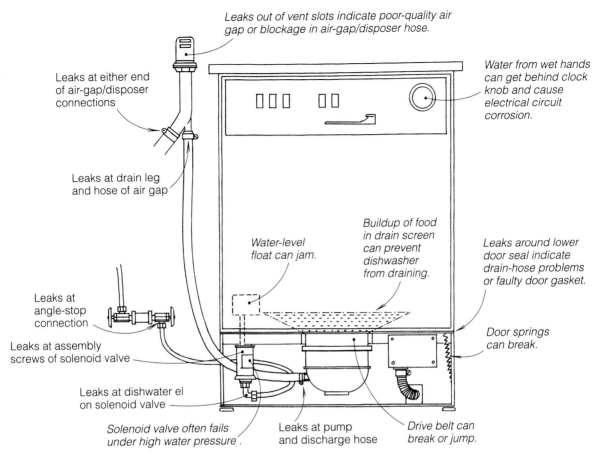

Leaks out of vent slots indicate poor-quality air gap or blockage in air-gap/disposer hose.

Leaks at either end of air-gap/disposer connections

Water from wet hands can get behind clock knob and cause electrical circuit corrosion.

Leaks at drain leg and hose of air gap

Water-level float can jam.

Buildup of food in drain screen can prevent dishwasher from draining.

Leaks around lower door seal indicate drain-hose problems or faulty door gasket.

Leaks at angle-stop connection

Leaks at assembly screws of solenoid valve

Door springs can break.

Leaks at dishwater el on solenoid valve

Solenoid valve often fails under high water pressure.

Leaks at pump and discharge hose

Drive belt can break or jump.

ply connection on the solenoid valve, back up the compression nut and reapply pipe dope. Also make sure that the dishwasher elbow on the solenoid valve is threaded in securely. The vibration generated by the dishwasher can also cause leaks at the angle-stop connection under the kitchen sink. A leak here can run down the supply tube and drop onto the floor under the dishwasher, confusing you as to the true source of the leak.

Standing water under the dishwasher may also be the result of leaks in the drainage system (which usually show up only when the appliance is running). Water draining out of the dishwasher is pumped under pressure up to the air gap, and leaks can occur at the connection between the discharge hose and the pump, and at either hose connection at the air gap. These leaks may be caused by loose or corroded hose clamps at the connections (replace plated-steel clamps with all-stainless, worm-drive clamps) or by cracked hoses (replace hoses).

If water escapes through the vent slots in the air-gap cap, suspect a blockage in the air gap (especially with cheap plastic models) or in the ⅞-in. air-gap-to-disposer drainage hose. To remove the blockage, pop off the chrome cap and dislodge the food dam with a pair of needle-nose pliers, or take down the drainage hose. A clogged (or kinked) hose or clogged air gap can also cause leaks around the lower door seal of the appliance (see p. 174).

If a leak is dripping out of a factory-installed component — for example, at the assembly screws on the solenoid valve, or at the pump seal — you'll have to call in the repair person.

MECHANICAL PROBLEMS

If your dishwasher won't fill, run or drain, there's a good chance that one of the mechanical components has failed. In my experience, the solenoid valve is the component that's most likely fail, especially if the building's water pressure is 80 psi or more. In normal operation the solenoid valve bangs open and slams shut to allow water in and out of the appliance. One day it slams shut for the last time, and no more water enters the dishwasher. You can have the valve repaired or replaced, but the most effective fix is to install a pressure-reducing valve on the house line (see Chapter 2).

If your dishwasher fills with water and goes through the cycles but it's evident that the water was not thrown around (there's still soap on the dishes), the spray arm probably didn't rotate. This may be the result of a broken or jumped motor drive belt (some dishwasher pumps have a drive belt, others are direct-shaft driven). Remove the lower panel and check the belt. Even if the belt is in place, it could be so stretched that it's not doing its job. If this is the case, replace the belt.

Another common complaint is standing water left in the machine after the completed cycle. While a broken pump could be the culprit here, it could merely be the result of a buildup of food scraps in the drain screen in the bottom of the machine or a plugged hose between the pump and the air gap. These areas are certainly worth investigating before calling the service person.

As explained above, if the appliance overfills to the point that water comes out passed the door seal, the drain hose or air gap could be clogged. However, this condition could also be caused by failure of the water-level float. If there's food scum or grease on the shaft of the float, the float can get hung up and admit too much water to the dishwasher cabinet. Lift the float out and clean off the side of the shaft; also, gently ream out the hole that the shaft fits into (using a pipe cleaner). On dishwashers that have a lower roll-out shelf close to the float, there's also the risk that the float can be broken by items hanging down from the wire shelf when the shelf is pulled out.

On older machines, broken door springs are a fairly common occurrence. If one breaks, don't put off replacing it or you could end up badly damaging or breaking a hinge and ruining the entire appliance. For most brands, it's a simple procedure of hooking one eye on the spring's end to a catch on the frame and the eye on the other end of the spring to a notch on a leg hanging down below the door, behind the lower panel.

One final potential mechanical problem is the timer/cycle control. If you are constantly turning the control knobs or pushing buttons with wet hands and fingers, enough moisture may eventually get behind the panel to cause corrosion on the electrical contacts or connections. In this case you'll need to call a service person to replace the timer.

WATER HEATERS

Water-heater problems include leaks in the tank, pressure leaks at threaded connections, and burner-control failures. Of these, tank leaks are the most serious because they require replacement of the entire water heater.

LEAKS

It used to be that you could count on a water heater lasting as long as 30 years. Nowadays, the quality of construction tends to be poor, and the bottom of the tank may rust out after only ten years or so. One way you can get more life out of your water heater is to drain off a gallon of water each month (starting when the heater is new). Draining this amount carries off the rust and sediment that settle on the bottom of the tank before they can cause serious damage. (Removing the rust also makes the water heater run more efficiently, since the debris blocks the transmission of heat to the water.) If you live in an area with high water pressure (80 psi or above), your water heater will last a lot longer if you have a pressure-reducing valve installed on the main water supply for the building.

If a tank leaks immediately upon installation, it's most likely the result of a manufacturing defect — typically a failed weld seam. Call the manufacturer for a replacement. Leaks may show up later at the drain cock at the bottom of the tank. At one time, water heaters came with brass drain cocks, but more common nowadays are plastic drain fittings. The bibb-type plastic cock is usually fairly trouble-free,

WATER-HEATER PROBLEMS

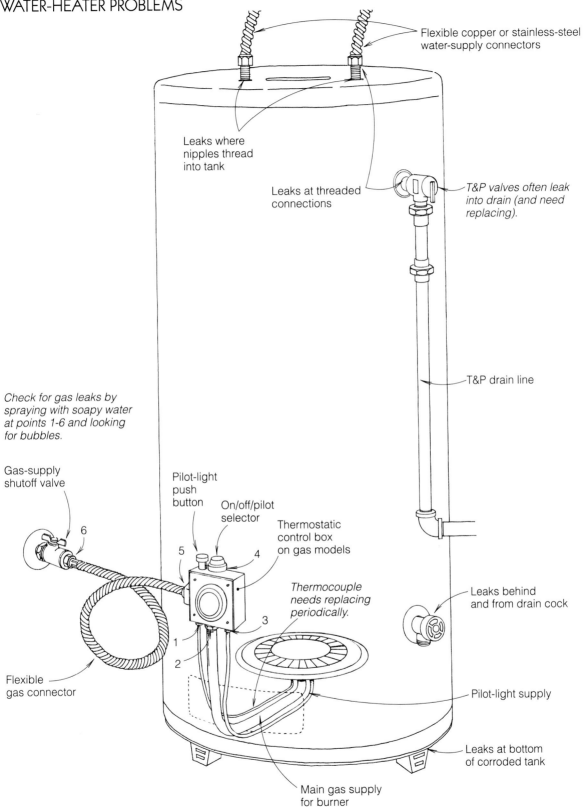

Flexible copper or stainless-steel water-supply connectors

Leaks where nipples thread into tank

Leaks at threaded connections

T&P valves often leak into drain (and need replacing).

T&P drain line

Check for gas leaks by spraying with soapy water at points 1-6 and looking for bubbles.

Gas-supply shutoff valve

Pilot-light push button

On/off/pilot selector

Thermostatic control box on gas models

Thermocouple needs replacing periodically.

Leaks behind and from drain cock

Flexible gas connector

Pilot-light supply

Leaks at bottom of corroded tank

Main gas supply for burner

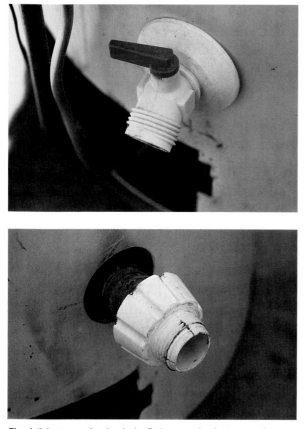

The bibb-type plastic drain fitting on the bottom of a water heater (top) is a big improvement over the round fitting (above). (Photos by Bill Dane)

but the round plastic fitting often leaks behind the outer skin and out the male-threaded sleeve in the center (see the photos above). If you get a leak behind the round fitting, drain the heater and pull out the fitting. Unthread the ¾-in. metal sleeve that's left in the heater and install a ¾-in. long-shank hose bibb (see p. 25). You can buy a brass cap to thread over the sleeve to contain a leak from the center of the fitting.

Pressure leaks can occur at any of the threaded connections on the water heater (see the drawing on p. 175). It's fairly common to find a leak between the nipples and the water-supply connectors on top of the heater, especially on the hot nipple, which expands and contracts. Leaks may also appear at the nipple-to-flex connector at the wall. If you have a leak at any threaded connection, shut off the water supply and reapply Teflon tape and pipe dope at the connections. Water heaters installed with galvanized nipples are far more prone to pressure leaks at the threaded connections than heaters installed with brass nipples, so you might want to replace any galvanized nipples, too.

Leaks may also occur at the male-threaded T&P connection to the water heater and at the threaded connection to the valve discharge. The T&P valve itself may leak (and sometimes the leak will go undetected if the valve is properly equipped with a drain line to the outside of the building). T&P valves are usually set to release at between 125 psi and 150 psi, but poorly constructed heaters will leak at much lower pressures. When the spring-loaded valve comes off the seat inside the T&P's housing, you'll often hear a chattering noise throughout the house's piping system. To check the T&P valve, put your hand on the drain line from the valve about 6 ft. away from the heater: If the pipe is hot, the valve is leaking and you'll need to replace it. (Note that a T&P valve will last longer if you install a pressure-reducing valve on the main line.)

MECHANICAL PROBLEMS

Residential water heaters, both electric and gas, have few mechanical parts other than moving electrical contacts. Problems on electric water heaters generally require the services of an electrician rather than a plumber. Problems on gas-fired water heaters — most commonly a lack of hot water because the burner is not firing — can be tackled by the home owner.

If a gas water heater with a conventional pilot light is not producing hot water, it's probably because the pilot has gone out — either because it's been blown out or because the thermocouple has failed. The thermocouple sits in the pilot flame, producing a tiny electrical current that is sufficient to make the thermostatic gas-control valve operate. A safety control feature shuts off the flow of gas if the pilot light goes out, but it can malfunction so always shut off the gas valve on the supply line and wait about ten minutes before attempting to relight the pilot.

If the pilot will not relight, the thermocouple probably needs replacing. However, before you buy a new one, first make sure that the connection into the thermostatic control box is tight. Many times if you just unthread the end of the thermocouple at the

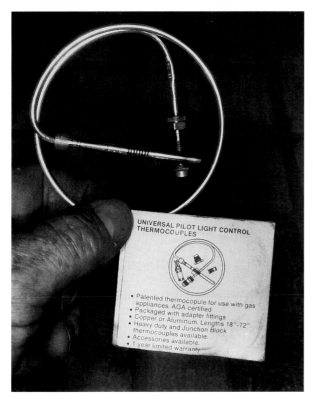

If the pilot light on a gas water heater goes out, you may need to replace the thermocouple. (Photo by Bill Dane)

control valve and polish the end of the thermocouple fitting with a fine nail file, the pilot will relight when you reinstall the thermocouple.

If the thermocouple needs replacing, I usually find it easier to take loose the burner-supply tube and pilot-supply tube from the control box and remove the whole burner (with pilot attached). This way I can get the thermocouple loose without slicing my hands on the edge of the access-panel opening. Test all the gas connections after reassembly with soap and water in a spray bottle. Any leaks will show up as bubbles.

SOURCES OF SUPPLY

ALSONS CORP.
42 Union St.
Hillsdale, MI 49242
(517) 439-1411
FAX (517) 439-9644
Hand-held shower heads and bidet fittings

AMERICAN STANDARD
P.O. Box 6820
Piscataway, NJ 08855
(800) 223-0068
FAX (800) 442-1905
Plumbing fixtures; tub waste and overflows

AQUAFLO
(DIVISION OF SPECIALTY PRODUCTS)
3689 Arrowhead Drive
Carson City, NV 89706
(800) 854-3215
FAX (702) 884-4343
Braided stainless-steel supply tubes

BLACKSWAN MANUFACTURING CO.
4540 West Thomas St.
Chicago, IL 60651
(800) 252-5796
FAX (312) 227-3705
Plumber's putty

BRASS CRAFT CO.
100 Galleria Officentre
Southfield, MI 48034
(313) 827-1100
FAX (313) 827-1368
Chromed-brass supply tubes

CASPER'S INDUSTRIES
(DIVISION OF OATEY)
6600 Smith Ave.
Newark, CA 94560
(510) 797-4672
FAX (510) 790-3442
Tub waste and overflows; brass drain fitting

CHICAGO SPECIALTY
(DIVISION OF MOEN)
25300 Al Moen Drive
North Olmsted, OH 44070
(800) 532-3377
FAX (800) 289-6636
*Rimster rim-clip wrench; strainer wrench;
seat wrench and valve seats*

CHICAGO VALVE CO.
2100 South Clearwater Drive
Des Plaines, IL 60018
(708) 803-5000
FAX (708) 298-3101
*Plumbing valves (including polished-chrome
washing-machine bibbs)*

CLOROBEN CORP.
1035 Belleville Turnpike
Kearney, NJ 07032
(800) 631-9550
FAX (201) 998-4953
Flow-improving agent for garbage disposers

DELTA FAUCET CO.
55 East 111th St.
P.O. Box 40980
Indianapolis, IN 46280
(317) 848-1812
Faucets and valves

DIAMOND TOOL & HORSESHOE CO.
(DIVISION OF COOPER GROUP)
Cameron Rd.
Orangeburg, SC 29115
(803) 533-7862
FAX (803) 536-6632
Diagonal-cutting pliers

EASTMAN CO.
(DIVISION OF U.S. BRASS)
P.O. Box 879002
17120 Dallas Parkway
Dallas, TX 75287
(800) 872-7277
FAX (800) 525-7213
*Chromed-brass supply tubes; CD-3 copper
air gap (for dishwashers)*

ELJER CO.
(DIVISION OF U.S. BRASS)
17120 Dallas Parkway
Dallas, TX 75248
(800) 423-5537
FAX (800) 333-4547
Plumbing fixtures

ELKAY MANUFACTURING CO.
2222 Camden Court
Oakbrook, IL 60521
(708) 574-8484
FAX (708) 574-5012
Self-rimming stainless-steel sinks

FLORESTONE PRODUCTS CO.
2851 Falcon Drive
Madera, CA 93637
(209) 661-4171
FAX (209) 661-2070
Terrazzo shower pans

FLUIDMASTER
P.O. Box 4264
1800 East Via Burton
Anaheim, CA 92803
(714) 774-1444
FAX (714) 774-5764
Toilet-repair kits

GENERAL WIRE AND SPRING CO.
1101 Thompson Ave.
McKees Rocks, PA 15136
(412) 771-6300
FAX (412) 771-2771
Hand-held mechanical snake; closet auger

GERBER PLUMBING FIXTURES CO.
4656 W. Touhy Ave.
Chicago, IL 60646
(708) 675-6570
Tub waste and overflows

GREAT NECK SAW MANUFACTURERS
165 East Second St.
Mineola, NY 11501
(516) 746-5352
Mechanical fingers

GREENLEE/TEXTRON
4450 Boeing Drive
Rockford, IL 61109
(800) 435-0786
Chassis punch for stainless-steel sinks

HERCULES CHEMICAL CO.
29 West 38 St.
New York, NY 10018
(212) 869-4330
Pipe-joint compound; bowl waxes

HOMER'S BRASS
P.O. Box 6541
Albany, CA 94706
(510) 524-1506
Brass washers

JABSCO PRODUCTS/ITT
1485 Dale Way
Costa Mesa, CA 92626-3998
(714) 545-8251
FAX (714) 556-4206
Brass hand pump

KIRKHILL
12021 Woodruff Ave.
Downey, CA 90241
(310) 803-3421
FAX (310) 803-3713
Rubber plumbing parts (stem washers, reinforced tank-bolt washers); reinforced flat rubber stock

KLEIN TOOLS
7200 McCormick Boulevard
P.O. Box 599033
Chicago, IL 60659-9033
(708) 677-9500
FAX (708) 677-4476
Aviation snips; diagonal-cutting pliers

KOHLER COMPANY
44 Highland Drive
Kohler, WI 53044
(800) 772-1814
(414) 457-4441
Plumbing fixtures; tub waste and overflows

MCGUIRE MANUFACTURING CO.
P.O. Box 7015
Prospect, CT 06712
(203) 758-4424
FAX (203) 758-4585
Kitchen-sink basket strainers

MILL ROSE CO.
7995 Tyler Boulevard
Mentor, OH 44060
(216) 255-9171
FAX (216) 255-5039
Pink Teflon tape

MILWAUKEE ELECTRIC TOOL CO.
13135 West Lisbon Rd.
Brookfield, WI 53005
(414) 781-3600
Hole Hawg right-angle drill; Sawzall

MISSION RUBBER CO.
P.O. Box 2349
Corona, CA 91718-2349
(800) 854-9991
FAX (800) 637-4601
Rubber couplings for joining pipe

MOEN
25300 Al Moen Drive
North Olmsted, OH 44070
(800) 553-6636
(216) 962-2000
Faucets and valves

OATEY CO.
4700 West 160 St.
P.O. Box 35906
Cleveland, OH 44135
(216) 267-7100
FAX (800) 321-9535
Pipe cements

PASCO
11156 Wright Rd.
Lynwood, CA 90262
(310) 537-7782
Four-in-one screwdriver (model #4208); no-hub coupling wrench (#7020); cast-iron hangers for wall-hung sinks (Z-Hanger, #1221)

PERFECTION SCHWANK CO.
P.O. Box 749
Waynesboro, GA 30830-0749
(706) 554-2101
Direct-vent heaters

PRICE PFISTER
13500 Paxton St.
Pacoima, CA 91331
(818) 896-1141
Plumbing fixtures; tub waste and overflows

RADIATOR SPECIALTY CO.
425 Huehl Rd., Suite #9
Northbrook, IL 60062
(800) 243-0050
FAX (708) 498-9958
Toilet plunger (#C-107); faucet-repair accessories

RECTORSEAL CORP.
2830 Produce Row
P.O. Box 14669
Houston, TX 77021
(713) 928-6423
FAX (713) 928-2039
Pipe-joint compound

RIDGE TOOL CO.
400 Clark St.
Elyria, OH 44036
(216) 323-5581
Ridgid-brand plumbing tools

J.R. SMITH MANUFACTURING CO.
P.O. Box 3237
Montgomery, AL 36193-2201
(205) 277-8520
FAX (205) 272-7396
Carriers for wall-hung toilets

STERLING/POLAR
920 East Lincoln Ave.
Searcy, AR 72143
(800) 558-7782
FAX (800) 237-9314
Bar and other sinks

WATER MASTER CO.
P.O. Box 1186
New Brunswick, NJ 08903
(908) 247-1900
Toilaflex plunger

WATTS CO.
815 Chestnut St.
North Andover, MA 01845-6098
(508) 688-1811
FAX (508) 794-1848
Water-hammer arrester (model #150HA); pressure-reducing valves

WILLIAMS FURNACE CO.
225 Acacia St.
Colton, CA 92324
(909) 825-0993
FAX (909) 370-0581
Direct-vent heaters

INDEX

A

ABS. See Pipe, ABS.
Acrylic, as fixture material, 35-36
Air gaps:
  clogs in, 136
  copper, recommended, 136
  in dishwasher drainage, 135, 138-139
  leaks at, 173
  mounting, 136, 139
  See also Dishwashers.
Aluminum, as fixture material, 41
Angle stops:
  adapters for, 103
  compression vs. threaded, 18-19
  connections for, diagrammed, 21
  described, 16
  for dishwasher supply line, 135
  for hot-water dispenser, 128
  for ice-maker supply line, 134
  installing, 22
  kitchen-sink configuration of, 22, 23
  leaks in, at supply connection, 158,
    173
  old-style, 19
    adapters for, 20
  purging, 68, 69
  raw-brass vs. chrome-plated, 18
  repositioning, 23
  supply-tube connection at, 19, 100-101
  two-outlet, 22, 134, 135
  See also Nipples. Supply tubes.
Augers:
  closet, for toilet clogs, 12, 154
  drain, described, 12

B

Back supports, recommended, 14, 15
Ballcocks:
  brass, 156-158
  leaks in, 156-158
  plastic, 157, 158
Basket strainers:
  for bar sinks, 113
  desirable features of, 112
  installing, 110-111, 113
  leaks at, 166
  See also Sinks, kitchen.
Bathtubs:
  acrylic, 35
  cast-iron, 31-33
  clogs in, 166-167
  enameled-steel, 36-37
  framing for, 48, 49
  installing,
    off ground, 43, 52-53
    on slab, 43-52

leaks in, at W&O mounting, 167, 168
setting on finish floor, 42-43
/showers, combination, 33-34
  fiberglass, material defects in, 34-35
  framing for, 57
  installing, 56-58
spouts for, 60-61
trap box for, 43
traps for, recommended sizes of, 49
valves for, 59-60
See also Traps. Valves. Waste and
  overflows.
Bibbs:
  hose, 16
    installing, 25-26
    standard vs. long-shank, 25
  washing-machine, 16
    vs. hose, 24
    installing, 24-25
Bidets:
  designs of, 29
  hand-held attachments for, 29
  installing 74-75
Bowl waxes:
  installing, 66
  for toilets, sizes of, 65-66
  See also Closet flanges. Toilets.
Brass:
  as faucet-hardware material,
    recommended, 95
  as faucet material, recommended, 95
  as fixture material, 41
  as pop-up waste material,
    recommended, 106
  as W&O material, recommended, 43
Bronze, as fixture material, 41

C

Cast iron, enameled, as fixture material,
  31-33
Caulk:
  adhesive, for self-rimming sink
    installation, 84-85
  silicone,
    for leaks around sink edge, 164
    for pedestal-sink installation, 127
    for shower-drain-fitting repair, 169
    for underhung-sink installation, 88
Ceramics, as fixture material, 40
Chalk lines, plumbing uses for, 3
Chisels, plumbing uses for, 2
Closet flanges:
  bolts for, 64
  installing, 64-65
  materials for, 64
  See also Bowl waxes. Toilets.
Closet supplies. See Supply tubes, toilet.

Cooktops, gas:
  electronic ignitions of, 148
  flex connectors for, 146
  installing, 146-147
  regulator for, 146
  vented, 146-147
  See also Ranges, gas.
Copper, as fixture material, 41
Copper tubing:
  for dishwasher supply, 139-140
  as faucet-supply-tube material, 103
  for hot-water dispenser connections,
    129
  for ice-maker supply line, 134-135
Countertops:
  and faucet compatibility, 99
  and sink compatibility, 78-80
  sink openings in,
    cutting, 81-82
    laying out, 81, 85
  with sink rim clips, compatibility of, 86
  /sinks, combination, 40-41
Couplings, rubber:
  for shower drainage, 53
  on trap arms, 116, 117, 127
  for tub drainage, 51

D

Dielectric corrosion, defined, 17
Dishwashers:
  angle-stop connections for, 22, 23
  clogs in, 174
  door springs, repair of, 174
  drainage through garbage disposers,
    139
  electrical problems with, 172, 174
  installing, 137-140
  leaks in,
    in drainage system, 173
    testing for, 140
    in water supply, 172-173
  leveling, 137
  locating, 135
  supply line for, 139-140
    elbow for, 139-140
  waste system for, 137-139
  See also Air gaps.
Drain cleaners, chemical, disadvised, 162
Drains, clogged, 167
  tools for, 12, 152, 163
Drills:
  cordless, plumbing uses for, 11
  right-angle, plumbing uses for, 11
Dryers, gas:
  flex connectors for, 149
  installing, 148-149
Drywall, repairing holes in, 11

EDITORS: JEFF BENEKE, PETER CHAPMAN

DESIGNER/LAYOUT ARTIST: CATHERINE CASSIDY

ILLUSTRATOR: FRANK HABBAS

PHOTOGRAPHER, EXCEPT WHERE NOTED: JEFF BENEKE

TYPEFACE: ITC STONE SERIF

PAPER: MEAD PAPER, 70 LB., MOISTRITE MATTE WEB

PRINTER: ARCATA GRAPHICS/HAWKINS, NEW CANTON, TENNESSEE